THE SOUTHERN TOUR

ASIAN ARGUMENTS

Asian Arguments is a series of books which explores life in Asia today. Written by experts from the fields of journalism, academia and politics, all of whom have considerable experience of living and working in Asia, the books reveal how citizens across the region – from China to Vietnam – are confronting problems such as environmental crisis, economic development and democracy.

Series Editor: Paul French

Available now in the series:

The Trouble with Taiwan by Kerry Brown and Kally Wu Tzu Hui
China and the New Maoists by Kerry Brown and Simone van Nieuwenhuizen
North Korea by Paul French
A Kingdom in Crisis: Thailand's Struggle for Democracy in the Twenty-First Century by Andrew MacGregor Marshall
China's Urban Billion by Tom Miller
Ghost Cities of China by Wade Shepard
Return of the Junta: Why Myanmar's Military Must Go Back to the Barracks by Oliver Slow
Myanmar's Enemy Within: Buddhist Violence and the Making of a Muslim 'Other' by Francis Wade
Thailand: Shifting Ground between the US and a Rising China by Benjamin Zawacki
Leftover Women: The Resurgence of Gender Inequality in China, 10th Anniversary Edition by Leta Hong Fincher

THE SOUTHERN TOUR

Deng Xiaoping and the Fight for China's Future

Jonathan Chatwin

BLOOMSBURY ACADEMIC
LONDON • NEW YORK • OXFORD • NEW DELHI • SYDNEY

BLOOMSBURY ACADEMIC
Bloomsbury Publishing Plc
50 Bedford Square, London, WC1B 3DP, UK
1385 Broadway, New York, NY 10018, USA
29 Earlsfort Terrace, Dublin 2, Ireland

BLOOMSBURY, BLOOMSBURY ACADEMIC and the Diana logo
are trademarks of Bloomsbury Publishing Plc

First published in Great Britain 2024

Copyright © Jonathan Chatwin, 2024

Jonathan Chatwin has asserted his right under the Copyright,
Designs and Patents Act, 1988, to be identified as Author of this work.

For legal purposes the Acknowledgements on p. 149 constitute an
extension of this copyright page.

Cover design by Grace Ridge
Cover image: Statue of Deng Xiaoping © ViewStock via Getty Images

All rights reserved. No part of this publication may be reproduced or
transmitted in any form or by any means, electronic or mechanical, including
photocopying, recording, or any information storage or retrieval system,
without prior permission in writing from the publishers.

Bloomsbury Publishing Plc does not have any control over, or responsibility for,
any third-party websites referred to or in this book. All internet addresses given in
this book were correct at the time of going to press. The author and publisher
regret any inconvenience caused if addresses have changed or sites have
ceased to exist, but can accept no responsibility for any such changes.

A catalogue record for this book is available from the British Library.

Library of Congress Cataloging-in-Publication Data
Names: Chatwin, Jonathan, author.
Title: The Southern tour : Deng Xiaoping and the fight for
China's future / Jonathan Chatwin.
Other titles: Deng Xiaoping and the fight for China's future
Description: London ; New York : Bloomsbury Publishing, 2024. |
Includes bibliographical references and index.
Identifiers: LCCN 2023043096 (print) | LCCN 2023043097 (ebook) |
ISBN 9781350324053 (hb) | ISBN 9781350435711 (pb) |
ISBN 9781350324077 (ebook) | ISBN 9781350324060 (epdf)
Subjects: LCSH: Deng, Xiaoping, 1904–1997. | Deng, Xiaoping, 1904–1997–Travel–China. |
China–Politics and government–1976–2002. | China–Economic policy–1976–2000. |
China–Description and travel. | Politicians–China–Biography.
Classification: LCC DS778.D46 C383 2024 (print) | LCC DS778.D46 (ebook) |
DDC 951.06/1092 [B]–dc23/eng/20240110
LC record available at https://lccn.loc.gov/2023043096
LC ebook record available at https://lccn.loc.gov/2023043097

ISBN:	HB:	978-1-3503-2405-3
	PB:	978-1-3504-3571-1
	ePDF:	978-1-3503-2407-7
	eBook:	978-1-3503-2406-0

Typeset by Integra Software Services Pvt. Ltd.

To find out more about our authors and books visit www.bloomsbury.com
and sign up for our newsletters.

For Clara and Iris

Chapter 11
THE STORY OF SPRING   111

Chapter 12
THE NEW ERA   121

EPILOGUE: A SOUTHERN TOUR   133

Timeline   144
Acknowledgements   149
Notes   150
Select bibliography   168
Index   172

CONTENTS

List of illustrations   ix

PROLOGUE: 'TIME IS MONEY'   xi

Chapter 1
BEIJING, 1989   1

Chapter 2
UNFINISHED BUSINESS   15

Chapter 3
THE SOUTHERN TOUR   29

Chapter 4
DEPARTURE   37

Chapter 5
THE THOROUGHFARE OF NINE PROVINCES   43

Chapter 6
THE EAST WIND BRINGS SPRING ALL AROUND   53

Chapter 7
WELL WATER AND RIVER WATER   75

Chapter 8
'WHOEVER IS AGAINST REFORM WILL BE DRIVEN OUT OF POWER'   85

Chapter 9
THE YEAR OF THE MONKEY   93

Chapter 10
RETURN TO THE CAPITAL   103

ILLUSTRATIONS

Figures

1	The Hankou 'Bund' or embankment, Wuhan	67
2	Swimming in the Yangtze, Wuhan	67
3	Statue of Deng Xiaoping, Lotus Hill Park, Shenzhen	68
4	View from Lotus Hill Park, Shenzhen	69
5	Billboard of Deng Xiaoping, Shenzhen	69
6	Steps up Luo Sanmei Hill, near Zhuhai, where Deng Xiaoping famously declared he would not turn back	70
7	Statue of Deng Xiaoping, Luo Sanmei Hill	71
8	The 'Fisher Girl' statue and cityscape of Zhuhai	71
9	Detail from an oil painting titled *The Vision*, showing modern-day Pudong in Shanghai, on display at the Longhua Martyrs' Cemetery	72
10	View from the peak of Mount Tai	72
11	The Wordless Stele, Mount Tai	73
12	Front page of the *Shenzhen Special Zone Daily*, 26 March 1992, featuring 'East Wind Brings Spring All Around – On-the-spot Report on Comrade Deng Xiaoping in Shenzhen'	74

Picture courtesy: All, except Figure 12, taken by Jonathan Chatwin, 2019

Map

1	Map of Deng's Southern Tour	x

MAP

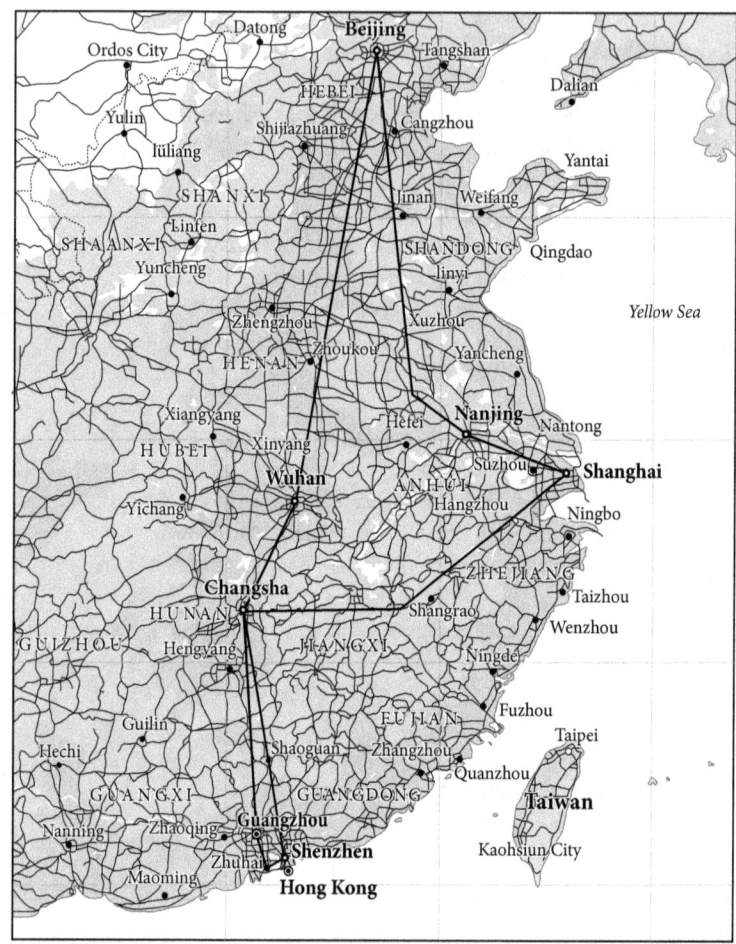

Map 1 Map of Deng's Southern Tour.

PROLOGUE: 'TIME IS MONEY'

On an overcast afternoon in the latter days of January 1984, China's seventy-nine-year-old paramount leader Deng Xiaoping stood high above the city of Shenzhen. From the balconied roof of a twenty-storey office building, the most notable interruption to his view was the adjacent concrete skeleton of what was becoming China's tallest skyscraper. Clad in bamboo scaffold and safety netting, with two enormous cranes pinned to its side, the International Trade Centre dominated the skyline of the new city of Shenzhen.

The rest of the city spread modestly below and around this new landmark. Shenzhen in 1984 was a grid of perpendicular roads, seemingly too broad for the low-rise white buildings, factory sheds and dusty, empty lots that flanked them. Occasional new office towers and apartment blocks stood proud of the sprawl, but this was an urban landscape still in search of a clear form, its ordered streets and the International Trade Centre itself offering the merest suggestion of what the city's future held. Liang Xiang, the mayor of Shenzhen, told Deng as they stood surveying the city that there were currently more than sixty buildings under construction that would exceed eighteen storeys – and that more than one hundred were planned for the coming years.[1]

To the south from Deng's viewpoint was the curving Shenzhen River, and beyond it, Hong Kong. Unseen to the north was the so-called 'Second Line' – an 80-kilometre fence and barbed wire internal border, still being built, which would separate this part of Guangdong province from the rest of mainland China, effectively making Shenzhen a separate territory within the borders of the People's Republic.[2]

As the light began to fade, the breeze picked up on the rooftop; even here in China's far south, January brought a winter chill. Deng stood at the front of a small crowd on the rooftop edge, the officials next to him leaning down to compensate for his poor hearing. According to contemporary accounts from state media, cadres accompanying Deng, who was dressed in a buttoned-up grey jacket and no hat, asked him twice to put on a coat, but he waved them away; he was focussed on his survey of the city – his city, as it would come to be seen – below.[3]

Deng was at the very beginning of a month-long tour around China's south. His private train had, that morning of 24 January 1984, crossed the border into Guangdong province, which arcs its back around the southern coast of China. It had passed through the provincial capital of Guangzhou, and headed southward through the second line to the city of Shenzhen. After a brief meeting with officials, first on Deng's itinerary that afternoon was his survey of the International Trade Centre.

It would be capped off at fifty storeys in September of that year: a stocky square-bodied building, banded with vertical lines of blue-mirrored windows and topped with a circular revolving restaurant. It was a building symbolic not just of China's reaching ambition, but also of the pace at which that ambition should be realized. Deng was told during his visit that a new floor was added every three days: a pace that became known as 'Shenzhen Speed' – though in fact the rate of building early on in the project had been far slower than this, partly due to a lack of proper equipment.[4]

The next morning, Deng took a short minibus ride to a village just visible from that vantage point of the previous day, perched on the very edge of China. Thirty-two pristine white two-storey houses sat along parallel streets, clustered together on a semicircle of land bordered by water-filled rice fields on one side and the Shenzhen River to the other. Beyond the rice fields, to the north, were the hollow-eyed towers and cranes of the city, with the International Trade Centre a punctuation mark on the inarticulate skyline.

The name of the village was Yumin Cun – 'Fishermen's Village' – and the inhabitants of the village were settled descendants of the 'boat dwellers' or Tankas who had for centuries plied the seas and rivers of southern China and were sometimes pejoratively called 'sea gypsies'.

Deng, dressed in a padded blue Mao jacket, was escorted down the main street by a smiling group of officials, his relative status in such groups in inverse proportion, as always, to his diminutive form. They stopped and entered one of the houses. The downstairs rooms were capacious and bright, and fitted with modern appliances: two refrigerators, an electric cooker, a hi-fi, a washing machine and a large colour television in the lounge.

'You have everything now?' Deng asked Wu Bosen, the local leader who lived in this capacious villa. 'Yes, everything,' Wu replied. He went on to say that this was all thanks to 'uncle' Deng. 'This is the policy of the Party Committee,' Deng replied. 'You have to thank the Party'. According to one account, Wu said his only worry was that the policy that had led to this economic success would change. Deng told him it would – but only for the better.

Wu told Deng that last year the household income in Fishermen's Village had exceeded 10,000 yuan (nearly US$5,000), making it the richest village in the country. Average per capita income in rural China was, as reported in official figures for 1983, 309.8 yuan (around US$150).[5] In 1979, the villagers had begun to develop small businesses and factories, supported by investment from across the border in Hong Kong, and the increasingly permissive rules that applied to Shenzhen. The village exemplified Deng's assertion of the previous year – that some people in China should be allowed to get rich before others.

'It will take one hundred years for the whole country to reach this level,' Deng lamented to his accompanying officials after seeing Fishermen's Village. After some challenged this bleak estimate, Deng revised it down, but said that such levels of affluence would still take at least seventy years to achieve given the size of China's population.[6]

By January 1984, Deng had been in charge of the country for just over five years. After decades of stagnation, China was now, he asserted, 'full of vitality and [...] thriving in every sector'.[7] But division and debate over how to pursue China's modernization had dogged these early years of his leadership, and those economic reforms that had been introduced were initial, tentative experiments.

Following his inspection of Shenzhen, Deng would cross the Pearl River to the city of Zhuhai, before heading back to Guangzhou, into next door Fujian province and, finally, north to Shanghai. The increasing prosperity and rapid pace of development evident in the cities he visited during this journey – particularly Shenzhen – convinced him that they offered both a model and inspiration for China's future. He would return to Beijing to advocate for rapid development of China's economy, and greater opening to the outside world.

The journey would become known as Deng Xiaoping's first *nanxun*, or Southern Tour. The denomination was derived from the title given to the lavish journeys made by emperors of centuries past to inspect their expansive realm and exhibit their imperial grandeur – and which were rendered into myth by the artists and historians who recorded them. It was a title that would come later, when this journey to the south had been eclipsed in significance by a second such tour made in its image, eight years – almost to the day – later; a journey that would crucially influence China's future and consciously gild a complicated legacy.

*

Deng had become China's *de-facto* leader in late 1978, two years after Mao Zedong's death. In the intervening two years, Deng had manoeuvred against the successor Mao had anointed: the fifty-five-year-old former provincial leader Hua Guofeng. Over the course of these two years, Deng demonstrated the patience that had been forcibly cultivated over the prior decade of the Cultural Revolution (1966–76), during which he had been purged twice. With a political ruthlessness that would become familiar during the next fourteen years, Deng successfully, and unfairly, caricatured Hua as representing a continuation of the ideology and economic policy of the latter Mao era, and lined up political and military support behind him.

There was no doubt that, after the long decade of the Cultural Revolution, the country's economy remained in a parlous state and a drive towards modernization was needed. 'Better to be poor under socialism than rich under capitalism', had run one slogan from the era; it was an ambition that had indisputably been achieved by the time of Mao's death.

Initiated partly as a means for Mao to re-establish himself in unassailable power, the Cultural Revolution had unleashed swirling social and political forces which no one – even Mao himself – had full control over, and which upended the lives of ordinary Chinese people. The revolution targeted those values and behaviours that contradicted, or appeared to contradict, socialist dogma, and terrible violence was directed towards those accused of representing bourgeois values; in Fishermen's Village one resident recalled his fear of eating bread and drinking soda water brought over the border from Hong Kong as they were 'products of capitalism'.[8] Millions of young people were uprooted from their lives and sent to the countryside to 'learn from the peasants'. Universities and schools were shuttered. Work became a secondary concern as ideology dictated all aspects of life. 'Many work units were paralyzed,' wrote Kang Zhengguo in his memoir of growing up in Maoist China. 'Production at the brickyard had come to a virtual halt. [....] While the militants made revolution, the rest of us loafed quietly on the sidelines, still drawing our state salaries'.[9]

The lethargic economic growth which attended the chaos of the Cultural Revolution meant that China had continued to fall behind the developed world. Deng would later question how socialism could be considered superior, if those living under it faced such chronic difficulties. He criticized those ideologues of the Cultural Revolution who 'clamoured for "poor socialism" and "poor communism"', those who believed that communism was a 'spiritual thing'. In 1978, the average monthly salary for workers was still only 45 yuan, he noted, and most rural areas remained mired in poverty. 'Can this be called the superiority of socialism?' he asked.[10] 'There was usually enough to eat,' wrote Lijia Zhang of the Cultural Revolution years, 'though the cicadas we roasted revealed a craving for meat not sated by the one gram of pork rationed monthly for each of us. Everyone was poor, and we were only a little poorer than our neighbours. We didn't have any toys, but we didn't know to miss them.'[11]

Though other socialist countries had tried to reform and modernize, China, an agrarian country of just under a billion people, a hundred times the size of Hungary, and with a very different history and society to that of the Soviet Union, was unhelpfully unique, and any lessons China's leaders might be able to take from other socialist economies were often, as with those of the Cultural Revolution, negative rather than positive. That most of China's trained economists had been sent down to the countryside to learn from labour only exacerbated the collective lack of certainty of how China might modernize in the aftermath of Mao's death in September 1976.

During his brief tenure, Hua Guofeng resurrected an economic plan that Deng himself, alongside Premier Zhou Enlai, had outlined in 1975. The idea was to drive economic growth by importing billions of dollars' worth of new foreign technology to build new steel plants, power stations and oil refineries, with funding for this lavish expenditure – one projection had the cost of twenty-two plants at $12.4 billion – provided by loans to be repaid by increasing exports and (unfeasibly, as it turned out) the production of petroleum. Deng was initially an enthusiastic supporter of the plan, but by the time he wrested authority from Hua in December 1978 the underlying principles of the so-called 'Great Leap Outward' had become subject to criticism by influential leaders as too risky and hasty. Deng understood that, politically, he needed to establish a clear contrast between his new leadership and what had come before: the plan was scrapped and blame for its excesses assigned, conveniently, to the marginalized Hua.[12]

Now began the first phase of what would become known later as 'reform and opening'. It was a neat title for a messy process: overseen by Deng, administered by others, and always subject to the push and pull of politics and ideology. Deng emphasized pragmatism: adopting a Maoist phrase, he encouraged party officials to 'seek truth from facts' and to be focussed on practical outcomes rather than ideology. In trying to improve these outcomes, Deng advocated a system in which there was more individual economic freedom and accountability.

The socialist model that China had followed since 1949 saw the state take ownership of the nation's resources and means of production, and responsibility, via a series of five-year plans, for directing resources, planning production and setting prices. The reward for the individual in such a system is, at least in theory, a guarantee of a basic level of economic security; for urban workers in state-owned enterprises, who received education, housing and healthcare as part of their employment, this was known as their 'iron rice bowl'. But, exacerbated by the chaos of the Cultural Revolution, this economic system, with its inefficiencies and discouragement of enterprise or innovation, had resulted in economic stagnation. 'Socialism cannot endure if it remains poor,' Deng said in 1979. 'If we want to uphold Marxism and socialism in the international class struggle, we have to demonstrate that the Marxist system of thought is superior to all others, and that the socialist system is superior to the capitalist'.[13]

The impact of the gradual shift away from centralized control that Deng and his leadership began to permit was most palpably felt first in the countryside, through what became known as the 'household responsibility system', which saw a higher fixed price paid for crops, a reduction in the proportion of grain required to be sold to the state, and ultimately, over the early years of the 1980s, the resurrection of family farming, with those tending the land able to profit from what they produced above the required quota. The development of the policy was a prime example of the complex interplay of different forces during the initial years of reform and opening, with local experiments ultimately trumping the initial plan put forward by the party.[14] 'During this major policy change, the central government did not apply uniform standards and issue unified directives,' wrote Zhao Ziyang later. 'Local governments were free to choose whether to implement and how'.[15]

China also began to look elsewhere for lessons in how to develop. During Hua Guofeng's tenure, officials had already begun to be dispatched abroad to study other forms of economic development. Leaders set out for Switzerland, West Germany, Hong Kong, Japan; in 1978 alone, top leaders took twenty trips to more than fifty countries. 'The more they see,' Deng confessed to North Korean leader Kim Il Sung, 'the more they feel we have fallen behind.'[16] That same year, Deng himself had visited Japan. On a tour of a Nissan car plant, he was told that it produced ninety-four cars per worker per year. In China's most productive plant, the rate was one car per worker. 'We are very backward. We have to recognize that,' he would say later in his trip. 'We have a lot to do, a long way to go and a lot to learn'.[17]

That life was better abroad had long been an open secret in Guangdong. 'Good situation; many problems' was how one official summarized the post-Cultural Revolution status of a province that had the longest coastline of any in China and had for centuries previously functioned as the country's gateway and window to the world.[18]

The neglect across the province was palpable in the late 1970s, particularly in towns and cities: roads and railways were in a parlous state; there were frequent energy blackouts; and housing was ramshackle and overcrowded.[19] During the Cultural Revolution years, Mao Zedong had instituted a policy which deliberately moved investment out of Guangdong and other coastal provinces, with the government instead pumping money and resources into areas in China's west and southwest, building new industrial zones far inland as part of a programme known as the 'Third Front', which was intended to protect the country in the event of invasion from the coast. The 'Third Front' initiative was even more economically damaging to the country than the political chaos of the Cultural Revolution,[20] and severely restricted investment in coastal areas like Guangdong.

The political atmosphere of the Cultural Revolution years had also been particularly hostile in Guangdong; those with relatives abroad had been targeted for persecution – and some estimated that 60 per cent of Guangdong cadres had close family or friends overseas.[21] Political and economic forces built to become unendurable for some, and throughout these years the bodies of those who tried, and failed, to cross the bay to reach Hong Kong next door regularly washed up on the shore, rotten and bloated. They were known as Freedom Swimmers, and they set out in their thousands each year. 'We wanted to go to Hong Kong, not just to fill our stomachs, but for freedom,' says one former Cultural Revolution Red Guard who fled from Shenzhen in 1973, swimming for six hours to reach Hong Kong.[22]

In the spring of 1979, officials presented a proposal to Deng Xiaoping which they thought might rejuvenate the economy and stem this flow of mainlanders crossing the border from Guangdong. They suggested establishing areas in the south that would have special rules allowing for foreign investment, from Hong Kong and beyond: to draw a circle by the South China Sea within which a more experimental approach could be taken.

A leading advocate of this idea was the Guangdong provincial party secretary, a sixty-five-year-old party veteran named Xi Zhongxun. Xi Zhongxun and Yang Shangkun, another key Guangdong official who would later become president of China, told Deng that Guangdong should become a battlefront and demonstration zone in national reform and opening-up: 'We need to reform China and implement these economic zones even if it means that we have to travel a bloody road ahead,' they said.²³ (One of Xi's sons, Jinping, was at the time studying chemical engineering in Beijing. 1979 would be a pivotal year for Xi Jinping, too: that autumn, he would begin his career in politics.)

These Special Economic Zones (SEZs) would be special in two significant ways. Firstly, they were run by local officials, free of direct control by state planners back in Beijing. Secondly, they were established to allow, and indeed encourage, foreign trade and investment, offering favourable terms to businesses from abroad. Both represented significant diversions from the old way of doing things in communist China, where central planning dictated the economic life of the country, and trade with the capitalist world had, for a long time, been ideologically objectionable.

In July of 1979, authorities in Beijing approved the establishment of the first two SEZs in Shenzhen and, just across the river, Zhuhai. In 1980 the trading city of Shantou, a little further northeast on the Guangdong coast, would be approved as a SEZ (along with Xiamen in next door Fujian province).²⁴

Guangdong was an obvious choice for the establishment of these areas. The Pearl River, which flows through the provincial capital of Guangzhou, drains much of the province, and broadens into an estuary flanked by Hong Kong and Macau. When, in 1583, the Italian Jesuit missionary Matteo Ricci travelled up the Pearl River, he observed that the whole of the estuary was so busy with trade it resembled one long harbour; the sixteenth and seventeenth centuries saw the river delta become the economic centre of Southern China.²⁵

The provincial capital of Guangzhou would subsequently become the site of the so-called 'Thirteen Factories' – a series of warehouses set in twelve acres on the banks of the Pearl River, which from 1757 to 1842 were the sole sites of legal foreign trade with China. The city became the main site of entry for foreign visitors, and the impressions recorded almost universally note its industrious, mercantile character:

> The rush of coolies with their burdens; the whir of the jade-cutting wheels; the din of the brass founders; the clang of the forge; the clatter of the silk loom, worked by hand; the monotonous thud of the gold-beater's hammer; the patient stitching of the embroiderers [...]; the markets, with hurrying throngs bringing in fruits of every variety, vegetables and live fish; and the thousand other employments carried on in shops opening full on the street, impress us strongly with the fact of their great industry.²⁶

In the communist era, Guangdong had played a crucial role in international trade; the twice-yearly Canton Fair – known officially as the 'Export Commodities Fair' – began in 1957; held at an exhibition hall on the north bank of the Pearl River in Guangzhou it provided the opportunity for western wholesale buyers to scrutinize Chinese goods.[27] And there were those powerful links of family, too: a majority percentage of the Chinese diaspora internationally have family roots in Guangdong.

Deng's trip of 1984 had been undertaken in order to assess the development of the Special Economic Zones, for which he took both credit and responsibility. He commented during the tour that the idea of the SEZs had been his suggestion, though he wanted to see for himself whether they were a success.[28] By the time he had finished his tour, however, and having witnessed the emerging prosperity and growth, Deng was unequivocal. 'In establishing Special Economic Zones and implementing an open policy, we must make it clear that our guideline is just that – to open and not to close'.[29] He wrote an inscription during his visit: 'The development and experience of Shenzhen prove that our policy of establishing the Special Economic Zones is correct'. Of the Zhuhai SEZ across the Pearl River he wrote in more modest but still complimentary terms that: 'The Zhuhai Special Economic Zone is a success'.

Deng's first Southern Tour would draw a line under the initial phase of China's economic reform. Upon his return to the capital, Deng gave a talk to top party leaders affirming the pace of change he had witnessed in Shenzhen, endorsing the motto that 'Time is Money, Efficiency is Life' and encouraging the establishment of other, similar areas around China. 'As we develop the coastal areas successfully, we shall be able to increase people's incomes, which accordingly will lead to higher consumption,' he told the assembled leaders. He repeated his belief that this development would, for now, be unequal: 'We shall allow some areas to become rich first; egalitarianism will not work'.[30]

There were, however, many in the party who remained deeply sceptical about such an approach, concerned that, in releasing the state's grip on the economy and encouraging private enterprise, free markets and foreign investment, the Chinese people would potentially become subject to the corrupting appeal of bourgeois ways of thinking. The chaos of the Cultural Revolution had been awful, but a gradual drift towards capitalism could be even more destructive, the sceptics argued. One critic had commented the previous year that 'nothing in Shenzhen is socialist except for its five-starred flag,' adding that the city was 'practically like Hong Kong'.[31]

The most prominent critic of the approach represented by the Special Economic Zones was Chen Yun. A year younger than Deng, and, with his lupine face and imposing stature, a notable physical contrast, Chen was one of the so-called 'Eight Elders' of the party.

Chen had grown up in the farmland out to the west of Shanghai, and as a teenager became a committed organizer for the Chinese Communist Party (CCP) in the city, with which he would retain a close association for the rest of his life. Chen was central to the planning of China's economic development for most of the first decade of CCP rule, and opposed Mao's policies of the late 1950s which led to the Great Famine, resulting in forced self-criticism and his later persecution as a 'rightist'.

Chen had been key in rousing support for Deng's political rehabilitation in the years after the Cultural Revolution, and would be central to developing and promoting economic policy in the early years of Deng's rule, having been appointed as head of the Economic and Financial Commission in 1979. Chen did not object to the market having a role in China's economy – indeed, in the 1950s, Chen had argued for the importance of the market. But he believed that markets should be corralled within a state-controlled plan which emphasized steady but not excessive growth, and invoked a famous metaphor to describe his approach, in which he argued that the socialist economy was like a bird in a cage. If the cage was too small, the bird would not survive; if the cage was left open, the bird would fly away. Chen did not specify the size of the cage, saying that it should be appropriate, and be readjusted from time to time, but he argued that 'enlivening the economy and regulation through the market can only operate within the framework of state plans, and must not depart from the guidance of planning'.³²

Chen's views, and the loose coalition of leaders seen to be allied with him, came to be defined by their critics as 'leftist' or 'conservative', after their desire to retain the key principles of the old Leninist system: 'Chen Yun's economic thinking is characterized by emphasizing the planned economy, although it does not exclude the importance of market regulation,' one journalist reported his sources within the party leadership as observing in 1984. 'But some people in the party who are more emancipated have attached greater importance to the market economy'. The article went on to quote a party leader who implicitly criticized Chen's adherence to old models, such as those he had overseen in the 1950s: '[S]ome methods and policies at present, which are the continuation of those of the 1950's and 1960's, do not suit the present situation'.³³ By 1984, as Deng and his leadership lauded the success of Shenzhen, and embarked on policies encouraging faster growth, and more marketization and foreign investment in the Chinese economy, the gap between Chen and Deng had widened irrevocably, and Chen and his allies began to openly question whether the reforms being pursued could be considered socialist at all: 'Chen Yun held that phenomena not in conformity with, and even running counter to, socialist principles had emerged in Shenzhen, which would exert very bad influence on the economic life of the whole country', one journalist noted in 1985.³⁴

The objections put forward against the Special Economic Zones were not just ideological, however. With money and lack of central control had inevitably come corruption. Business deals in the SEZs became predicated on relationships – with other businessmen, customs officials, local cadres, the military – which were cultivated by offering favours: gifts of luxury items, expensive meals and often cash bribes. Meanwhile, smugglers ran televisions, cassette players and pocket calculators into Guangdong: the unlikely haul of fishing vessels in the South China Sea. A report from 1979–80 recorded the illegal importation of 180,000 wristwatches, 250,000 televisions, nearly 500,000 cassette players and 1.1 million calculators.³⁵ At various points in the 1980s, campaigns would be launched to address such malfeasance – including the building of the fence and barbed wire 'Second Line' – but the problems never truly went away.

Despite the cautioning voices, in the months after his Southern Tour of 1984, a further fourteen cities would be designated as Open Coastal Cities, offering similar possibilities of economic experimentation (though the choice of name acknowledged just how controversial the Special Economic Zones remained, and the rules applying to them were less permissive). As an editorial in the *People's Daily*, the official newspaper of the central committee of the CCP, would explain in May 1984, 'Comrade Deng Xiaoping has pointed out that there is a guiding ideology in instituting the open-door policy that must be explicitly stated, and that is, we are opening up, not retracting. Further opening up the 14 coastal port cities to the world is precisely a major new step taken to this end'.³⁶

During the grand celebrations for the thirty-fifth anniversary of the People's Republic of China in October 1984, one float carried the slogan he had endorsed during his trip: 'Time is Money, Efficiency is Life'. In October of that year, after the party had adopted a resolution which supported a move towards freer markets and reduction in central planning, Deng gave a speech welcoming the document, and reiterating a call for the country to quadruple its GDP by the year 2000. 'This is something feasible, tangible and within our grasp,' he said. 'But we shall not be able to reach this new target without the policy of opening to the outside world'.³⁷

*

Today, from the revolving restaurant at the top of Shenzhen's International Trade Centre, the view is of skyscrapers all around, many of which tower above it: the city's current tallest building is nearly 400 metres higher than this earlier monument to vertical aspiration. Ruling off the grid of the city are the same perpendicular highways, though far broader and busier, leading the eye off in each direction to a horizon that resolves itself from city to countryside only where low hills spring up, or where to the south the view across the river shows the almost unchanged farmland of Hong Kong's New Territories. Shenzhen is home to over 17.5 million people; Guangdong is China's most populous and economically important province. If it were a country, it would rank thirteenth globally in terms of GDP.

From the top of the International Trade Centre, it is two short lift rides and a twenty-minute stroll along those busy highways to Fishermen's Village. The village itself is now entirely unrecognizable from the orderly grid of low houses Deng saw in 1984. On his first visit, Deng had viewed the village as a model for the rest of China: an example of the *xiaokang* or 'moderate prosperity' he wished to encourage. By the time of his second visit to Shenzhen, its symbolism had become more complex: in 1992, Fishermen's Village had become a dense mass of so-called 'handshake' buildings, built cheaply by locals to rent to the migrant workers who would, for low wages and in punitive conditions, drive the city's economic transformation. The name was derived from the fact that the buildings were so cramped and close together that one could hang out the window to shake the hand of the occupant of the building opposite. Today, land reclamation projects have channelized the Shenzhen River; where once were rice fields are high rises and a multi-lane highway. The centre of the village is dominated by obliquely set pink pastel apartment towers of varying height with small shops and restaurants at their base.

In the winter of 2012, China's new leader Xi Jinping would make a visit to this shrine of reform and opening, in knowing homage to Deng. Official figures from 2019 recorded the average household income for villagers – now owners of valuable rental property in one of the most prosperous cities in the world – at 600,000 yuan or about 90,000 US$.

Leading from the entrance of Fishermen's Village to its centre there is a 350-metre pillared corridor, presenting a series of murals which set out sequentially the story of Deng's visit, the village, and its place in the official chronology that has been imposed upon the city – the story of how Shenzhen got from there to here. In this official version, Shenzhen grew exponentially and straightforwardly from small fishing village – from *this* small fishing village – to miracle city and global economic powerhouse. It is a narrative smoothed and shaped to fit the bigger, equally worked story of reform and opening the party likes to tell itself and others – in preference to a tumultuous reality far harder to relate in such linear simplicity.

In the party's version of this story, Deng's second Southern Tour of 1992 is generally presented devoid of context. A 2014 editorial for the *Global Times* remarks euphemistically of the Tour that 'reforms were not carried out smoothly, and Deng was surrounded by all kinds of differing opinions and complexities. But he was able to prove that he was right. Heroes like Deng are products of their times, and they also shape history'.[38]

Deng's tour would certainly shape history, but the cause and effect of his journey in 1992 is far more complex. By the time he set out that January, China's economy had undoubtedly seen rapid progress towards the ambitious goal he had set out in 1984 of quadrupling GDP, with growth averaging around 12 per cent in the initial years after his visit. But the fragile – some might say superficial – consensus that had briefly seemed to have been established after his first Southern Tour had fractured once more.

The growth the country had seen in the intervening years had been geographically and demographically uneven, and was stalked by the pernicious duo of corruption and inflation as the economy began to overheat. The Special Economic Zones themselves had endured vocal criticism and even accusations of failure, as internal factional debates raged about China's policy of opening to the outside world. Deng himself was frailer, deafer, eight years older, and had lost his two chosen deputies and potential successors: Hu Yaobang and Zhao Ziyang. Most significantly, and tragically, the streets of China's cities had witnessed a night of unprecedented, unforgettable violence, sanctioned by Deng, in the early summer of 1989.

Beginning in late 1988, Deng Xiaoping had been forced to watch on as leaders began to change course, more stridently and openly questioning the controversial policies he had advocated over the course of the prior decade, and consequently putting in place significant countermeasures, rolling back his reforms and slowing China's economic growth.

When Deng arrived back in the Special Economic Zone of Shenzhen on his Southern Tour of 1992 he was there not to bestow his approval on the city, but rather to employ it as rhetorical example and practical manifestation of the policies he believed were essential to safeguarding the country's and party's future – as well as his own legacy. His visit would attempt to shore up support for his approach, and aim direct criticism of the faction, with Chen Yun as the figurehead, who had long opposed Shenzhen and all it represented. 'Nobody is listening to me now,' Deng had complained the previous year.[39] Like Mao before him, he would set out from his capital in order to make himself heard.

Chapter 1

BEIJING, 1989

Above Beijing's imperial centre rises Prospect Hill. Its eponymous view was once reserved for members of the emperor's household; today you can buy a cheap ticket and climb a steep, short incline on well-laid steps through pine trees to the pagoda which crowns it.

From this busy terrace, you can look out to the cardinal points of the city. To the south, the dull gold roofs of the Forbidden City crest and fall, pulling the eye southward to Tiananmen – the Gate of Heavenly Peace – and the vast Square just beyond. To the east are the smooth metallic skyscrapers of the Central Business District, which seem to glare at the old, low-rise version of Beijing and say: this is how you build a city. To the north, just off a busy main road, you can almost make out the archway entrance to Miliangku Hutong, or 'Rice Depot Alley', on which Deng Xiaoping's old house still stands.

Stretching all along the western periphery are the calm-grey, willow-lined waters of the lakes which gifted the city this view. Drawing water from the Jade Spring high in the hills to the city's northwest, they were dug by hand for the pleasure of the emperors. Soil from the lakes was piled in a great heap to form this solitary peak on the otherwise frying-pan flat plain of Beijing.

This view is one that China's leaders would prefer you did not see – though even they cannot subvert geography. For the two most southerly of this chain of lakes, and the expansive grounds and buildings which surround them, have, since 1950, formed the leadership compound of the CCP. These are *Zhongnanhai* – meaning 'middle and southern lakes' – a name that has now become metonymic of China's ruling elite. Around the two lakes are scattered a mixture of repurposed imperial pavilions, temples, houses and grey modern offices. Zhongnanhai was once part of the protected space of the Imperial City, a vast pleasure park and escape from the sometimes claustrophobic courtyards of the Forbidden City. Today, the whole site is off-limits once again, ringed by a high red-ochre wall and patrolled assiduously by uniformed and plain-clothed police.

After the communist victory of 1949, Mao Zedong was initially suspicious of establishing himself in the imperial heart of Beijing – it is said that he refused ever to enter the Forbidden City – but, after a brief stay in a villa out in the hills to the west of the capital, he moved into Zhongnanhai in late 1949, establishing the former imperial garden as the nexus of China's fledgling administrative apparatus.

Over the subsequent decades, the pavilions, offices and gardens of Zhongnanhai were stage and scenery for much of the political drama of China's late twentieth century. Mao's two residences within the compound were the focal point for much of this: the cut and thrust of internal party debate, as well as key meetings with foreign leaders; in the book-lined rooms he moved into in 1966, which adjoined Zhongnanhai's indoor swimming pool, he met with Kissinger and Nixon to discuss the resumption of harmonious relations between the United States and China.[1]

Many of the most historically significant political events to occur at Zhongnanhai, however, have taken place in Huairen Hall: the 'Hall of Cherished Compassion'.[2] The hall, which sits on the western bank of the long, lozenge-shaped Middle Lake, was an addition to the imperial park during the late Qing dynasty, but was then extensively remodelled by the CCP in the early 1950s to impart a more august socialist grandeur. It is a broad, imposing ceremonial hall with staggered roofs of glazed green tile falling in curved lines to upturned corners; the facade is of austere grey brick interrupted by red wooden pillars, windows and doors. The building's capacious interior houses a large auditorium, as well as numerous smaller meeting rooms. These chambers have seen interminable party meetings, vitriolic debate, political ambush, accusations, arrests and heart-attacks.

On Friday, 9 June 1989 Deng Xiaoping arrived at Huairen Hall after a short car ride from his house. Deng Xiaoping had long preferred to avoid meetings at Zhongnanhai; his hearing had been poor for many years, and he favoured intimate conversations at his house, sending a trusted surrogate to the leadership compound. But this was a meeting with a very public purpose: portions of Deng's speech to an assembly of military leaders would be broadcast that night on the national television news across China – and subsequently relayed all over the world.

The summer heat had yet to properly set in, though barely a breeze caught the stooping branches of the willows around the middle and southern lakes. Inside Huairen Hall, dressed in a light grey-blue Mao suit, Deng greeted tiered ranks of uniformed military leaders, shaking hands and receiving broad smiles. He began his address by expressing a deep grief at the loss of soldiers and police on the night of 3 June – without a mention of the hundreds, possibly thousands, of Chinese civilians who had been killed by those forces – many of them on the streets immediately outside the compound of Zhongnanhai. Together, they stood in silence as a 'tribute to the martyrs'.[3]

Deng declared that the protests had been inevitable – that, given what was happening both in China and the wider world, they would have occurred sooner or later: better now, because there were enough veterans in the party who understood how best to deal with them. He praised the People's Liberation Army (PLA) for their approach. 'In short,' he said, 'this was a test and you passed it'.

Deng expressed little contrition or sympathy for the protestors. He portrayed those who had turned out in their thousands in cities across China as a mixture of the misguided and the dissolute. In his speech it was asserted that a small minority were responsible for the unrest – the 'dregs of society', as he described them, whose aim was to overthrow the state and the party. A report three days previously similarly divided those wounded in the military crackdown into two categories: a handful of lawless ruffians, and 'the onlooking masses who do not understand the situation'.[4] These were categorizations that helped the CCP avoid confronting the realities of mass protest, but both in terms of the constituencies involved and their aims, it was a misreading of the facts. Deng and most fellow party elders had not visited the square; some had been escorted to a room on the third floor of the Great Hall of the People, a Socialist-Realist wedding cake of a building on the western flank of Tiananmen Square, where all they could see was crowds and tents and litter: a visual echo for those veterans of the disorder of the Cultural Revolution, when Tiananmen Square had also been filled with raucous students. From a distant quiet room on the top floor of the Great Hall of the People, the distinction was difficult to discern.[5]

Two months earlier, in April 1989, another, fairly routine, meeting had been taking place at Huairen Hall. This gathering of the Politburo was notable, however, for the attendance of seventy-three-year-old former General Secretary of the party, Hu Yaobang.

Hu had become party leader, and thus one of Deng's key deputies, in 1981, and was in post for six tumultuous years as the reform and opening process variously stuttered and accelerated forward. He had, though, been forced to resign from his post early in 1987; on 16 January, a state media announcement had declared that his resignation had come after making 'a self-criticism of his mistakes on major issues of political principles in violation of the party's principle of collective leadership'.[6] Hu had failed to act decisively enough, in Deng's view, in suppressing student protests that had erupted the prior December in support of political liberalization. Ever since, he had been held in great regard by those eager for political change in China, though Hu had reportedly spent the subsequent two years reading books, refining his calligraphy and generally avoiding meetings of the Politburo, of which he remained a nominal member.[7]

On the agenda that morning of 8 April was the question of reforms in education. Rumour has continued to swirl around what happened during the course of the discussion.[8] In an officially contested version of the meeting, the debate became heated, with Hu becoming 'overagitated' before ultimately passing out and suffering a heart attack. He was rushed to hospital. On Saturday 15 April, one week on, he suffered another heart attack and died.

Though Hu was not the political radical some construed him as, his death would be the spark that ignited protests in Beijing and across the country. As one student would later reflect: 'In Chinese culture, there's a phenomenon I'd call the cult of the dead. After death, all the man's flaws are forgotten and his memory is enshrined in a halo of glory. Then people use the dead man to vent their anger and express their hopes'.[9]

After Hu's death on 15 April, it was initially students from Beijing's universities who had gathered, both on their campuses and in the imperial heart of the city around Tiananmen, to commemorate the former party chief and rail against a range of issues they felt they and the country faced.

'Mourners placed wreaths in front of the Monument to the People's Heroes in Tiananmen square,' state media reported two days after Hu's death. 'A veteran communist among the mourners told *Xinhua* that Hu contributed a lot to the rehabilitation of veteran cadres and made frequent visits to poor people in grassroots units. "He always thought of the people and I have come here to express my respects from the bottom of my heart"'.[10]

This initial groundswell of public feeling would grow, as would the numbers drawn to Tiananmen Square. Many were inspired by the promise of rejuvenating China, modelling themselves on the intellectuals of the May 4th Movement, who seventy years previously had protested in front of Tiananmen with a desire to renew and intellectually strengthen the country. (Indeed, 1989 was a significant revolutionary year, being the 200th anniversary of the French Revolution as well as the 40th anniversary of the Chinese Communist revolution.) Later the movement in the capital would grow to incorporate – sometimes awkwardly – students from across the country, as well as ordinary Beijingers from all manner of professions and walks of life.

Given the fluctuating make-up of the protestors, it is unsurprising that the aims of the protests were so compellingly heterogeneous, defined by a collection of nouns which meant different things to different participants. Whilst democracy and freedom were the most abstractly aspirational of these, the fact was that the iniquities of China's economy had become a significant source of discontent over recent years.

Unemployment was on the rise, and the jobs that were available tended to be low-wage, low-skill – and thus unappealing to university graduates. Inflation had been running in double digits, meaning those on fixed salaries were struggling to make ends meet. Government officials, on state-determined wages, turned with increasing frequency to corrupt methods to bolster their income, breeding resentment and distrust. Rumours abounded about party cadres, and their children, making illicit fortunes from the black market. One survey of the student movement at Tiananmen found that ending corruption was the most widely shared goal of the protestors.[11]

Deng acknowledged in his 9 June speech that mistakes had been made in not dealing with this issue.

> In the early 1980s when the Special Economic Zones were established, I told comrades in Guangdong that we should do two types of work at the same time: carrying out the policies of reform and opening on the one hand and cracking down on economic crime on the other, including ideological and political work. […] But looking back over the years, we can see obvious deficiencies in what we did.

Though Deng invited those listening to ponder the best path forward, he was clear in his conclusions. 'The important thing is that we must never turn China back into a country that keeps its doors closed,' he said. 'Our basic ideas […] including the policies of reform and opening to the outside, are correct'.

Deng had been seen in public with decreasing frequency over recent months. Observers in the outside world were struggling to discern where power now lay in the upper echelons of the CCP, and there was continued speculation around the state of Deng's health. His speech at Zhongnanhai on 9 June was an assertion of authority. His choice of audience was telling: Deng's only official position was as Chairman of the Central Military Commission – effectively Commander-in-Chief – and his speech was intended to offer a reminder to those watching on, both in the party and country, that Deng still retained the all-important support of his military leaders.

One person conspicuously absent from the 9 June meeting at Huairen Hall was the second most important politician in China: Zhao Ziyang, former Premier and now General Secretary – the man who had replaced Hu Yaobang at the top of the party in 1987.

Ten days later, another meeting would formalize Zhao's political disappearance. He would spend most of the rest of his life – nearly sixteen years – as a self-described 'prisoner of the state', in a modest courtyard house to the east of the old city. His ouster would mean that, within two and a half years, Deng had seen his two chosen deputies, Hu and Zhao – his left and right hands, as he once called them – removed from the key leadership positions he had elevated them to.

Zhao's charge sheet was short and simple: he had offered his public support to the protestors at Tiananmen in the weeks before the final massacre. As the later judgement of the party put it, 'Comrade Zhao Ziyang committed the serious mistake of supporting turmoil and splitting the Party, and had the unshirkable responsibility for the shaping up and development of the turmoil'.[12]

On 23 April, the day after Hu Yaobang's memorial service at the Great Hall of the People, Zhao had left Beijing on the overnight train for Pyongyang on a state visit to North Korea. By the time he returned a week later, the government response to the protest had substantially toughened, with the publication of a front-page editorial in the *People's Daily* on 26 April entitled 'It is necessary to take a clear-cut stand against turmoil'. In the intervening week, and in Zhao's absence, Deng had apparently heard reports from Li Peng and President Yang Shangkun which led him to label the student demonstrations as 'anti-Party, anti-socialist turmoil'.[13] A small number of people, the editorial argued, had taken advantage of the grief of young people at the death of Hu Yaobang. But however small the number, the editorial projected malign motives to the protests' current form: 'This is a planned conspiracy and a disturbance,' it read. 'Its essence is to, once and for all, negate the leadership of the CPC [Communist Party of China] and the socialist system'.[14]

Once he was back in Beijing, Zhao attempted to repair relations, stating his belief that the protestors were patriotic, and assuring them that the Party shared their desire to end corruption.[15] According to Soviet leader Mikhail Gorbachev, Zhao saw the issue as one of generational difference: 'Right now there is the sense of a lack of mutual understanding between Party and state institutions on one side and young people and students on the other,' he told Gorbachev during a visit which coincided with the protests. 'We don't understand their moods well, and they don't really understand us'.[16]

Zhao's sympathetic perspective was not shared by others in the leadership, however – including Deng Xiaoping. The inevitable conflict came on 17 May. Zhao had asked that day to see Deng alone at his house; when he arrived, he found the rest of the Politburo Standing Committee already there.[17] 'I realized,' he wrote, 'that things had already taken a bad turn'. The group sat in a horseshoe of comfortable armchairs with Deng at the centre, positioned in front of a table displaying the trophies he had won playing bridge. Zhao addressed the group, pleading for a more moderate approach. 'If we take a confrontational stance with the masses,' he concluded, 'a dangerous situation could ensue in which we lose complete control'.

As Zhao spoke, Deng grew visibly displeased. He had made the decision to bring the PLA into Beijing and declare martial law; if they were to back down, Deng said, the situation would spiral completely out of control.

Two days later, in the early hours of the morning, Zhao made a visit to the protestors in Tiananmen Square. With his greying hair neatly brushed back, oversized dark-framed glasses and blue Mao suit, his appearance stood in stark contrast to the dishevelled and exhausted students who crushed around him in one of the buses parked on the square. Holding a red and black megaphone, he pleaded with those on hunger strike to cease, and believe in the possibility of ongoing dialogue. They were young, he said, and should look forward to the modernization of China. Yet, in many ways, the opening words of his speech had said it all. 'Students, we have come too late,' he had begun.

Those on the square, Zhao wrote later, did not understand what he meant: 'Even less could they imagine the treatment in store for them'.[18] On 20 May, martial law was publicly declared, and military units advanced on the city, only to find the roads blocked by protestors who had learnt of their impending arrival. The army would end up having to retreat, though this was but a temporary reprieve.

On the night of 3 June, the army returned, moving determinedly along the main avenues leading to Tiananmen Square. In the late hours of summer darkness, Zhao sat in the courtyard of his family home on Fuqiang Hutong and listened to the echoes of gunfire across the city.

Zhao Ziyang was a generation younger than Deng Xiaoping, born in 1919 to a well-to-do family in land-locked Henan province. He joined the CCP in 1938, and remained committed to its ideals even when his father was murdered by party forces in the 1940s for being a 'rich landlord'. Zhao did not suffer through the Long March of 1934–5 – the epic journey undertaken, at great human cost, to relocate the communist headquarters from southern to northern China – a journey in which Hu Yaobang had proved his revolutionary credentials by nearly dying.

Zhao's rite of passage, like so many others in this story of reform, had been the Cultural Revolution. In 1967, during the revolution's most savage phase, he was purged and sent to work in a Hunan factory for four years, having been paraded before his exile through the streets of Guangzhou wearing a dunce cap, and labelled a 'stinking remnant of the landlord class'.[19] Zhao had been high in the leadership of Guangdong Province, where he had experimented with reforming the economy. In total, Zhao spent nearly two decades of his career in Guangdong; this gave him, in his own words, 'an earlier and deeper understanding of the international market and foreign trade'.[20] In the early 1960s, Zhao had written to the Central Committee to ask for permission to increase foreign trade in Guangdong – an experiment that helped the economy there recover from the punishing years of the Great Leap Forward.

In 1975, at the tail end of the Cultural Revolution, and after his political rehabilitation, Zhao was sent to Sichuan, China's largest province, where he pioneered policies which rewarded productivity and offered greater autonomy to farmers and factory managers. Conditions were so trying when he arrived in Sichuan that there were stories of peasants offering to exchange their children for ration cards. Zhao's policies increased industrial output by 81 per cent within three years.[21] As one Sichuan saying put it, playing on his family name, '*Yao chi liang, zhao Ziyang*' – 'If you want to eat, find (*zhao*) Ziyang'.

In 1979, his career in the party now firmly in the ascendancy, Zhao travelled to Europe, visiting the UK, France, Greece and Switzerland. In southern France he noticed that, rather than fighting the hot and arid climate, local people had established vineyards. Likewise, in Greece, hilly regions that in China would have been made into terraces – difficult to irrigate and maintain – were instead given over to profitable olive groves. Why were they able to do this, Zhao asked himself? 'Because they were not living in an autarky,' he wrote later, 'but instead relied on trade with the outside world and utilized their strengths to export their goods in exchange for what they needed'.[22] Adopting a policy of self-sufficiency had meant that China was not doing what it did best. He recognized that being integrated into the international marketplace was essential.

Deng, impressed by Zhao's work in Sichuan, promoted him to the national leadership after his own elevation in 1978; in 1980 Zhao became China's premier, and essentially second-in-command.

Zhao Ziyang oversaw many of China's key economic reforms during the 1980s, and pioneered the policies that saw the coastal areas of China – Guangdong in particular – become engines of prosperity. 'I am a layman in the field of economics,' Deng said in 1984. 'I have made a few remarks on the subject, but all from a political point of view. For example, I proposed China's economic policy of opening to the outside world, but as for the details or specifics of how to implement it, I know very little indeed'.[23] Deng, though, created and sustained the political space in which Zhao was able to fill in those details and specifics. It was Deng's first Southern Tour of 1984 that allowed Zhao to move more purposefully forward with his vision of developing the cities that studded China's coastline. In 1987, Zhao told a meeting of party cadres that he wanted to 'throw [*shuai dao*] the coastal areas into the international market, [where they] would rely on the international market to develop'.[24]

In early 1988, Zhao put forward a new strategy for China's coastal areas, which consolidated his ideas of using them to drive prosperity across the whole nation. 'I came to believe,' Zhao wrote, 'that the international market provides the right conditions for our coastal regions to accelerate their development, because labor-intensive production will always shift to places where labor is abundant and cheap'.[25] Deng immediately approved it.

By the end of June 1989, however, Zhao had become unmentionable, banished to his courtyard home. He never saw Deng Xiaoping again, and he would be functionally erased from the party's history – with direct credit for many of his policies later handed to Deng, whose centrality in the official narrative of the 1980s is partly a consequence of the political perils of foregrounding Zhao in any discussion of the era.

Early in his confinement, Zhao attempted to test the ill-defined restrictions under which he was living. In the autumn of 1990, he declared that he intended to play a round of golf at Changping Golf Course, to the north of the city. (His love of the bourgeois game had always raised eyebrows amongst his more austere colleagues.) His secretary was told to advise Zhao against it; when Zhao persisted, the authorities ordered his assigned chauffeur not to drive him. Zhao replied by telling them he would take the bus. After frenzied discussion, it was decided that his chauffeur could drive him – but only if accompanied by a police car. The golf course was part-owned by a Japanese company, and word of Zhao's reappearance quickly got back to the Japanese Embassy. The news was reported internationally, much to the frustration of China's new leaders, who preferred to keep the man who might have been China's Gorbachev firmly out of frame. 'After this disturbance,' wrote Zhao, 'they notified me [...] that I was prohibited from going out during the investigation'.[26]

During the summer of 1989, Deng made the decision that at the age of eighty-five he would imminently relinquish his last official post as Chairman of the Central Military Commission and retire. He had talked about doing so for years, though his plans had been derailed by the ousting of Hu Yaobang in 1987; the recent purge of Zhao Ziyang had also not made the decision any more straightforward. 'At the time, given their experience in struggle, their achievements in work and their political and ideological level, [Hu and Zhao] were the best choices I could make,' Deng said in a talk with party leaders a week after his 9 June speech to the military at Huairen Hall. 'Besides,' he added pointedly, 'people change'.[27]

Retirement – and the transitions of power it implied – was a fraught concept for the party. Previous leaders had either been ousted, generally forcibly, or continued in post until they died; Mao Zedong and Premier Zhou Enlai had followed the old communist edict of working for the revolution 'with their last breath and last drop of blood'.[28] Such lifelong terms did 'not facilitate the renewal of leadership or the promotion of younger people', Deng said in 1980. 'It is an institutional defect which was not evident in the sixties because we were then in the prime of life'.[29]

In order to address this issue, he established the 'Central Advisory Commission' in 1982: a means of moving the old guard out of key positions of power, whilst still allowing them a say on the country's direction (often these happened to be party elders whom Deng felt were opposed to the reform agenda; Chen Yun would be tactically moved to become the commission's Chairman in 1987). Those who became members of the commission kept their salaries and ranks from their previous positions, and retained influence – often a great deal of influence – over the new generation who had replaced them.[30] The commission was an imperfect solution to the question of what to do with ageing cadres – and reflected the reality that authority in the country and party often had much less to do with official position than it did with political and military connections.

Deng told leaders in that June meeting that he planned to step back from decision-making, though he remained happy to help if needed – 'but it won't be the way it used to be'. As with the positions of those who had ascended into the Central Advisory Commission, there was a creative ambiguity to his framing – this was no straightforward transfer of power.

In part, this was because he knew that the man he had chosen to succeed him, sixty-two-year-old former mayor and party secretary of Shanghai Jiang Zemin, lacked a secure power base. Jiang was a newcomer to Beijing – indeed, he was initially billeted in modest temporary quarters in Zhongnanhai, constituting just a bedroom and an office. Jiang's strength, one observer commented, was 'his popularity, but in China that's not enough. He has no organisations behind him like the military or the state security organs'.[31]

The technocratic Jiang had established himself as an effective administrator at provincial level, but, most pertinently for Deng, had demonstrated resolve in dealing with dissent. He had quelled the student protests of late 1986 with a combination of characteristic showmanship – he recited the Gettysburg Address in English to a crowd of angry students, telling them they did not understand Lincoln's speech – and the deployment of party and security apparatus. He had also shuttered the *World Economic Herald*, China's most liberal newspaper, in the first phase of the Tiananmen protests of 1989, after it had planned to print speeches in support of Hu Yaobang and against state crackdowns on free expression.

There was however widespread scepticism at whether Jiang was adequately prepared for the job. 'We don't like him because we don't believe he has the qualifications to be General Secretary,' said a Chinese intellectual after his official promotion. 'He's only had municipal experience'.[32] He would later describe taking over the leadership at this fraught moment in the country's history as feeling like standing at the edge of a deep canyon.[33] Many assumed – some overtly hoped – he was simply a placeholder. Jiang would need, initially at least, Deng standing behind him.

In the rest of his 16 June speech, Deng had offered the leadership, including Jiang, a didactic itemization of what he believed China's future should look like. Economic development should continue – though the rate of growth, he acknowledged, shouldn't be as high as previously planned. Reform and opening to the outside world, however, should in general be pursued with 'greater daring', whilst simultaneously tackling corruption. In a dig at those who said the policies of economic reform had caused the protests, he told the leadership: 'In this incident there were no slogans against reform and opening to the outside world, but one of the slogans frequently chanted was the demand to combat corruption'.

In September, he spoke once more to leaders about his retirement at a meeting at his home. Part of his speech referenced the seismic changes unfolding in Eastern Europe. In Poland, in Hungary, in Estonia, Latvia and Lithuania, people were coming together to protest communist rule. 'The problem now is not whether the banner of the Soviet Union will fall – there is bound to be unrest there – but whether the banner of China will fall,'[34] Deng said. What was most important was avoiding similar turmoil in China – and continuing 'genuine' reform and opening to the wider world. As a supportive editorial in the *People's Daily* would put it that same month, 'We must continue to practice the open policy, to bring foreign capital, technology, advanced management experiences, and so on into China for our own use, so as to speed up our country's modernization. We will be unswerving in this respect. We certainly must not stop eating for fear of choking'.[35] Deng went on to reaffirm his support for Jiang Zemin, telling them that the collective of the party leadership must have a core. The past few years had seen, he noted, two leaders in need of replacement and problems with inflation. 'Because we had a core,' he said, 'it was easy to solve those problems'.

On 9 November, the temperature dropped in Beijing: a harbinger of a long winter to come. Sleet blustered in the north wind which swept through the narrow lanes of the grey capital. Deng Xiaoping rose that morning as normal and worked through a pile of papers. He took lunch with his family, and then, at around 4 pm, he was driven the short journey south past Zhongnanhai to the Great Hall of the People.[36]

After a short speech, accompanied by photos and rousing applause, the retirement ceremony was over; he had requested a simple event without too much eulogizing. Deng said his goodbyes to the smiling leaders who crowded around him, and returned to his motorcade for the journey back home: the house was brightly lit for his arrival.

His grandchildren had made him a card, with four butterflies on the front, and a written message: 'Wish Grandpa to be as young as we are, for ever and ever.' The family's cook of thirty years prepared a banquet of Deng's favourite dishes; the adults drank red wine and joined together to celebrate his six-decade career. On the wall of the dining room was a bright red poster made to commemorate the occasion: '1922–1989– Eternity,' it read.

That night East German border officer Harold Jaeger defied the orders of his superiors and opened the barrier in the Berlin Wall at Bornholmer Street. Tens of thousands of East Berliners crossed into West Germany. By the time Deng awoke in the cold dawn of 10 November, the world had changed.

The front page of the Friday 10 November edition of *The New York Times* featured a banner headline: 'East Germany Opens Frontier to the West for Emigration or Visits; Thousands Cross'. The second most prominent story, above a photo of Deng Xiaoping shaking the hand of a smiling Jiang Zemin, carried the headline: 'Deng is Resigning Last Formal Post with China Party: Senior Leader is Replaced on Military Commission but He Still Holds Power'.

Chapter 2

UNFINISHED BUSINESS

As deep cold thickens water, winter slowed the pace of life in Beijing. Along Rice Depot Alley, behind the high blue gates of Deng Xiaoping's house, life settled into a gentler rhythm now official responsibilities were dispensed with – though Deng had always been one for routine.

He rose at eight and after breakfast – often fried dough sticks, or *youtiao*, accompanied by warm soy milk – he would read for an hour or two: newspapers, official reports, books. Deng generally worked reclined in his study, with his grandchildren often playing nearby on the hard wood floor. His study was a large, high-ceilinged room with tall windows. Four comfortable beige armchairs arced underneath the window, and a chaise-longue was pushed up against the wall. There was a desk, adjacent to the door and beside some glass-fronted bookshelves, but he almost never worked behind it.

In late morning, he would set out for his morning constitutional, walking the paved path around his garden: 188 metres anticlockwise. In his early seventies, he set his goal at twenty laps of the courtyard. As he got older, he reduced his quota to ten, though still set a fierce pace. The garden was dense with trees: cedar, lacebark pine, Chinese flowering crab-apple, walnut and cherry. In 1977, when Deng and his family had first moved into this two-storey house, the garden had been filled with crops grown by soldiers; growing flowers and plants for decoration had been thought inappropriately decadent during the years of the Cultural Revolution. Deng had kept some of the original trees, got rid of the crops, and planned and planted this well-ordered garden.

His morning routine was replicated after a midday lunch and nap – reading, and a walk. For his 6.30 pm dinner, Deng's preference was for 'four dishes and one soup' – a modest spread, normally drawing on the cuisine of his home province, Sichuan, enlivened by dried chilli and Sichuan pepper. Leftovers would be kept for the following day. After dinner, Deng would play bridge or billiards, or watch television. 'His way of living was too regular, too common,' his daughter commented.[1]

For those who had taken part in the protests of May and June that year, life had been stripped of any regularity.

In the months following the massacre on the night of 3 June, security forces had scoured the country for those involved. Many fled abroad, often escaping by a long overland trip to Guangdong, and then across the border to Hong Kong. For those who stayed, however, precarious weeks or months almost inevitably concluded with their arrest. The authorities endeavoured to track down anyone involved in the protests, no matter how tangentially, with public security bureaus told not to be too fastidious in their approach to these mass arrests.[2] The government attempted to sway public opinion against the protestors by publishing photos of dead PLA soldiers in national newspapers; a hotline was set up to allow members of the public to report known participants. On the day after Deng's 9 June speech at Huairen Hall alone, the Beijing authorities reported the arrest of more than 400 people.[3]

Once detained, protestors were beaten, tortured with tasers and crammed together into tiny cells. In the Beijing prisons, scabies became rife; at night you could the sound of dozens of prisoners scratching their raw skin. Denied meaningful legal process, their extended confinement was a certainty: the only question was how long they would be imprisoned for.

Those sentenced to over ten years in prison were being held that autumn and winter in Beijing Municipal Prison No. 1, out in the anonymous suburbs of eastern Beijing. One protestor tells of being immediately sent into solitary confinement upon his arrival there: 'The summer passed and fall arrived. From a crack in my door, I could see the withered branches and fallen leaves everywhere. I saw prisoners assembling in the yard, singing, "The stars surround you and the moonlight goes with you"'.[4]

On 10 January 1990, Beijing's television news announced that 'In accordance with the order of the State Council of the People's Republic of China signed by Premier Li Peng', the authorities had, after 236 days, decided to end martial law in the city.[5] Tiananmen Square was reopened – with every square metre now surveyed by newly installed security cameras.[6] For those travelling by car past the square, along the Avenue of Eternal Peace which slices the centre of the old city, there was still an audible reminder of the events of June 1989: the faint rumble of car tyres running over the marks of tank tracks still engraved on the surface of the road.

2. Unfinished Business

Eleven days after the lifting of martial law, on 21 January, Deng set out southward from the capital. He would pass the lunar new year holiday in Shanghai, staying for nearly a month. This too was part of his routine – he would spend new year there every year from 1988 to 1994. And his association was long-standing; he had first visited the city in 1920, aged sixteen years, when he had disembarked in Shanghai after eight days aboard a steamship travelling down the Yangtze River.

His arrival in 1920 had marked the end of the first stage in a longer journey: along with eighty-two other students from his home province of Sichuan, the teenage Deng was on his way to France as part of a work-study programme organized by his school in Chongqing, one of Sichuan's major cities. He would not return to China until 1927. Deng had a week to explore Shanghai before the French ocean-liner, the *André-Lebon* set sail for Marseille.[7]

Deng had already docked at the great river port of Wuhan as he progressed down the Yangtze, where, as in Shanghai, the river front was lined with the offices of international trading firms, consulates, hotels and banks: bombastic erections of grey stone which loomed over the river, their columns, domes and balustrades reflected in its filmy waters.

This was the architecture of the so-called Treaty Ports – cities handed over to foreign powers for the purposes of trade, following the enforced legal settlements after the Opium Wars between western nations and China in the mid-nineteenth century – the so-called 'Unequal Treaties'. In Shanghai's case, the signing of the Treaty of Nanking aboard *HMS Cornwallis* in August 1842 declared that British citizens, their families and establishments shall be allowed to reside in Shanghai, 'for the purpose of carrying on their Mercantile pursuits, without molestation or restraint'.

Shanghai had been divided up by colonial powers into separate zones. Stretching across the northern half of the city, and wrapping around the eastbound bend of the Huangpu River, was the International Settlement, established by the British, though incorporating many other nationalities by 1920. The French Concession was a rectangle of shaded streets to the south of the International Settlement into which the Chinese city, walled until 1912 and looking like a squashed circle, pushed north. Foreigners were in the minority in terms of Shanghai's population, though they squarely claimed the economic success of the city as their own: the unmistakable result of their civilizing influence in the years since the city was officially opened to foreign trade under terms of the Treaty of Nanking in 1843. 'Shanghai was nothing but a swamp through which flowed innumerable creeks connecting the large fertile plains beyond and forming a breeding place for the mosquito and malaria', one correspondent observed in 1919. 'With true British characteristics this place was turned from a useless swamp until to-day, boasting magnificent roads, and every modern convenience, except sewerage, priding itself on its local government and the modernity seldom excelled either in Europe or America, it is a city which might have been transplanted from any Occidental country'.[8]

Unlike other Chinese cities, with their enforced symmetry, the colonial version of Shanghai had spread messily along an asymmetrical web of roads stretching away from the screen of neoclassical and art-deco buildings along its already famous Bund – the name derived from the Hindustani word for embankment.[9] On the opposite bank of this clockwise river bend was Pudong – literally meaning 'east of the Huangpu River'.

By the time of Deng's visit in 1920, this flat semi-circle of land facing the Bund formed the functional obverse to its ostentatious architectural performance, which was still evolving into its most imposing form: many of the Bund's grandest buildings would be thrown up over the course of the next decade. The view across the murky water to Pudong showed planked wharves stretched into the river, dense with sampans and small, steam-powered cargo boats; low-rise brick warehouses and workshops spread out in plots belonging to trading firms and manufacturers. Behind this barrier of noise and industry were miles of small villages and rice fields stretching eastward to the sea.

Shanghai existed under foreign control for almost precisely a century. The dividing lines which segmented the city were shaded in contrasting colours on contemporary western maps of the city – with areas under Chinese control often simply left blank. By the time the communists took over in 1949, these internal boundaries no longer pertained, but the legacy of Shanghai as a divided city constructed in the image of western metropolises, and where Chinese people were subjugated by colonial rule, would shape its prospects for the next four decades.

Deng saw Shanghai in 1990 as a symbol of unfinished business. The city had not been a significant beneficiary of the policies of reform and opening piloted in the 1980s; indeed, its development had been consciously held back. In the early years of Deng's rule, there had been plans mooted for Special Economic Zones in Shanghai and nearby, but those suspicious of this new policy, including Chen Yun, argued that the area was 'famous for its concentration of opportunists who would, with their consummate skills, emerge from their cages if given the slightest chance'.[10] Others worried that Shanghai would become merely a foreign concession once more. The city was also communist China's greatest source of revenue – so was not a place where experimentation could be easily risked.

During his twenty-three-day visit in 1990, Deng met with various party and military leaders, pushing for faster development of the city, telling them that they should 'consider taking some major steps to raise the flag of "reform and opening up" to the international community'.[11] On a cold and snowy Lunar New Year's eve, he and his wife Zhuo Lin attended a celebration at the Jinjiang Hotel along with party and military officials, telling the assembled crowd 'I have come to Shanghai for Spring Festival, and I wish you New Year's greetings; and through you send New Year's greetings to the people of Shanghai'.[12]

On the evening of 13 February, the date of his planned return to the capital, Deng took a car through the busy streets to Shanghai's train station in the north of the city accompanied by Zhu Rongji, Mayor of Shanghai. Zhu was tall, with sharp, hawk-like features and nearly twenty-five years younger than Deng. But both shared a forthrightness and an ability to shift the political temperature through sheer force of will. The relationship they developed in Shanghai would shape China's economic future.

As they wound through the traffic, Deng and Zhu discussed the proposed development of Pudong, which remained a working landscape of low-rise buildings and farmland, not greatly dissimilar from that which the teenage Deng had seen seventy years ago on his first visit to the Bund.

'You've started late. But you can move quickly now,' Deng reassured him. 'The conditions in Shanghai are better than those in Guangdong, and your starting point can be higher'.[13] Zhu was at the time deeply concerned about the lack of modernization in the city, then home to around eight and a half million people. Due to the low growth of the last decade, the city had been notably outpaced by the SEZs, but Shanghai's neglect predated the era of reform and opening; the older parts of the city had outwardly altered little since the treaty port days, with overcrowding rife in cramped, tumbledown accommodation, whilst narrow congested roads and a lack of subway system meant traffic was a persistent problem (Shanghai's subway would finally open in 1993; Beijing's first line had opened to the public in 1971).

A couple of weeks later, Zhu would relate his thoughts on this conversation with Deng: 'We truly can only take the path of opening up and developing an externally oriented economy – this is the only way out,' he told Qiao Shi, another leader with long Shanghai associations. 'Otherwise, it will be impossible to solve a whole series of problems we face, such as housing, traffic, and pollution, and people's grievances will grow greater and greater. [...] I feel there is actually only one option, namely the policies used in the Shenzhen Special Economic Zone, but I didn't dare say so in my report'.[14]

On a spring day at the beginning of March, having been back from Shanghai for a little over two weeks, Deng summoned key leaders, including Jiang Zemin and Premier Li Peng, to his house on Rice Depot Alley to take them to task for what he saw as an existential problem with the current economic trajectory of the country.

'Why do people support us?' he asked them pointedly as they sat around him. 'Because over the last ten years our economy has been developing and developing visibly'.[15] They needed to pay closer attention to the drop in economic growth over the last two years, he told them. The slowdown in economic growth since 1988 had been substantial: in 1989, industrial growth had gone backwards for the first time in a decade, and economic growth was about one-third of the previous year. Wages fell; unemployment rose. Some workers said that the situation reminded them of the early 1960s, when China was recovering from the Great Leap Forward.[16]

This economic slowdown had resulted from policies that were implemented following rampant inflation and panic buying in 1988. As the summer heat had set in that year, Chinese people, troubled by reports that Zhao Ziyang and Deng Xiaoping planned to remove state controls on prices, had descended on their local banks to withdraw savings, determined to buy goods at today's prices. As radio stations in Beijing had reported that August, 'people who were oversensitive to prices and in a constant state of anxiety would associate any unusual sign in their economic life with a price hike. They brought along bags, buckets, and other kinds of containers, and lined up and waited in front of stores or markets.' It went on to report how at one store, in the aftermath of the removal of price controls on cigarettes and alcohol, customers 'assaulted the knitwear and textile products counter'.[17] Inflation, which had become a growing problem over the last few years, would hit well over 20 per cent over the course of the summer of 1988.[18]

Though the specific issue of price rises was dealt with fairly swiftly, those conservatives in the leadership who had long harboured concerns about Zhao's economic approach – those who said it was too capitalist, that it encouraged bourgeois thinking, that it gave away too much control, that it neglected the old state-owned firms at the expense of new private businesses – pressed home their advantage and continued to push for austerity, and a gradual undoing, or at least slowing, of many of the policies of the preceding decade. Zhao Ziyang would be sidelined; his mistake of not anticipating the psychological effect of merely discussing price reform allowed others opposed to overall reform to effectively defenestrate him, despite his nominal role as General Secretary. At an official photo session at Huairen Hall, Deng would ask him 'Why did Hong Kong newspapers report that you no longer manage economic affairs? How can you not be managing the economy anymore?'.[19]

There had seemed potential to loosen some of the new economic strictures in early 1989 – but then came Hu Yaobang's death and the protests of the spring and early summer – which would also lead to the definitive end of Zhao's political career. Leaders such as Premier Li Peng and Chen Yun, who had backed Li in becoming premier, would draw a direct causal connection between the economic approach of the 1980s, and in particular the corruption and bourgeois liberalization it had encouraged, and the events of June 1989. A journalist for Hong Kong's *Sing Pao* would report Chen's alleged view of the 'incident'. 'The central authorities and policy decision-makers should be responsible for the turmoil which took place in Beijing [...] For the people to hate and protest against corruption, bureaucracy, and decadent practices of the party and government is beyond reproach'.[20]

The strategies employed across 1988 and 1989 were broad. Price controls were reimposed; credit was restricted; government spending and provincial power were reined in; interest rates were raised; growth targets were lowered. 'They restored the old methods,' Zhao wrote of Li Peng and First Vice Premier Yao Yilin, who took charge in the aftermath of that chaotic summer, 'making major cutbacks through administrative means. Powers that had been handed down to lower levels were reclaimed, measures that had relied significantly on market mechanisms were abolished'.[21]

The feeling was that the state had, over the course of the last decade, gradually ceded too much control, and chased overly ambitious growth. As a new plan introduced in autumn of 1989 would put it, 'These difficulties did not just emerge suddenly in the last year or two; they are a concentrated reflection of deep-rooted problems that have accumulated over many years'.[22] In March of 1990, the economist Wan Dianwu would write similarly; that in the years after Deng's first

Southern Tour, 'with overheated economic development, swollen accumulation and consumption, salient contradictions between supply and demand, plus all contradictions in the course of the change from the old to the new structures, serious currency inflation and chaotic economic order emerged'. It was necessary, he wrote, to 'firmly establish the guiding ideology for sustained, steady and coordinated economic development and to overcome the tendency toward being overanxious for quick results'.[23]

There was regular repetition of this formula – 'sustained, steady and coordinated development'. Li Peng would use it frequently in articles and speeches; in October of 1989, he would give a speech emphasizing the need for restraint in economic development, in which he lauded the achievements of the last year in reducing demand, increasing levels of savings and reducing industrial growth: 'The growth rate is dropping in those areas which used to have an excessively high rate, such as the provinces of Guangdong, Fujian, Shandong, Jiangsu and Zhejiang'. He framed the 'rectification' process, as it became known, as a necessary period of austerity: 'Only by tightening our belts for several years, uniting as one, and struggling hard can we pass the barrier', he said.[24] In February of the following year, he would be in Shenzhen, telling leaders there that the province should 'guard against impatience for success. Guangdong should earnestly summarize its experience in reform and opening to the outside world and readjust its economic structure so as to develop the provincial economy at a more sustained, steady, and coordinated pace'.[25]

Deng, conversely, continued to fundamentally believe that rapid economic growth was the only way of avoiding instability: that rising unemployment and a lack of visible progress would leave party leaders with little by way of reassurance for a restive population. 'If the economy stagnated for five years or developed at only a slow rate […] what effects would be produced? This is not only an economic problem but a political one,' he told the leaders arrayed around him on that March day.[26] 'The people can tell very well what their standard of living is. We leaders can never calculate it so well as they do; their judgment is most accurate'. He implicitly rebuked Li Peng's target of 6 per cent growth, implying that it would not be enough to meet his lauded target of quadrupling gross national product by the year 2000. He went on to encourage the leaders to seize opportunities, adding that 'only when people have felt the tangible benefits that come with stability and with the current systems and policies will there be true stability'.

Deng also returned to the question of Shanghai. He was, as always, plain spoken, and did not soften his instructions with rhetoric or persuasion: 'It is of prime importance to develop Shanghai,' he told them, and then invoked a metaphor which belied his love of bridge: 'That city,' he said, 'is a trump card. By developing Shanghai we shall be taking a short cut'.

He ended with an unsubtle reminder of the larger undertaking they were embarked upon: that goal of quadrupling the country's gross national product by the year 2000 – this was, he said, a question he thought would keep the leadership up at night for the next decade. 'It is crucial for us to achieve rapid economic growth,' he said. The challenge was clear: a couple of years of more limited growth had been acceptable; now, however, he wanted to see an acceleration of those policies that had driven China's fast-paced expansion in the first decade of his rule – and for the development of Shanghai to spearhead this reinvigoration of reform.

On 18 April 1990, Premier Li Peng attended a ceremony in Shanghai celebrating the fifth anniversary of the Shanghai Volkswagen Corporation and gave a speech where he confirmed that 'some policies of the economic and technological development zones and the Special Economic Zones can be implemented in the Pudong area'. He welcomed future investors from Hong Kong, Macau and Taiwan: 'We will provide preferential conditions for cooperation and improve the investment environment,' added Li.[27]

But for all the Dengist rhetoric of this announcement, often touted as Pudong's 'birthday', progress remained slow in developing the eastern bank of the Huangpu during the rest of 1990. In October of that year, Zhu Rongji admitted that funding for the ambitious plans remained a problem; the government had given some money for the city's development, but 'to complete these projects quickly, we will still be in urgent need of large foreign investments'.[28] Some of this would come in the form of loans, but the city also needed to attract financing from foreign companies and banks – both in those places Li had referenced and further afield – all of which required convincing foreign investors that Shanghai had the right rules and regulations in place to safeguard their investment – and that the political situation in the country had stabilized sufficiently after the events of 1989.[29]

With progress, both in Shanghai and nationally, not as rapid as Deng would like, he was back in the city again at the beginning of 1991, leaving the capital aboard his private train on 27 January. He would stay for just over three weeks, once again pushing local officials to move faster. On 18 February, Deng addressed Zhu Rongji and other local officials in the revolving restaurant on the forty-first floor of the Jinjiang Tower in

Shanghai – a futuristic silver bullet of a building, completed in 1988 and then still the tallest building in the city.

'It is late for us to be developing Shanghai, so we have to work hard,' he told the assembled audience. He lamented not having designated Shanghai a Special Economic Zone; they had not, he said, taken the intellectual advantages of the city into account at the time. His speech was more than just a call to develop Shanghai, though. He emphasized the need to continue the policies of reform and opening. 'Some people may have different views about this,' he said, before adding in a conciliatory tone, 'but they are still well-intentioned'. As they gently rotated through the cold Shanghai air, he overtly challenged those assembled to support him: 'If I am the only one to speak in favour of reform and opening,' he said, 'it won't be enough'. In concluding he recalled his departure from the city, all those years before: 'In 1920 when I went to study in France, I took a foreign packet of 50,000 tons. Now that China is opening to the outside world, we can make ships of 100,000 and 200,000 tons. If we hadn't opened up, we would still be hammering out automobile parts the way we did in the past'.[30]

After Deng's return to Beijing a few days later, Zhu Rongji gave a typically frank speech which seemed to capture the depths of Deng's frustrations. He discussed the flawed, self-interested nature of Shanghai people: 'They're like a basket full of crabs, biting into each other so that nobody can move,' he said. 'Perhaps we aren't quite that bad, but if I claw at you and you claw at me, we'll at least move more slowly'.[31] He went on to suggest that those in charge right now were ill-equipped to deliver change; that much more emphasis needed to be put on training new local officials with the right skills and character. It was a stern and public condemnation of the perceived inertia and incompetence that frustrated Deng deeply.

Deng leveraged Zhu's support to spread his broader message. Complaining that no one was listening to him in Beijing, Deng, with the help of his daughters, orchestrated the publication of four front-page articles over the course of February, March and April in the Shanghai CCP newspaper *Liberation Daily*, under a pen name of Huangfu Ping. Suggestive of both place (the Huangpu river) and person (the last character echoing that of Deng's given name) the name also had a double meaning; it could be translated as 'Shanghai Commentariat', but also – in the dialect of the journalist who helped put together the articles – as 'receiving the mandate of the people to aide Deng Xiaoping'.[32] Deng's articles offered the public a summary of the ideas he had expressed privately in his Shanghai meetings, arguing for greater pace and ambition in reform and opening, particularly with regard to Shanghai. They were confrontational; one headline asserted that 'Reform and Opening Requires a Large Number of Cadres with Both Morals and Talents', with the subsequent piece arguing that '"national demons" who "utter flowery words and do evil things", a role played by double-dealers and fence-sitters, should absolutely not be allowed to sneak into the ranks of our cadres'.[33] An observation in another of the editorials that 'China will lose a good opportunity if it becomes bogged down on worrying about whether something is capitalist or socialist' would later come to be seen as particularly contentious.[34]

However, despite the controversy the editorials generated – Li Peng would describe them later as 'terrible'[35] and unhelpfully disruptive – and a successful move to secure Zhu Rongji a job in the capital as Vice Premier, the summer of 1991 passed with the pace of reform still far slower that Deng would like. Chen Yun had intervened in July, directly criticizing Deng's famous formulation that reform was like crossing a river by feeling for the stones. 'In my opinion,' Chen said,

> this is applicable when the river is narrow and the water is shallow. But what happens when the river is wide and the water is deep? It does not matter when you swallow a mouthful of water, but it will be harmful when you drink too much. We have already suffered by one-sidedly regarding the growth in output value as the ground to judge the correctness of our policies.[36]

Political focus was also distracted by two major events that summer, one domestic and one international. In May and June, torrential rainfall caused major rivers across China, from Sichuan to Jiangsu, to overflow, creating a humanitarian disaster so severe that it compelled China to ask for international help. The floods made millions homeless, with many forced to set up tents on river levees for shelter. Agriculture in the provinces of Anhui, Shandong, Hubei, Shaanxi, Jiangsu and Henan was severely affected, with farmers racing to harvest their crops.[37]

And then on 18 August, the summer holiday of Soviet President Mikhail Gorbachev was interrupted by a small group of communist hardliners, who, having first cut his five telephone lines, arrived at Gorbachev's dacha at Foros in Crimea and demanded that he sign a decree declaring a state of emergency and transfer power. Gorbachev refused: 'I had promoted all these people,' he later wrote, 'and now they were betraying me!'.[38] After three days, the coup collapsed, with thousands coming out onto the streets of Moscow in support of

Gorbachev and his reform agenda. But he was politically wounded and weakened by the coup, and on Christmas Day of 1991, the hammer and sickle flag that flew from the flagpole atop the Kremlin in Moscow was lowered for the last time; Gorbachev had resigned earlier that same day. The Soviet Union was no more.

Deng had met with the Chinese leadership two days after the attempted coup against Gorbachev, on 20 August. He emphasized that China remained stable for two reasons: '[F]or one thing, we resolutely adhered to socialism when we quelled the unrest in 1989 and because, for another, we have persisted in the policies of reform and opening to the outside world'.[39] Though it was right to stress stability, he told them, it was important not to let opportunities slip by, reaffirming his belief that economic growth needed to move to a higher level to ensure China continued to narrow the still substantial gap between it and developed countries. For Deng, the unfolding situation in the Soviet Union reaffirmed his existing beliefs: only more ambitious, faster reform and opening could ensure the stability of the state and the longevity of the party.

The official list of Deng's activities that summer and autumn is sparsely populated, and rumours suggest that he may have been unwell. Ordinarily, the leadership would have decamped in late July to the beach resort of Beidaihe, just under two hundred miles east of Beijing on the Bohai Sea, for two weeks of political decision-making punctuated, for Deng at least, by a daily swim; in 1991, however, the meeting was cancelled.[40]

As the autumn turned to winter, there was a sense of inertia in Beijing. With the economy showing mediocre growth, debate continued to rage about what direction should be taken. Chen Yun had emerged once more to rail against opening further to foreign trade;[41] others argued that to return to the policies of reform was to allow a further drift towards capitalism. Jiang Zemin, who was stuck in the middle of the factional conflict, was demonstrating a notable aversion to risk.

The journalist Harrison Salisbury wrote in 1991 that the leadership's approach to the future was 'like a man trying to tiptoe into the twenty-first century without wandering into a minefield. There was not a single new idea in the first five-year plan of the nineties, not an upbeat prediction for the year 2000'.[42] Another commentator would describe 1991 as the year of living cautiously.[43]

Too cautiously for Deng Xiaoping, who despite the ever-regular routines which dictated life behind the high walls and screening pines of his house, was harbouring increasingly radical notions of how to forcibly disrupt the status quo that had set in and reinvigorate China's economic reform. One report suggests he was particularly motivated by a meeting that winter at which thirty-two party elders had called for the abolition of the Special Economic Zones.[44]

Time was of the essence for Deng. Scheduled for October of the following year was the 14th Party Congress, when around 2000 delegates would convene for six days at the Great Hall of the People on Tiananmen Square to approve key decisions and formalize positions in the party hierarchy. This would be Deng's third party congress as leader; the previous two had been key in establishing the trajectory of reform and opening, and he knew that the months before October, when Jiang Zemin and others would map out the agenda for the meeting, would be his last chance to materially influence China's future direction. The ground of his courtyard hard and bare; the December sky thick with the coal smoke from hutong braziers: his thoughts turned southward.

Chapter 3

THE SOUTHERN TOUR

In early November 1684, having successfully suppressed an eight-year revolt by some obstinate lords in distant provinces, the Kangxi Emperor set out for his first tour of the southern reaches of his empire. Kangxi was the second Qing emperor to rule over all of China, heir to a dynasty of north-eastern Manchus who had administered the country for only seventeen years by the time he was enthroned in the Forbidden City, just before his seventh birthday.[1] Kangxi would initially learn of the vast country which stretched south of Beijing – the city's name translates as 'Northern Capital' – through books, maps and the reports of his courtiers. At the age of thirty, he set out to see for himself.

On his first, sixty-day-long, tour Kangxi and his vast retinue would travel south to Suzhou, about halfway down China's long curving eastern coastline. He would return five more times on imperial Southern Tours, each time following a similar, if slightly more expansive, itinerary; visiting sacred sites as well the bustling commercial and intellectual centres of the area known as Jiangnan – south of the Yangtze river: then the cultural and economic heartland of China.

As the historian Michael G. Chang notes, as well as being a central source of tax revenue – just as it remained in the communist era, with Shanghai as the government's cash cow – and the nexus of the imperial literati, Jiangnan was also 'a bastion of Ming loyalism and anti-Manchu sentiment'.[2] The Southern Tours of Kangxi were showy political acts designed, in part at least, to establish and sustain legitimacy by both displaying the imposing glory of the court, and demonstrating the emperor's concern for, and interest in, this important region. 'Partly the trouble lies in failure of contact between top and bottom,' the emperor observed. 'After I began to make regular tours through Shandong, Zhejiang, and Jiangnan, then things got better there.'[3]

Those further distant provinces on China's southern edge – places like Guangdong and Fujian – were not on Kangxi's itinerary, partly because they were simply so far away – but also because his tours were so consciously and performatively emulating the imperial tours of great dynasties such as the Qin and Tang.

His first destination in 1684 was Mount Tai, the sprawling mountain which looms out of the plains of Shandong province to the south-east of the capital. Emperor Shun of Chinese legend – held to have ruled around the twenty-third century BCE – had apparently travelled during his reign to all the cardinal points of his kingdom – with his first journey made eastwards, to the sacred Mount Tai:

> In the second month of the year, Shun made a tour of inspection to the east as far as T'ai-shan [Mount Tai], the Supreme Mountain, where he made a burnt offering to Heaven and sacrificed to the mountains and rivers according to their importance. He received the eastern nobles in an audience and put their calendar in order, standardized the musical pitches and the measures of length and volume as well as the five kinds of rituals. He was presented with the five tokens of rank, three kinds of silk, two living animals and one dead one; he returned the five tokens of rank to the nobles.
>
> After finishing his tour, he returned to his capital.[4]

Shun's legend would be the originator of this tradition, but imperial history records seventy-two emperors journeying to Mount Tai to perform ceremonies and sacrifices to the heavens. The peak of Mount Tai, sacred to Buddhism, Daoism and Confucianism, became dense with physical relics of their imperial visits.

Kangxi would also visit the vast Temple of Confucius in the town of Qufu – the great sage's birthplace – as well as the tomb of Zhu Yuanzhang, founder of the Ming dynasty which preceded the Qing, just outside the city of Nanjing; there, he reflected on the fall of the Ming, attributing it to 'factional struggles [...] to the proliferation of taxes and the growth of banditry' – and resolved to learn its lessons.[5] Though the Qing (1644–1911) would be China's final dynasty, the reigns of Kangxi; his son, the Yongzheng Emperor; and his grandson, the Qianlong Emperor, would come to be looked upon as China's last imperial golden age. The three rulers were thoughtful and savvy in their deployment of traditional customs and rituals, and in their commitment to the art and culture drawn from their Manchu heritage as well as that of the – increasingly expansive – empire they now ruled over.

Though Kangxi's Southern Tour of 1684 was his first, his most well-known is his second of 1689.[6] For this tour, which again took in Mount Tai before heading further into Jiangnan, Kangxi chose the most renowned painter of the late seventeenth century, Wang Hui, to record his tour for posterity. Wang and his team took eight years to produce twelve painted scrolls of his journey, each about 27 inches high and measuring, collectively, more than three football pitches in length.[7] Stored in lacquer cases, they were not intended as public works of art, though their artistic influence would be significant; instead, these together constituted an official memorial of the Southern Tour, a work of careful historiography.

These scrolls functioned as proxies for the journey itself; unrolled from right to left, the viewer would travel with the emperor and his retinue through a landscape of muted greens and browns. The scrolls also provide a glimpse of the pageantry and social impact of the Southern Tour: the record of his arrival into Suzhou in Scroll Seven has the grey and dun rendering of the city walls and bridges eclipsed by the vibrant density of those officials and urbanites who had turned out to glimpse the emperor, cramming the streets and waterways. 'Those gathered along the route to greet the procession stretched on continuously for hundreds of *li*; however, they were most numerous in Suzhou,' a contemporary account recorded. 'The various local officials were in front. Government students and licentiates were behind them. Local elders were next, finally followed by ordinary residents. People came by water and by land'.[8]

As well as incorporating imperial pageantry and ritualistic pilgrimage, the Southern Tours also had a practical purpose: in particular, the inspection of the complex hydraulic infrastructure that kept the famously capricious Yellow River in check. If this was ignored – as it had been in the early decades of Qing rule – the integrity of the Grand Canal, the artery which connected Beijing to China's fertile south, supplying the north with millions of tonnes of rice each year, would be severely compromised. Kangxi knew well how severe the consequences could be if the people were not fed; substantial engineering works were embarked upon and inspected by the emperor on each of his Southern Tours.

Kangxi's grandson, the Qianlong Emperor (r. 1735–96), would share this commitment to ensuring that the Yellow River – famously known as 'China's Sorrow' – was kept in check: 'No task of the southern expeditions is more important than supervising the maintenance of the Yellow River,' he wrote.[9] In his six tours, Qianlong, like his grandfather before him, paid homage to Confucius in Qufu, performed rites on Mount Tai, and inspected his military during his tours: he even commissioned a twelve-scroll visual record of his first Southern Tour.

The later tours of Qianlong would come to be perceived as examples of imperial excess; certainly they demanded years of intensive preparation and, despite attempts to avoid obvious ostentation, were costly exercises in manifesting imperial power. Michael G. Chang has estimated the resources required at '18,000 carts [...]; 2,400 mules; 2,200 camels; 3,450 boats; 18,000-20,000 horses (approx. 6,000 for the immediate retinue); and some 300,000 boat trackers, porters, and construction personnel'.[10]

Qianlong ruled until the tail end of the eighteenth century, and as Qing dynastic power waned in the decades which followed his death, so too did the tradition of the Southern Tour.[11] Rebellions and wars began to roil across the south, as the imperial bureaucracy simultaneously scrambled to deal with existential military threats from outside China's borders. Expeditions in the model of Kangxi and Qianlong became both politically imprudent – and practically unfeasible.

*

In the late summer of 1971 – nearly two centuries after Qianlong's last imperial Southern Tour – the seventy-seven-year-old Mao Zedong set out southward from his capital aboard his private train.

Over the course of twenty-nine days, he would visit the cities of Wuhan, Changsha, Nanchang, Hangzhou and Shanghai; declaiming to military and party leaders at each stop on a topic that had come to obsess him: the stubbornness and perceived ambition of his *de facto* second in command and likely successor, the military leader Lin Biao. It was a journey that would change China's future, and the fate of Deng Xiaoping. It would subsequently become known as Mao's own 'Southern Tour'.

Mao Zedong was always ready to repurpose the old in service of his new China, and understood the political power of vacating his capital, which he came to characterize, particularly during the Cultural Revolution, as a bastion of political and cultural orthodoxy. He would establish the modern Southern Tour in the toolkit of China's communist leaders, with his 1971 trip just one of many journeys made aboard his special train to the provinces of the centre and south to shore up political support, demonstrate authority and appeal to constituencies beyond the red walls of Zhongnanhai; in the early 2000s, a book was published accounting with some hyperbole the *twelve* 'Southern Tours' of Mao Zedong. 'I've always advocated calling for local rebellions whenever Central Committee organs act badly,' Mao said in 1966, clarifying his enthusiasm for reaching out to the provinces when adequate political support in Beijing eluded him. 'All the localities should produce more Monkey Kings to create an uproar in the celestial palace'.[12]

In the first phase of the Cultural Revolution, which had been born in violence five years earlier, the Great Helmsman argued that representatives of the bourgeoisie had infiltrated the party, and needed to be ousted. Deng Xiaoping was, as the revolution began, one of a trio of party leaders who effectively administered the country under Mao's theoretical guidance; he would quickly be labelled the country's 'No. 2 Capitalist Roader': a response to Deng's earlier pragmatic economic attempts to mitigate a Mao-made national famine during the catastrophic years of the Great Leap Forward (1958–62), when absurd economic and industrial ambition had led to tens of millions of deaths from starvation, and his lukewarm support of the revolution itself. 'These so-called Soviet-style revisionists were alleged to be seeking to corrupt the masses by using old ideas to restore capitalism,' wrote the sinologist Roderick Macfarquhar.[13]

Deng was forced to participate in the first of a series of public denunciations, and compelled to admit his failings. Subsequently he and his wife would be held under house arrest, forbidden from seeing their children. In 1968, his son Pufang fell from the third storey of a Peking University building whilst being hounded by Red Guards: he would spend the rest of his life in a wheelchair. Deng's younger brother, Shuping, committed suicide after suffering weeks of torment. 'Of the many families assailed during the Cultural Revolution, ours was not the hardest hit' wrote Deng's daughter later.[14] She was, remarkably, right; perhaps most notoriously, President Liu Shaoqi, essentially the second most important politician in China when the revolution began – and the 'No. 1 Capitalist Roader' – would die from neglect in confinement in 1969.

In the autumn of that same year, Deng was expelled from Beijing and sent to work in a factory in Jiangxi province in China's southeast. In Deng and Liu's absence, Lin Biao was now positioned as Mao's heir apparent.

Lin, who at sixty-two was just a few years younger than Deng Xiaoping, was a hero of the civil war who still held enormous personal sway within the PLA. The American journalist Edgar Snow had met Lin in 1936, during the civil war, describing him as thin, handsome and oval-faced – and noting that he was one of the few commanders in the army not to have been injured. Shortly after the publication of Snow's account, however, Lin was shot by mistake by a Red Army soldier;

an injury that may have caused Lin's long-standing health problems. Mao's physician, Li Zhisui, met Lin in 1966, and offers a portrait of a weak, insular man which stands in stark contrast to the impression he cultivated publicly.

> Lin Biao was still so afraid of wind and light that he rarely went outside, often missing meetings. His fear of water was so extreme that even the sound of it would give him instant diarrhea. [....] Lin Biao was obviously mentally unsound but Mao was promoting him to the highest reaches of power. Soon he would be hailed as Mao's 'closest comrade in arms'.[15]

Lin secured his position as heir by publicly attacking and undermining the 'anti-revolutionary' Deng Xiaoping and Liu Shaoqi, and sycophantically encouraging Mao's cult of personality; his orders in the early 1960s that the PLA newspaper should accompany editorials with an apt quotation from the Great Helmsman resulted in the compilation of his sayings into a bound collection that would come be known as the *hongbaoshu* – the little red book – printed over one billion times during the first five years of the Cultural Revolution.[16]

By the time of Mao's Southern Tour in 1971, however, the relationship between Lin and Mao had become seriously strained. Mao would single out the actions of Lin and his associates at a meeting of the Central Committee in the mountain resort of Lushan in Jiangxi the previous summer as the source of his displeasure.

The committee had met at Lushan before, in 1959. At that dramatic meeting, then Defence Minister, Peng Dehuai, had openly criticized the calamitous policies of the Great Leap Forward, and had subsequently been purged from the party. Lin Biao had replaced him; now he too would face a decisive conflict. As party leaders gathered at the cluster of villas at the foot of Lushan in 1970, the issue that would divide Lin and Mao was already a source of debate. A new constitution was in the process of being drafted and included, apparently against Mao's will, the requirement that there be a State Chairman (sometimes referred to as President): effectively a ceremonial head of state. Mao resented the duties of head of state: meeting foreign dignitaries, hosting official ceremonies and meetings, signing treaties; he had previously handed the role off to Liu Shaoqi, and the post had been left vacant after Liu's ousting. So Mao did not want the role, but he seems to have seen Lin's proposal as a power-grab; a step too far from his anointed successor.

At Lushan, these debates were played out, with Mao eventually siding against Lin and his supporters who seemed to have overplayed their hand. 'They mounted a surprise attack and carried out covert activities,' Mao would say later. 'Why didn't they dare to do it openly? That shows they had ill intentions'.[17] Mao would not publicly criticize Lin, but instead chose a surrogate and one-time favourite of Mao, Chen Boda, to be the subject of his ire: he hoped, one account says, that Lin would come to realize that he was also in the wrong and submit a 'self-criticism' to Mao. It was not forthcoming.

On 14 August 1971, the summer after the Lushan confrontation, Mao's train departed Beijing, cutting south. He would stay in Wuhan until the 27th, before heading to his home province of Hunan and its capital Changsha: the most southerly of his stops. On 31 August he travelled east to Nanchang, and then spent a week in Hangzhou – always one of his favoured escapes from Beijing, in the heart of Jiangnan. After briefly pausing in Shanghai, he arrived back to Beijing in the afternoon of 12 September. Everywhere he went, he reiterated the same message: 'Some people are eager to be the president, split the party, and seize power,' he said. He referenced his displeasure at Lin's actions at Lushan and, according to state media, warned military leaders against supporting any split in the party.[18]

Exactly what happened next is still the subject of some uncertainty. The most widely believed explanation is that Lin's twenty-five year-old son, aware of the growing hostility evidenced by Mao's Southern Tour speeches, and perhaps also conscious of his unpredictability, began to put together a plan for a *coup d'etat*, in which Mao would be assassinated by attacking his train either with flame throwers, heavy artillery or by blowing up a bridge. The official version of the story has Lin Biao himself as the originator of this plot, which was titled 'Project 571', though its military naivety, and indeed the fact that it so whimperingly failed, seems to suggest that Lin – who despite his lack of vigour did not lack military astuteness – did not likely have oversight.

Either way, shortly after midnight on 13 September – the night after Mao's return to the capital from his Southern Tour – a British-built Trident plane took off from the north-eastern town of Shanhaiguan, where the Great Wall meets the sea, with Lin, his wife and son on board. According to one account, Zhou Enlai asked Mao if he should have the plane shot down. 'Rain has to fall, girls have to marry, these things are immutable; let them go', he replied.[19] Seemingly heading for the Soviet Union – an initial plan to establish a rival political centre in Guangdong province having seemingly been abandoned – the plane reached only as far as eastern Mongolia, crashing during an emergency landing, necessitated by lack of fuel, with all nine passengers killed.

News of Lin's death would not be publicly communicated until November: the 1 October military parade through the heart of Beijing, in which Lin had taken on a prominent role during the Cultural Revolution, was abruptly cancelled.

Listening to news of the 1971 National Day celebrations from his exile in Jiangxi, Deng Xiaoping silently noted the absence of any mention of the hated Lin, who, along with Mao's wife Jiang Qing, had campaigned so vociferously against Deng during the first phase of the Cultural Revolution, who had vilified and usurped the now-dead Liu Shaoqi, who had so sycophantically cultivated Mao's approval. Just over a month later Deng and his wife would hear at their factory the official news of Lin's attempted flight and the subsequent plane crash first hand. After dinner that evening, with his children around him, the taciturn Deng offered his assessment of the death of Lin: 'It would have gone against Heavenly Reason for Lin Biao not to die!' he said.[20] It was not just personal for Deng, however; he recognized that, with Lin's death, there was one fewer obstacle blocking his return to the capital – and political power.

Chapter 4

DEPARTURE

Just east of Tiananmen Square, two clock-tower pagodas cast their shadows across a vast plaza, perched atop the shoulders of a building that otherwise would not look out of place in Soviet Moscow. Beijing Railway Station was built in the late 1950s, when China still looked north to the Soviet Union for guidance on matters architectural and otherwise. From its fourteen platforms, trains leave for all over China, and beyond: four times a week a locomotive still departs for Pyongyang.

On a freezing January afternoon in 1992, a convoy of vehicles led and followed by police cars sped along the Avenue of Eternal Peace past Tiananmen Square, and took a right turn towards the station's broad buff frontage. The plaza was busy with the bustle of arrivals and departures – and some, hunkered down amongst plastic plaid bags packed to bursting, who appear to have made the unforgiving flagstones a temporary home. Circling the frontage and its massed ranks, the cars and minibuses came to a halt at the private entrance to Platform One.

A group emerged and quickly bustled their way on to an ordinary looking train, painted in the green and yellow livery of all China's rolling stock. They would be the only passengers. And although the train was, apart from its lack of an official identification plate, externally identical to the hundreds which passed through the station each day, inside it was something quite different: an eight-carriage house on wheels, with a lounge, dining room, bedrooms with proper beds and bathrooms with full-sized baths.

At 3.35 pm, as the passengers settled bags, the train pulled gently away from the platform, clanking over switch points southwards. Rolling slowly past the last relics of the Beijing city wall, it crossed the Tonghui River and cut through the expansive southern suburbs of Beijing, gradually acquiring speed as the city was spread more thinly.

Arrayed around Deng as he sat in an armchair were three generations of his family. Four of Deng's five children had accompanied their father; only his businessman youngest son Deng Zhifang did not join the tour.

His wife of fifty-three years, Zhuo Lin, had long been an unvarying presence at Deng's side on his trips away from the capital. Zhuo was twelve years younger than Deng, and they had met in the summer of 1939 in the revolutionary wartime headquarters of the CCP in Yan'an and married that September. As a young man, Deng had been married twice before; to Zhang Xiyuan, a 'rare beauty' who had died in 1930 from complications in giving birth to Deng's daughter, who also did not survive.[1] Having remarried shortly after Zhang's death, his second wife, Jin Weiying, would desert him in 1933 as he suffered severe political criticism. She would go on to marry one of Deng's political enemies whilst he, according to one account, never forgave her for her betrayal.[2] In Deng's daughter's biography of her father's early life, Jin is not even mentioned.

It was this youngest daughter, Rong, or Mao Mao as she was known within the family, who would be the most publicly prominent family figure during the Southern Tour. Rong, who with her spectacles and round face was the image of her mother, had become a regular companion of her father in recent years, tending to his practical needs, and ensuring that his failing hearing did not inhibit his ability to take part in discussions. There were grandchildren, too, as well as Wang Ruilin, his loyal and long-serving secretary.[3]

The family's living quarters were hauled by a German diesel locomotive built in the 1970s: frog-eyed and green liveried, with sweeping white racing stripes, the NY6 was known in Chinese as the *da mali*, or great horsepower, for its ability to conquer steep inclines. It travelled on a line established in the late nineteenth and early twentieth century by a Belgian company supported by French money. China could simply not afford the expense of such endeavours in the latter days of the Qing dynasty, nor did its government have the requisite experience in constructing railways – but they recognized the importance of establishing a north-south line to ship grain from the fertile south. Opened fully in 1906, this first line south from Beijing covered 1214 kilometres, had 125 stations and crossed the Yellow River on a three-kilometre-long bridge. It ended, however, at the city of Hankou, on the northern bank of the Yangtze River in central China. The connecting line to the far south, which was not completed for another thirty years, could only be reached by ferrying the trains across the broad river: it was not until 1957 that a bridge was opened, with much attendant fanfare celebrating communist engineering prowess, across the Yangtze at Hankou – finally joining this vital north to south thoroughfare between Beijing and Guangdong.

The route took Deng and his family southwest from the capital, out through the flat frozen farmland of the North China Plain, the grey working cities of Baoding and Shijiazhuang, across the curling mudflats of the Yellow River. Then more flat squares of agricultural land, defined by yellow-white dirt roads – and not a hill in sight until, just north of Hankou and the Yangtze, the rising line of mountains disrupts the monotony of the landscape.

Deng liked to travel by train 'so that he could look out the windows and see how people were living,' his daughter said. Like all Chinese leaders he would go on regular 'inspection tours', and he carefully noted the implications of what he saw: the northern houses still roofed with thatch, versus those further south of two solid storeys, how crops were growing, whether houses had television aerials on their roof or not.[4]

What was Deng thinking as his train rumbled southward? His trips to Shanghai over the last two years had not resulted in the reinvigoration of reform and opening he was advocating – without which, he had told Jiang Zemin in September, the country would have no future.[5] This journey was a bigger, more directly confrontational, undertaking, but it remained a political gamble. At the forefront of his mind was surely the tour of 1984, when he had last visited the far southern provinces and affirmed the progress of the Special Economic Zones. Then, he had seen and endorsed the country's nascent transformation, and that year had begun the second phase of reform.

Now, he knew, greater economic freedoms, rapid growth and consequential improvements in living standards had moved from novelty to expectation amongst many in China. Growth rates through the middle years of the 1980s had hovered around or above 10 per cent annually, according to the World Bank.[6] Urban per capita income rose from 500 yuan in 1981 to nearly 1400 yuan in between 1981 and 1989, whilst rural income rose, from a lower base, at a rate of 9.2 per cent each year.[7] And this statistical increase was reflected in the everyday: what people ate, what they wore, how well they could support their children. In Maoist China, families had valued the acquisition of the so-called *si da jian*, or 'four big items': in the 1950s and 1960s, these had been a Flying Man brand pedal-driven sewing machine, a Flying Pigeon bicycle, a Shanghai brand wristwatch and a Red Star radio. By the 1980s, this list was transformed, reflecting the new purchasing power of the Chinese consumer: it now included a refrigerator, a colour television, a washing machine and a tape recorder, with imported brands such as Panasonic most highly prized. The rise in living standards was profoundly unequal but was evident, if not accessible, to all.

Alongside greater freedom to farm for individual gain, government approval of small industrial enterprises, known as Township and Village Enterprises, or TVEs, had allowed local people in parts of rural China to engage in profitable manufacturing, with some filling gaps left by the big state-run firms by manufacturing consumer goods like rubber bands or buttons, whilst those in provinces like Guangdong engaged with the international market, making consumer goods for export. 'In the end,' writes the economist Barry Naughton, 'TVEs transformed virtually every aspect of the Chinese economy'.[8]

In towns and cities, smaller-scale entrepreneurship had also been encouraged with a policy that allowed private businesses employing no more than eight people in total – Marx had written that a greater number of employees leads to exploitation. These *getihu*, as they were known, set up road-side stalls or small shops to cater for consumer demand; sometimes looked down upon as 'peddlers' by professional people they nevertheless often became enormously prosperous.[9] '*Getihu* were the new breed of private businesspeople running the market stalls and changing the country,' wrote Lijia Zhang of the emergence of this new economic force in her hometown of Nanjing. 'Rows of stalls [...] sold anything and everything of use: cooking pots, padded trousers, straw brooms, pickled pig tails, dried persimmon, frogs on skewers, and crickets in tiny bamboo cages. With better service and cheaper prices than the state run shops, such markets had sprung up all over the city, like mushrooms after spring rain.'[10] The rise in private and collective enterprises was, alongside the reforms in agriculture, a key feature of the reforms of the 1980s. 'By the end of the 1980s,' writes Susan Shirk, 'less than 40 percent of China's national income originated in the state sector'.[11]

The new economic expectations of Chinese people were one reason that Deng felt he could rely on popular opposition to the current approach that had dialled back growth and focussed more on the centrally planned sections of the economy. Perhaps even more significant to his sense of leverage, however, was the power that was now held by leaders outside Beijing. Effectively, in their gradual and piecemeal attempts at reform, the central leadership had, on a whole range of important matters, ceded control to provincial officials.

During one key meeting in Beijing in 1990, Premier Li Peng had told local leaders that he wanted to change the system by which tax revenue was returned to central government. Previously, the percentage of tax that had to be sent back to Beijing varied from place to place; Guangdong, for example, was allowed to keep 90 per cent of the tax it collected in order to encourage growth. On being told that this advantageous system might be taken away, a row broke out, and local leaders simply refused to give it up. In the end, it was agreed that the system would remain in place – a remarkable defeat for the central government, and a demonstration of the strength of feeling facing China's conservatives as they tried to roll back the reform agenda.[12]

Deng knew that he could rely on support from those in the regions of China that had most benefitted from the changes introduced before 1989 and it was there he was headed. Officials in Guangdong province had begun to hear rumblings as early as July of the previous year that an 'important guest' might be coming to Shenzhen. In mid-December, preparations had begun in earnest, and by early January were so advanced that one company Deng would visit had set about repairing a corridor they thought might be troublesome for their elderly visitor.[13] An official three-person delegation, which included Zhang Baozhong, Deng's bodyguard, had been dispatched from Beijing on 3 January to inspect preparations and formalize the route. This was no secret trip; his arrival in the south was anticipated with fervour by the officials awaiting him there – just as it was contemplated with nervous uncertainty by the leaders behind the high red walls of Zhongnanhai.

Chapter 5

THE THOROUGHFARE OF NINE PROVINCES

On a narrow street in Hankou – one of the three old cities now bound together as Wuhan – a broad buff and white three-storey building of bland neoclassical style hides behind leaning plane trees. Fixed above its pillared portico is a red sign embossed with gold characters announcing that this is the site of the '8–7' meeting, an historic gathering of the leadership of the then six-year-old CCP which took place on 7 August 1927. The sign is in the handwriting of one of the lowliest of the attendees of the meeting, twenty-two-year-old Deng Xiaoping.

The original copy of his calligraphy, written during a visit in 1980, hangs above the entrance to the modest room upstairs where the meeting took place. It was in this small room, with its dark hardwood floor and shuttered windows, that, on that hot August day in 1927, Deng Xiaoping met Mao Zedong for the very first time. Mao would say later that he didn't recall their meeting.[1] He was certainly the more senior of the two, both in political status and age – he was thirty-three at the time – and there is little reason that he would have noted the lowly party cadre who sat in the corner taking notes.

Shortly beforehand, Deng had changed his name to become known as Xiaoping: his given name was Xiansheng, but he had been known by the name given to him at primary school in Sichuan, Xixian.[2] 1927 was a tough year to be a member of the CCP. Founded in 1921 on the principles of Marxism-Leninism, the Party had initially sought to unify with the Nationalists, or Kuomintang (KMT), against warlord rule. The two parties were allied in a 'United Front' from 1924 to 1927; a facade under which ideological discord and suspicion festered and eventually, in April of 1927, exploded into open conflict when Nationalist leader Chiang Kai-shek initiated a violent purge of leftists in Shanghai, which became known as the Shanghai Massacre. For the rag-tag group that constituted the CCP – intellectuals, workers, peasants supported by Soviet advisors sent to support the nascent party – pseudonyms and disguise became essential to evade detection in the aftermath of this brutal crackdown.

In an official, modern painting of the 1927 meeting, held to discuss the way forward for the CCP in a period of profound existential crisis, Mao Zedong is presented as the dominant figure of the scene; standing, bathed in almost beatific light, as he addresses the other twenty-four attendees – including a blonde-haired, big-nosed Soviet advisor. Mao certainly did speak during the meeting – it was at this meeting that he first asserted that 'political power grows out of the barrel of a gun' – but it would not be until the next decade that he emerged as the truly dominant figure in the party.

Until his arrival on the Southern Tour of 1992, Deng's 1927 stay in Wuhan – he would leave in the autumn of that year – would be the most significant of his seven visits to the city. Mao, though, established a far stronger connection with the city. Across the river from Hankou, in the city of Wuchang, is a museum on the site of the house Mao occupied in 1927, where he lived with his wife, Yang Kaihui, and children. A display tells of the more than fifty times he came to the city. 'His brilliance dazzles and his lustre shines in Wuhan. [...] His revolutionary activities and theoretical creation in Wuhan are treasures that will be cherished by generations of people in the city'.

During his years as leader of the People's Republic, Wuhan became an escape for Mao; a regular part of his itinerary on his southern sojourns from the capital, offering the opportunity for him to demonstrate his physical strength by swimming in the broad Yangtze – he did so eighteen times between 1956 and 1966. In a 1956 poem, 'Swimming', he would contrast the physicality and freedom of taking to the waters of the Yangtze with the limitations of Beijing.

> I have just drunk the waters of Changsha
> And come to eat the fish of Wuchang.
> Now I am swimming across the great Yangtze,
> Looking afar to the open sky of Chu.
> Let the wind blow and waves beat,
> Better by far than idly strolling in a courtyard.

In the winter of 1965, Mao embarked on an eight-month-long escape from a capital he had come to perceive as full of intransigent officials. Were it not for the party's later desire to shift responsibility for the Cultural Revolution away from Mao Zedong, this journey would doubtless have been co-opted by Chinese historiography as another 'Southern Tour': it has all the trappings of the modern incarnation of this imperial tradition. Mao's itinerary was extensive, taking in

5. The Thoroughfare of Nine Provinces 45

ten different stops in total, but it centred on three cities that he was intimately familiar with: Hangzhou, Wuhan and Shanghai.³

He arrived in Shanghai in November of 1965. Shortly before his arrival, he had encouraged the publication of an article designed to further his radical agenda and circumvent editors in Beijing – just as Deng would in Shanghai in 1991 with his 'Huangfu Ping' articles which criticized those cadres who 'have not sufficiently emancipated their minds' and pursued reform too slowly. Published in a city newspaper called *Wenhui Bao*, the article was, rather remarkably, a theatrical review of a play that Mao saw as a criticism of him, titled *Hai Rui Dismissed From Office*. The play was an historical drama written by Wu Han, the intellectual Vice Mayor of Beijing, which told the story of an official of the Ming dynasty court who is dismissed by the emperor for criticizing him; few could miss the allegorical nature of the play's narrative, which directly alluded to the treatment of former Defence Minister Peng Dehuai at Lushan back in 1959. The publication of the scathing review, a targeted attack on 'bourgeois' elements in the party that Mao felt were obstructive to his radicalism and wanted to remove, would 'light the fuse' of the Cultural Revolution. (Wu Han, like Liu Shaoqi, would die in prison in 1969.)

During his trip, Mao oscillated between preferred redoubts in Hangzhou, Shanghai and Wuhan, and even managed a short visit back to his hometown of Shaoshan in Hunan province. In the early summer of 1966, he stopped off in Wuhan to spend a few weeks staying in a guest house near the city's East Lake. At 11 am on 16 July, a typically cloying summer's day in a city known as one of China's 'four furnaces', Mao entered the fast-flowing waters of the broad Yangtze, which bisects Wuhan, climbing down from a motor launch and coasting with the current of the river for an hour and five minutes. According to official records, he managed fifteen kilometres in that time, leading the *South China Morning Post* to run a story headlined 'Mao Tse-tung for the Olympics?' – though his personal best was apparently set a few years earlier in 1961, when he was noted to have achieved twelve kilometres in just forty minutes. On the banks, crowds had gathered, waving red flags and chanting slogans. Two hundred young swimmers joined him in the water and sang a song: 'We are the communist successor generation'.⁴ Today, next to the Yangtze, enormous bronze letters spell out the date of this symbolic event: 66.7.16.

His swim was a demonstration of vigour and a showy return to public view. It prefigured his return to the capital later that month where he would immediately move into his new lodgings in Zhongnanhai adjoining his beloved indoor swimming pool. A month later, he would watch from the Gate of Heavenly Peace as more than a million Red Guards flooded Tiananmen Square – having centred himself once more on China's political stage.

The Yangtze River was white in the weak winter sun as Deng Xiaoping's train rattled across the bridge and pulled into Wuchang Station's Platform Number One at 10.31 am on 18 January 1992. Descending tentatively to the platform, Deng wore a smart peaked grey cap – not a Mao cap, but something far less utilitarian, Western even – a darker grey overcoat, and a cream scarf. The day was brisk but a few degrees warmer than the capital the family had left the previous day. Deng Rong accompanied him on to the platform, she in an identical cream scarf and bright red overcoat. The men who met them, most notably Hubei Party Secretary Guan Guangfu and Governor Guo Shuyan, were far more soberly dressed: white shirts under black jumpers and cheap looking winter jackets.[5]

'We will walk a little, and talk a little,' Deng told them. The platform was only about 500 metres long; during the conversation, they walked its length four times, stopping periodically, a photographer running ahead to capture their conversation.

Deng railed to the officials against empty talk – a recurrent preoccupation of his – saying that there was too much bureaucracy: too many meetings, reports which were too long, speeches which were too long. He tactically invoked Mao, mentioning his aversion to long meetings and ability to express himself concisely. Deng recalled how, when asked to draft a speech for Zhou Enlai for the Fourth National People's Congress of 1975, Deng had managed to keep it under 5,000 characters – but still, he said, it remained effective. It was a bold way to begin: the time for talking, he was declaring, had passed.

He told them not to be afraid of foreign investment – reminding them that the party always retained the political control. He criticized those on the left – adherents of the old planned economy – in perhaps the most directly confrontational aspect of his speech: 'The "right" can bury socialism,' he said, 'and the "left" can also bury socialism'. He asserted that while they should be wary of the 'right', they should mainly be guarding against the 'left'. Though couched in abstraction, the warning amounted to a direct condemnation of those who had been driving the conservative economic agenda over the last few years.

Deng went on, asserting that development was now the top priority; not to pursue reform and opening, develop the economy and improve people's lives, he said, was a dead end. To move slowly, he said, was the same as stopping – or even going backwards.

Rumours that emerged later in the year had suggested Deng, upon arriving at Wuhan – 'an area where the economy had not been invigorated or managed well' – simply refused to get off the train, telling officials that he would return when they had improved the economy.[6] Though later contradicted by the official account, the fact that Deng stopped at Wuhan for only half an hour – and did not leave the station – reflects the fact that he did not feel that this once thriving hub of central China was worthy of detailed inspection.

Positioned ideally at the junction of two rivers, the Han and the Yangtze, and right in the heart of central China, the city of Wuhan had long been famous as a centre of trade and industry, known as 'the thoroughfare of nine provinces', and later as the 'Chicago of China'. As the historian Chris Courtney notes, 'When the scholar-official Fan Chengda visited the Wuhan area in the twelfth century, he found thriving market cities, home to tens of thousands of households and rows of shops "as thick as teeth in a comb".'[7] In the era of the Qing dynasty, Hankou was, according to the poet Zha Shenxing (1650–1727), the '[g]reatest of markets, crossroads of land and river trade'.[8] The sinologist Stephen R. Mackinnon has written that Wuhan 'dominated the economic and political life of the central Yangzi region for well over a millennium'.[9]

In December of 1858, the British paddle steamer *HMS Furious* anchored off Hankou, as part of the first foreign fleet ever to have ascended the 636 miles of the Yangtze from the coast; those aboard were here to cast an appraising eye over a port they had just secured trading rights to at the end of what would turn out to be the first phase of the Second Opium War. They were initially unimpressed: the site, wrote Laurence Oliphant, private secretary to Lord Elgin, was 'eminently disappointing. We had heard so much of the congeries of cities that are situated at the junction of the Han and the Yang-tse [...] that we had formed grander expectations, and anticipated a nobler reward after all our anxieties and exertions.'[10] A few years later in 1861, the war having concluded in Britain's favour after Lord Elgin's forces torched the Summer Palace in Beijing and forced the Chinese into a further punitive treaty, the British government leased a concession area at Hankou from which to trade – and the city began its new life as a centre of international commerce deep in the heartland of China. The British concession would be joined later in the nineteenth century by those of France, Germany, Russia and Japan. Along the river front at Hankou emerged the foreign streetscape that Deng Xiaoping would see on his 1920 journey to Shanghai.

After the communists took charge in 1949, the city became once more an important centre of industry after years of war and Japanese occupation. Hundreds of factories were built and the population swelled to 2.5 million by 1966.[11] The most significant of its industrial enterprises was Wuhan Iron and Steel, which opened in 1958; the city had since the late nineteenth century been a centre of iron and steel production, and, under the first decade of communist rule, the region become a national capital of industry. During the years of the 'Third Front' policy, which moved industry deep into China's southwest, and the Cultural Revolution, Wuhan's development slowed, though it still ranked fourth as an industrial centre in 1981.[12]

The choice of Wuhan as the first stop of his Southern Tour was, as with everything Deng did, carefully made. By 1992, it languished as a resonant symbol of the iniquities and imbalances of thirteen years of reform and opening. Wuhan was of the old economy; stuck in the heart of China far away from coastal zones of development. Deng had repeatedly warned of the problems that might be caused by a greater divide becoming established between coastal and inland areas in China; inland provinces had seen only one tenth of the foreign investment in China between 1978 and 1991.[13]

It was not just a question of Wuhan's location, however. Change had been slow to come to all of China's established cities. Rural reform in the early 1980s had been relatively straightforward; a question of essentially getting out of people's way. Changing the economic structure of China's cities, whilst avoiding negative impact, at least in the short term, on those who lived in them, was far more challenging.

Change was needed, though. Decades of under-investment in infrastructure meant that roads and buildings of China's cities were crumbling; electricity and water supplies were unreliable; transportation was crowded and inadequate. Housing was often cramped and run-down. The sociologist Deborah Davies records that in Shanghai

> families rarely occupied more than two rooms; communal showers or bathrooms were the norm and kitchens were set up on the pavement, in hallways, or in alcoves built on porches and roofs. [....] In 1987, when most families had purchased a refrigerator, it stood in the inner room that served as bedroom and living room. Floors and walls were bare cement and thin curtains or bamboo shades offered a veneer of privacy.[14]

Housing, alongside other essential services like healthcare, education and food, was provided via your work unit, or *danwei* and by the state-owned enterprise or institution you worked for. Despite the rise of entrepreneurship – the *getihu* who set up small businesses to serve the everyday needs of city dwellers – state-owned enterprises, predominantly engaged in heavy industry and manufacturing, still dominated the economic life of Chinese cities in the late 1980s and early 1990s. In 1985, 70 per cent of all urban workers were employed at a state-owned enterprise; by 1992, despite the rise in the urban population, this had dropped by little more than half a percentage point.[15]

State-owned enterprises were hulking symbols in steel and smoke of the planned economy; what they made, and in what quantity, was dictated by the state, rather than the market, and they were coddled like a favourite child, via subsidies and insulation from real competition. Though the lifestyle these companies supported for workers via the *danwei* system was far from luxurious, those who worked for them were often suspicious of changes that might lead to the removal of their 'iron rice bowl'. 'Urban reform is [...] complicated and risky,' Deng Xiaoping acknowledged. 'Every step we take in urban reform will affect tens of thousands of families'.[16]

Urban reform was launched in 1984, and, as well as successfully encouraging greater individual enterprise, incorporated attempts to free state-owned enterprises from the strictures of centralized state planning and give greater autonomy to local managers. In tandem with this, changes to the mechanisms for setting prices for the goods the factories and workshops produced were proposed. In the past, the government had set the prices of all goods, not always realistically. Now, prices were to be gradually allowed to level at whatever the market dictated:

> As for the price of consumer goods, except for an extremely small minority of crucial products that will remain under state price controls, the price of ordinary products will be gradually decontrolled as market conditions permit. The proportion of producers' goods for which the central government determines the price will progressively shrink, and the proportion determined by the market will increase.[17]

State-owned enterprises would subsequently be allowed to sell products at market prices, once state quotas had been fulfilled, providing incentives for greater efficiency. But freeing prices inevitably saw inflation spiral following this decision in 1984, and many state-owned enterprises were less than prudent with their newfound freedoms, paying out government money in bonuses and wages, thus encouraging demand. The so-called 'dual track' pricing system, which saw goods being sold at both state-set prices and market prices simultaneously, created fertile conditions for hoarding and corruption to thrive, where those on the inside could buy at the cheaper state-set price, and sell on the open market.

In the aftermath of the inflation crisis of 1988, and the protests of 1989, urban reform stalled, as rectification set in. Ironically, despite conservatives extolling the importance of state-owned enterprises, their policies, and the economic slowdown they created, fundamentally weakened them. Demand and prices for goods fell, leading to layoffs at state firms which itself fuelled social unrest. By the time of Deng's Southern Tour, China's state-owned enterprises were losing significant amounts of money, 'and were increasingly seen as financial liabilities'.[18]

During his tour Deng would argue that places like Shenzhen should support inland areas by generating revenue and helping with technology (some of Wuhan's textile factories were still using equipment left behind by British manufacturers in the 1940s).[19] This had long been Deng's thinking: 'To let some people and some regions become prosperous first is a new policy that is supported by everyone. It is better than the old one,' he had said back in 1983.[20] But by 1992, despite the remarkable economic growth of the last fourteen years, the imbalances remained and the question of how to enliven the economies of cities like Wuhan remained central to China's economic future. 'Don't argue; try bold experiments and blaze new trails,' Deng would assert during his tour. 'That's the way it was with rural reform, and that's the way it should be with urban reform.'[21]

Time passed quickly on the platform at Wuhan, and before they knew it, nearly half an hour had elapsed. Deng concluded his talk by encouraging the local officials to select and develop younger members of the party, and reminded them of the importance of seeking truth from facts, as Mao had instructed.

Deng said a hurried farewell to the beaming party officials and boarded the train. At 11.02 am, the train pulled away from the station, heading south once more. The three party cadres who had spoken with him retired into a room in the station to record Deng's words during the precisely 29 minutes he was on the platform; the report would be sent back to Beijing that evening, and scrutinized by Jiang Zemin and Li Peng, who both responded quickly to Deng's comments on bureaucracy, acknowledging the need to streamline meetings and devote the party's energy to practical problems.²²

Deng's train followed the line of the Yangtze south, pulled along the flat, red-soiled plains, past villages of low white houses and red-tiled roofs set amongst rice-fields and small fishing lakes. At 4 pm, it arrived into the station at Changsha, the capital of Mao's home province of Hunan, about 210 miles south of Wuhan. The station was a low, spreading 1970s box of a building, with neoclassical pillars and a central clock tower, rising to a red torch – symbolizing the fact that it was in Changsha where Chairman Mao had supposedly first ignited the revolutionary fire.

Deng again briefly descended; this time the train would stop only for ten minutes. As they walked in the cool shade of the platform, he chatted to provincial party secretary Xiong Qingquan about last year's terrible agricultural conditions, and the flooding that had inundated much of central and eastern China; in Hunan, the Yangtze had burst its banks and 700,000 acres of farmland had been underwater.²³

Xiong asserted that despite this, the agricultural output and oil production for the province had been exceptionally high. 'Only China, relying on the strong leadership of the Communist Party, relying on the superiority of socialism can fight such a big disaster,' Deng said – overlooking the international help the country had had to rely upon, and the fact that more than two million people remained homeless in the affected provinces. One report from 27 January that year told of the misery of the poor rural residents in affected provinces who had seen their homes and livelihoods washed away – in some cases entire villages had disappeared – and were now having to endure an exceptionally cold winter, planting crops in the snow.²⁴ Xiong's propagandizing spin on the floods was very much of a piece with the national media coverage; a *People's Daily* front page asserted that same month that 'In the struggle against the floods, Anhui witnessed courageous sacrifice and selfless contribution from heroic people who left a record that inspires tears of sadness and odes of praise [...] This provides vivid teaching material for the rural socialist education activities now under way'.²⁵

Xiong, over the past year, had given a number of speeches which were cautiously supportive of Deng's agenda, arguing in June of 1991 against 'formalism', and saying there were too many meetings, too many documents, too many performative acts of leadership within the party.²⁶ On the issue of the economy, he had commented that 'we must continue to strengthen agriculture, invigorate industry, enliven circulation, and maintain proper growth', which, he said, would be over 6 per cent.[27] He was clearly a leader receptive to Deng's point of view.

During their conversation, Deng also referenced Hunan's history of producing revolutionary leaders: leaders who had the courage and knowledge to create miracles, he said.[28] The province certainly had a strong pedigree: President Liu Shaoqi and Peng Dehuai, Defence Minister in the 1950s, were from the province – Peng, like Liu, had died in terrible circumstances during the Cultural Revolution. Zhu Rongji had grown up in Hunan, as had ideological firebrand and leading party propagandist Deng Liqun, born into a wealthy family there in 1915.

But the reference was, of course, to Mao Zedong who, like Deng, had wearied himself waiting for bureaucrats to act on his – very different – political demands. It was a tactical invocation, particularly in Hunan; Mao's statue stood in the entrance hall of the railway station, and his hometown was just an hour and a half southwest of the city. And it was an allusion that was made more explicit when, just before his departure, Deng encouraged Xiong that now was a good time to seize the opportunity and develop Hunan more quickly, and repeated once more the Maoist dictum that they should continue to 'seek truth from facts'. Calling together those assembled on the platform, he posed for a final photograph, and with the help of his daughter clambered back aboard the train. The doors clanked shut, and with a low rumble the diesel locomotive pulled slowly out of the station.

Chapter 6

THE EAST WIND BRINGS SPRING ALL AROUND

All night the same rattling and creaking of the train, the Doppler fade of its horn, the occasional slowing as they passed through another station. This was Deng's second night aboard his special train; the journey from Beijing to Shenzhen in 1992 was a near two-day slog, no matter how important you were.

The interminable winter flatness of the North China Plain had been replaced. Outside the train's windows now flashed a landscape of Guangdong's more limited horizons, defined by thickets of bamboo and egg-shaped hills that seemed to emerge unexpectedly from tiered farmland. Clusters of single-room, single-storey stone cottages sat asymmetrically amongst this vibrancy; and where there were not homes or hills or vegetation there was water: terraces, rivers, lakes and ponds. As the train moved closer to, and then past, the provincial capital of Guangzhou, signs of the new China became more evident, roads and bridges, low-rise factories and accompanying accommodation blocks, modern houses of the white tile that covers a multitude of construction sins. Further south, the train slipped through the 'Second Line' that separated the Shenzhen Special Economic Zone from the rest of China.

At 9 am on 19 January the train pulled into the platform at Shenzhen Station, and Deng descended to the platform to be greeted once more by a phalanx of officials. 'We have really missed you!' one said. Another added 'The people of Shenzhen look forward to seeing you, and have been looking forward to it for eight years!'.[1]

It was a cool spring day in Shenzhen and the officials were dressed in lightweight suits and grey jumpers; Deng likewise had shed the heavy overcoat and scarf he had needed at Wuhan. The group bustled from the station and into waiting minibuses, driving the five minutes north to the Shenzhen Guesthouse where Deng and his family would stay. They had a hotel villa to themselves, newly renovated with cream furnishings and floral fabrics. Deng's room featured a large pine desk complete with inkstone and brushes: a hopeful suggestion, made in the knowledge of his calligraphic efforts during his last visit to Shenzhen. In front of the ornate faux-marble fireplace, cream leather sofas had been arranged; there was even a small ornamental bar built into the room's corner.

Deng was encouraged by the party officials and his family to rest after the long train ride; 2000 kilometres in just under two days. After briefly retiring to his room, however, Deng re-emerged. He declared that he didn't want to just sit still – he wanted to see the city for himself.

Officials scurried to prepare the minibus, and Deng walked in the courtyard of the villa with his daughter, Deng Nan, and recalled that famous inscription he had written during his Southern Tour visit of January 1984: 'The development and experience of Shenzhen prove that our policy of establishing the Special Economic Zones is correct,' he had written. He was here, in part, to try to evidence this assessment once more.

He clambered into the white Toyota minibus with his family and local officials, including Xie Fei, the local provincial leader; Li Hao, former mayor and current party secretary; and current mayor Zheng Liangyu. Also accompanying Deng and the party was local journalist Chen Xitian. Chen was the only print reporter permitted to record Deng's visit; he would spend the next five days following the leader around the city, transcribing his utterances on a small notepad – no audio recording was permitted – and relying on the second-hand accounts of officials when he was unable to squeeze into Deng's minibus. Despite the obvious newsworthiness of Deng's visit, however, Chen's report would not be published until 26 March, two months after his departure, when his 11,000-character article, titled 'East Wind Brings Spring All Around', was printed on the front page of the *Shenzhen Special Zone Daily*, headlined in decorative red characters and accompanied by a photo of a grey-jacketed, relaxed Deng.[2]

The narrow road away from the hotel was shaded by overhanging trees and hemmed in by buildings, but soon they emerged onto one of the city's broad perpendicular highways. Deng recalled how some of this part of the city had, in 1984, been rice fields, fishponds, narrow paths and low houses; today, the road was flanked by medium-rise buildings of white and pastel render and a few taller of mirrored glass. 'Eight years have passed, and Shenzhen is developing so fast. It exceeds my expectations,' Deng said.[3] When Deng had last visited, the total population of the Special Economic Zone was just shy of 350,000 people; now it was well over a million. In the much larger geographic area of the city of Shenzhen there were now around 2.3 million people.[4]

Deng asked party secretary Li Hao about the recent economic performance of Shenzhen, and expressed specific interest in the rates of foreign investment – one of the issues that had made Shenzhen's establishment so contentious. 'There were different opinions on the operation of the SEZ from the beginning and worries about whether it was capitalist,' Deng said. But, he argued, the development of Shenzhen had answered those critics: the SEZ was surnamed socialism, not capitalism – evidenced by the fact, he argued, that only a quarter of investment was from abroad.[5] He advocated for more foreign investment, reaffirming that the political control remained in China's hands. He declared that those who thought this meant a slow move towards capitalism 'lack basic knowledge'.

It was a characteristically blunt assessment by Deng, but the accusation had haunted the SEZs for the twelve years since their establishment for the simple reason that the model they had largely followed – of a geographical area delineated to allow for different rules and aimed to encourage investment from abroad – had no socialist pedigree.

The origins of the concept can be traced back to the late 1950s and an airport in southwestern Ireland. Shannon Airport served as a stopover for transatlantic flights in the era before aeroplane fuel capacity was sufficient for the whole journey between Europe and America. In an effort to maintain the economic growth of the airport as newer, more capacious, aircraft came to market and threatened to render the stopover obsolete, the Irish Government established the Shannon Free Zone to encourage foreign investment by providing various tax incentives, creating a thriving international hub that also served to support local industries. That the new town of Shannon built in the subsequent decades remained small – its population today is around 10,000 – and the initial site of the Free Zone was a modest 2.5sq/km did not stop Shannon becoming a site of pilgrimage. Following Jiang Zemin's visit in 1980, Shannon would host Zhu Rongji, Premier Wen Jiabao and even Xi Jinping, shortly before he became leader.[6] The idea of such separate zones would be replicated in different forms around the world, and became a fixture of countries seeking to develop their economy through manufacturing in the 1970s. That it originated in capitalist countries, however, and was a model explicitly designed to attract money from abroad remained deeply troubling to many in the CCP.

In particular, it conjured the powerful memory of the era of treaty ports and foreign concessions: places like Hankou or Shanghai, or the 'island' of Shamian, just up the Pearl River in Guangzhou, which was given over to the British and French for trade in the nineteenth century;

the foreigners dug out a river to separate it from the Chinese city and stationed armed guards on its two bridges.

This debate over what the material difference was between Special Zones and these old colonial demesnes was fierce throughout the reform and opening period. One article published in 1985 articulated the distinction as one of control and intent:

> The goal of the imperialist countries in establishing concessions in the old China was to carry out aggression. They regarded the concessions as the bridgehead for military aggression, economic plunder and spiritual and cultural enslavement. The purpose of their making investment and running enterprises inside the concessions was to control China's economy and absolutely not to bring about economic prosperity in China.[7]

There remained, however, a persistent suspicion over who was benefitting most from the advantageous trading conditions of the SEZs, and whether the risk of foreign exploitation was worth the reward.

In the intervening years since Deng's last visit to the SEZs, the equation had not seemed at all balanced. After the initial successes of the first four years of their development, the achievements of the SEZs, at least against the ambitions set out at their conception, had been recently less satisfactory. By 1988, one American China-watcher, the scholar Suzanne Pepper, was noting Shenzhen's 'unimpressive performance': 'Hidden costs are created by an unskilled work force unused to factory labor. Infrastructure is inadequate despite the relatively large investment therein. Transport remains poor, communications are faulty and power shortages are regular occurrences. [….] Overseas Chinese investment, moreover, had not been of the desired quality'. The conclusion drawn by analysts in Hong Kong, Pepper wrote, was that the experiment with Special Economic Zones had 'essentially failed to achieve its intended aims', though she itemized the multifarious reasons why the Chinese leadership would never admit as much.[8]

The minibus buzzed slowly south, and the train station came back into view: a squat low-rise hunk of concrete and blue glass right on the Hong Kong border. Deng's daughter pointed out the station sign hanging in red from a concrete arch, the two characters copied in Deng's handwriting, and made a joke about the sign being his patented intellectual property – a persistent issue in Shenzhen which was notorious for its production of counterfeit goods.

They cut west, parallel with the river. They discussed the official opening of Shenzhen Stock Exchange in July 1991 (Shanghai's had opened in December the previous year) – another idea 'borrowed' from the capitalist world. Deng rhetorically verbalized the concerns many had about the idea of introducing such trading: 'Are securities and the stock market good or bad?' he queried. 'Do they entail any dangers? Are they peculiar to capitalism? Can socialism make use of them?' He had already formulated his response, however, saying that people can reserve judgement, but that China must try such ideas out. If they go well, they can be expanded; otherwise they can be stopped. 'What is there to be afraid of?' he asked. For Deng, the only test, as with the SEZs, was whether adopting and adapting such approaches could help drive prosperity.

But, later in 1992 would come a demonstration of exactly what critics were afraid of, when, in August, the Shenzhen authorities began their lottery of permits to buy shares the following year – a process that quickly devolved into chaos. The frenzied desire to acquire tickets, despite only one-in-ten odds of success, meant huge queues developed outside the city's banks two days before the lottery tickets went on sale. When the tickets did finally go on sale, all five million sold out within a few hours. Many suspected that local officials had kept tickets for themselves. On 10 August, 'tens of thousands of enraged investors rampaged through the city in protest', smashing windows and overturning cars. It was the worst unrest that China had seen since 1989. The police 'responded with water cannon, tear gas, and warning shots fired into the air,' reported journalist James Miles. A heavy rainstorm finally helped to dissipate the protestors.[9]

Later that year, Zhu Rongji would attribute the calamitous events in Shenzhen to China being an 'immature market economy', and urge caution and careful planning in developing China's stock markets; the subtext of his speech was that Deng's comments during his Southern Tour had encouraged a too-freewheeling approach to this sensitive issue.[10] Perhaps more predictably, Chen Yun would suggest that this 'turmoil' was another demonstration of the dangers of moving too fast with reforms.[11]

After little over ten minutes travelling through the city, the minibus arrived at Deng's first destination: the Huanggang Border Crossing Station on the very southern edge of the city.

Officials sporting smart peaked hats greeted Deng as he clambered with assistance from the minibus and escorted him, flanked by Zhuo Lin and Deng Rong, to the bridge across the Shenzhen River. This border post with Hong Kong had been completed in 1989, and around

7000 cars and 2000 people crossed each day. Deng walked slowly out onto the bridge, right up to the borderline and stood looking across into Hong Kong's New Territories: flat, water-filled farmland; the occasional village of white houses; low, rounded hills and curling alluvial valleys off into the distance.

After dinner that evening – despite being in the south, his daughter had ensured that there was plenty of Sichuanese chilli in the evening's meal – Deng set out for his regular walk on the streets near to his hotel. After nearly half an hour, as the walking party returned, one of the officials accompanying Deng suggested that, for convenience's sake, they might return along the same road that they had walked earlier. Deng turned and addressed him. 'I will not turn back!' he said, smiling.

It was a knowing comment, full of allusive power. It referenced a remark Deng had made during his 1984 Southern Tour, and which had since become famous, co-opted into the mythology of that journey and of reform and opening.

Shortly after his visit to Shenzhen that January, eight years ago, Deng had spent two nights at the lavish Zhongshan Hot Springs Hotel, just north of the city of Zhuhai on the other side of the Pearl River. Built by the pro-Beijing Hong Kong businessman Henry Fok, it featured one of China's first (post-revolution) golf courses, designed by Arnold Palmer. Behind the hotel rose a modest peak, named Luo Sanmei after a girl of local legend who was deemed a model of filial piety. The hill did not quite reach one hundred metres in height; its features softened by fractals of fern and azalea, and shadowed by a high canopy of pine, eucalyptus and sandalwood. A rough path ran to a pagoda at its peak.

Deng, setting out from the hotel on his morning constitutional, followed the path up the hill, flanked by a retinue of attendants. And though he was then seventy-nine-years old, he managed the 653 steps to the top without difficulty, so the story goes. As he began to descend on the far side, however, those accompanying him expressed concern about the steepness and unevenness of the loose gravel path. The way they had already walked was, perhaps, safer.

'*Bu zou huitoulu*' he told them: 'Do not turn back!'.

Deng's refusal to go back would be transmuted in party histories from banal utterance into resonant metaphor. What it pithily seemed to express was his determination to keep moving forward, no matter the challenges or objections. The political infighting, ideological zealotry and economic stagnation of the Cultural Revolution were what lay close behind them in 1984. As he had observed the prior summer:

Now that we are on the right track, our people are happy and we are confident. Our policies will not change. Or if they do, it will be only for the better. And our policy of opening to the outside world will only expand. The path will not become narrower and narrower but wider and wider. We have suffered too much from taking a narrow path. If we turned back, where would we be headed? We would only be returning to backwardness and poverty.[12]

His reference to that comment atop Luo Sanmei, here in Shenzhen eight years later, was a reassertion of his renewed faith in forward motion as an escape from the troubled past, and a reminder of the significance of that last Southern Tour in moving China's economic debates forward. It had a personal resonance too; Deng was not one to constantly revisit or discuss past events or traumas: his consistently muted response to the persecution of the Cultural Revolution years seems to testify to that.

But it was the nation's need for faster action that he was overtly referencing once more in 1992, the journey towards that self-set goal of quadrupling China's GDP by the year 2000. He would invoke another similar metaphor during this trip in expressing that need – drawing again on the imagery of travel, and emphasizing the risks of not continuing on: 'For a big developing nation like China, it is impossible to attain faster economic growth steadily and smoothly at all times [...] Like a boat sailing against the current, we must forge ahead or be swept downstream.'[13]

At ten o'clock the next morning, Deng Xiaoping was 160 metres above the crowded streets of Shenzhen, panoptically surveying the city from the revolving restaurant which perched like a spaceship atop the pinstriped International Trade Centre that he had watched being built on that visit eight years ago. He sat at a long banquet table, with a map of the city unrolled in front of him and upturned teacups positioned in anticipation; crowded around him were scores of local officials and even restaurant staff, eager to glimpse the leader. Party Secretary Li Hao narrated the view, with Deng Rong leaning forward to repeat his words to ensure her father understood. Accounts of this occasion relate his desire to 'stand tall and see far', in the idiomatic Chinese expression, and looking north he could just make out the low buildings and narrow lanes, adjacent to his hotel, that were relics of the old town of Shenzhen: the small provincial settlement which would lend its name to the city and Special Economic Zone that came to spread around it.

This old town owed the limited significance it had in the pre-reform era to the railway. Since 1911, the peninsula of Kowloon in Hong Kong had been connected to the Chinese city of Canton (Guangzhou) by a train line: the Kowloon-Canton Railway, or KCR. The first stop on the Chinese side of the border was a station just outside the market town of Shum Chun or Shen-Ch'uen. As a local trading centre serving the villages and people of the rural area surrounding it – you could buy sugarcane, birdseed, pears, dried oysters and peanuts in the town, amongst other goods – the appeal of this small town for those travelling across the border was limited; most passengers were heading further north to the busy metropolis of Canton.[14] In 1931, however, a casino was opened in Shum Chun, capitalizing on the ban on gambling in Hong Kong by offering a more convenient destination than Macau, which was a four-hour boat ride across the mouth of the Pearl River. The casino's five-year existence saw a brief but dramatic spike in those stopping off in the town; by the year after its closure in 1936, in any case, the Second Sino-Japanese War had begun, causing increasing disruption to the rail services.[15] By 1939, the area around Shum Chun had become a virtual no-mans' land as a result of Japanese bombing.[16]

Shortly after the CCP secured victory over the Nationalists in 1949, Shenzhen became the administrative centre for the county, replacing the old town of Nantou. It settled into life as a moderately sized, moderately prosperous Guangdong town, with two main roads: People's Road and Liberation Road. The railway station moved closer to the river in 1950, and Shenzhen remained significant as a site of first encounters for those crossing the 'Bamboo Curtain'. In 1980, London *Times* journalist Trevor Fishlock found a town of 'simple narrow streets' with firewood stacked outside and chickens in cages. 'The houses were small, humble and clean,' he continued. 'The streets of London were like this once. It was easy for me to feel that I had been transported in time. But then there would be a jolt: in one of these old, charming and winding streets I would look into a house and see the television screen flickering.'[17]

The old town was surrounded by countryside dotted with hundreds of villages, including Yumin Cun, the Fishermen's Village that Deng had so admired in 1984. When the SEZ was established in 1979 these, as part of the surrounding county, were incorporated into the expansive new 'city' of Shenzhen. Further complicating the question of what 'Shenzhen' connoted was the fact that the Special Economic Zone was a smaller subsection of this newly denominated city.

As the architect and academic Juan Du points out in her book *The Shenzhen Experiment*, this complexity also allowed those in charge to misrepresent the population figures: whilst 30,000 is the oft-repeated official figure of Shenzhen's pre-reform days, Shenzhen 'city' had a population of over 300,000 in 1979, and even within the smaller SEZ there were nearly 100,000 people.

Shenzhen's urban development in the 1980s would, though, be concentrated around the old border crossing and market town. The cluster of new buildings in this district would define the first centre of the city and be the site of its first skyscrapers. Gradually, the planned city would spread from this nucleus, developing new urban hubs, and incorporating the hundreds of villages incorporated by the SEZ.

The city pulled in young workers from all over China; about 70 per cent of all those living in Shenzhen at the time did not hold *hukou* – the official registration record which confirms a person as a permanent resident of an area and qualifies them for services including health and education. Annual economic growth rates had run at over 30 per cent for most of those years, driven by this abundance of cheap and transient labour who, on arriving in the city would find themselves cheap accommodation in one of the *chengzhong cun* – 'villages in the city' or 'urban villages' – whose original residents had taken advantage of rural land laws to build dense low-rise housing for rental.

As Li Hao and Deng Xiaoping took in the panorama of the city from atop the International Trade Centre, Li addressed not the physical transformation manifest in front of them, but some of the less visible change.

Li told Deng that the average salary in Shenzhen had nearly quadrupled over the last eight years, but he also stressed that the city had also ensured it promoted 'spiritual civilization' alongside this development of 'material civilization'. The comment referenced a model Deng had advocated in the earliest days of reform and opening, and which had been resurrected in various guises in the ensuing period. It linked the development of economic reform with the need for a focus on morality, patriotism, public order and adherence to socialist ideals.

In the course of the 1980s, two major campaigns had been launched to promote such virtues, and crack down on the perceived vices of the capitalist world. In 1983, the aim of eliminating 'spiritual pollution' would briefly come to dominate party rhetoric, whilst, beginning in 1986, 'bourgeois liberalization' was targeted. These terms had no universally agreed upon definition, however, and thus were often invoked tactically to characterize behaviours that were ideologically unacceptable to different factions of the party. Nor was there consensus about how to address them: whether such ideological work should be the primary focus of the party, dictating methods of reforming the economy and underpinning campaigns of education and propaganda, or whether the two elements – ideological and economic – should be separated, with the main focus on the latter.

Specifically, many argued that the policies of reform and opening – and, in particular, sites of foreign influence like Shenzhen – directly introduced malign forces which would chip away at China's spiritual civilization. The act of pursuing wealth was problematic enough – conservatives in the mid-1980s would argue that members of the party and PLA were being distracted by the consuming aim of making money – but cultural influences from abroad – including pornography – were also seen as eroding public notions of morality.

In an article written in 1990, Li Hao had attempted to address such criticisms emphasizing that, in the arduous construction of Shenzhen, ideological work had been a consistent focus: 'We promptly conducted education in the party on special topics, and theoretically distinguished right from wrong, sought a common understanding, and clearly stated that the SEZ implemented only special economic policies, not political ones,' he wrote. He went on to describe the city's approach to promoting spiritual civilization, in which primary and secondary school students were taught about the history of the nation, to help them understand that 'only socialism could save China, that the younger generation must bring credit to the Chinese nation and to the motherland, and that they must further develop the socialist economy with their own efforts'.[18]

Deng demonstrated a consistent belief in the need to forcefully respond when he perceived threats to public order and to the rule of the party. In 1978 he had, despite initial rhetorical support, suppressed the Democracy Wall movement, during which individuals had expressed their demands for political reform and democratic rights by posting critical essays and posters on a wall at Xidan intersection, just west of Tiananmen Square. In 1986 he had been eager to see student protests in Shanghai and other cities dealt with firmly. And in the aftermath of the Tiananmen massacre Deng had acknowledged that, though despite the campaigns and rhetoric, there had not been an active enough approach to educational and ideological work.

Here in Shenzhen, though, and throughout his Southern Tour, Deng's relentless focus was on economic development. He dismissed conservative concerns, by asserting that the stability of the period after 4 June 1989 'was precisely because we had carried out the reform and the open[ing up] policy, which have promoted economic growth and raised living standards'. To Li, Deng cited the importance of adhering to the idea of 'one centre' – economic development – and 'two basic points' – pursuing reform and opening, and upholding the Four Cardinal Principles, which addressed ideological requirements. This formulation – a favourite of Zhao Ziyang – emphasized the primacy of economic development, and separated the economic from the political.

Though he would acknowledge the importance of combatting the more material problem of corruption, ensuring good public order by 'stamping out' evils, economic progress trumped everything. 'The key is to develop the economy; development is the absolute principle,' he said. Risks should be taken; reforms should be bold. 'When we have enough material wealth,' he would argue, 'we shall have the initiative in handling contradictions and problems'.

During their discussion, Li Hao had referenced the several visits of Singapore's Prime Minister Lee Kuan Yew to Shenzhen, and his positive comments about the model the city could provide. Deng had already told Xie Fei that Guangdong needed to strive to catch up with the 'four little dragons' of Asia – commonly known in English as the Four Asian Tigers: Hong Kong, Singapore, South Korea and Taiwan. So the invocation of Singapore was apposite; Deng was a particular admirer of the public order of the city, and argued that China should strive to surpass it. This model – of economic liberality and experimentation, but with stringent boundaries and punitive responses restricting behaviour – was articulated by Deng in typically direct imagery: 'You have to use a two-fisted approach,' he said. 'With one hand, you grab reform and opening. With the other, you grab every kind of criminal behaviour. You have to have a firm grip with both hands'.[19]

After this centrepiece visit to the International Trade Centre, which neatly closed the circle after his 1984 scrutiny of its construction, officials had organized a visit to a high-profile factory in the north of the city, the Xianke Laser Company (known as SAST in English), a state-owned company established in 1984 which produced laser discs, CD players and speakers, having imported production technology from the European electronics company Philips. Xianke had been carefully chosen; established in only 1984, it was an example of the type of new high-tech industry Deng Xiaoping wanted to encourage in Shenzhen and beyond.

Deng was shown into the company's VIP room and played a film documentary about Deng Yingchao, politician and wife of Zhou Enlai (and foster mother of Li Peng). A singer demonstrated the company's speaker systems by performing a rousing rendition of 'On the Field of Hope' – a song about the generational and emotional ties felt by those who work the land, made famous in the 1980s by Xi Jinping's future wife, the folk singer Peng Liyuan. 'I heard it very clearly,' said Deng after the performance.

Deng praised the youthfulness of the workforce – 'the hope is with the young generation' he said – and was reassured that the company was legally purchasing the rights to the foreign films that they reproduced. Before his departure in late morning, Deng was presented with ten CDs, ranging from revolutionary songs to Peking Opera.

The technology Deng saw during his visit to Xianke seemed like the future, and the company would become famous as a result of his inspection of the factory, attracting international visitors. At its zenith, Xianke employed 4000 people, and had more than twenty subsidiaries. But its technology was ultimately superseded during the 1990s, and it racked up huge debts, meaning that, by the early 2000s, production had essentially ceased.[20]

'Shenzhen was the first "instant China" destination,' wrote *Fodor's Guide* in 1992. 'Since then it has developed at such a rapid rate that it's very like Hong Kong. Today most tourists to Shenzhen are Chinese from Hong Kong engaged in business or on family holidays at lavish but moderately priced resort hotels. Local and foreign tourists are drawn to the brilliant Mini Kingdom [Splendid China] and China Folk Culture Villages parks, and golfers head for the 18-hole golf course'.

The rest of Deng's stay would see the patriarch adopt the role of eager tourist. On the sunny, brisk morning of the 21st, Deng arrived at the adjacent 'Splendid China' and 'China Folk Culture Village' theme parks with his family in tow. The China Folk Culture Village offered whistlestop encounters with China's ethnic minorities: the fifty-five non-'Han' Chinese groups officially recognized by the PRC. Deng watched the prepared performance of song and dance before boarding an electric buggy for a tour of Splendid China which, in this new city of Shenzhen, offered a chance to encounter China's ancient heritage, presenting scaled-down 1:15 versions of China's most famous landmarks. The park was still open to tourists, and a group of Malaysian Chinese visitors spotted Deng and took his photo. The next day, a small version of the image was reproduced in a Hong Kong newspaper – the first public record of his visit to Shenzhen.

Deng took a tour of the sites, visiting the miniature Forbidden City and Tiananmen Square, the Giant Buddha of Leshan from his home province of Sichuan, the Three Pagodas of Dali in Yunnan, and the famous karst peaks along the Li river near Guilin. Eventually they arrived at the Potala Palace of Lhasa, perched high on an artificial hill. 'I have been to other parts of China, but I have never visited Tibet,' he said, posing for a photograph with the whole family. The image shows fourteen family members huddled together, with Deng centre-right – the most soberly dressed of any of them in a buttoned-up black jacket. It is an utterly ordinary picture of a family holiday. All are caught in mid-pose; Deng Rong has her hand half-raised seemingly in order to direct the group's attention to the relevant camera. Behind them rises the white and terracotta palace, with its countless windows and staircases like a sketch by Escher.

Deng would continue in a similar mode the next morning, visiting the Fairy Lake Botanical Garden, where, helped by his children and grandchildren, he planted a *ficus altissima*, or Lofty Fig, tree. Deng was not averse to playing the tourist; during his 1979 visit to America he had gamely eaten barbeque and donned a cowboy hat bought for him at a Rodeo in Houston: 'If the idea was to show that the Chinese visitors were just folks,' *The New York Times* reported, 'the rodeo was the place to put it across'.[21] The photo would be reproduced around the world; it was a moment that marked a new era in US-China relations, with Deng – voted as *Time* magazine's 1978 man of the year – breaking down prejudices of Chinese leaders as unsmiling, austere and inherently hostile to American values.

That this trip was so consciously adorned with the trappings of a family holiday was not any sort of attempt, as some have suggested, to obscure his purpose; the hastily transmitted account of his first stop at Wuhan had made his intention clear immediately to Jiang Zemin and the other leaders back in Beijing. It reflected a desire, encouraged by his children, to recast his post-Tiananmen image by portraying himself as an ageing patriarch and family man.

The official version of his Southern Tour would record crowds in Shenzhen addressing him in this patriarchal vein as 'yeye', Grandpa, or 'shushu', Uncle – expressing a very different public sentiment to those protesting in the aftermath of Hu Yaobang's death three years previously, who, far from viewing Deng as a benign, avuncular figure, argued that the wrong person had died: the 'hypocritical and false live on,' one poster read. 'One man is enough to make the country perish'.[22]

In his latter years and after his death, his children would continue to try to burnish Deng's image as a caring father, discussing in reverential terms Deng's family life. 'It seemed he lacked reactions when others talked to him,' his son Pufang said after his death, overtly addressing the public perception of Deng as emotionally guarded. 'But he had his own way of emotional expression. It was very fine and smooth not like the exaggerated kinds'.[23] 'It seemed to me that few people on earth loved children from the bottom of their hearts as Father did,' his daughter Deng Rong wrote of him.[24] She would publish two biographical accounts of his life: *Deng Xiaoping: My Father*, published in China in 1993, and *Deng Xiaoping and the Cultural Revolution* (2000). Neither comes anywhere near discussing the complicated latter years of reform and opening, and a mooted third volume dealing with the final phase of Deng's career is yet to appear.

At 8.30 am on 23 January, Deng Xiaoping shook hands with officials and hotel staff, before clambering into his minibus and setting off in convoy for the port of Shekou where he would board a boat across the Pearl River to the city of Zhuhai.

Deng sat, as the convoy drove westward, looking out on busy streets shadowed by the reaching buildings which paralleled them. Quite quickly, however, the city began to peter out into patchy countryside punctuated with building sites. To the north, a low hill rose out of the landscape. Eight years later, on 14 November 2000, a six-metre-high statue of Deng Xiaoping, cast in bronze and wrapped for its unveiling in swathes of red paper, would be revealed by Jiang Zemin; the statue had languished in a warehouse since 1997, the year of Deng's death, so uncertain were his successors as to how they should memorialize him.[25]

And even as he prepared to leave, Deng was still refining his final message to officials. 'The primary consideration is not to be afraid of making mistakes,' he said. 'The first thing we need to consider is to explore boldly, instead of first considering making mistakes. The second is to find the problem and correct it immediately'. When he got to the pier, he walked towards the waiting boat, before suddenly turning to Li Hao and saying: 'You carry on your work faster!'. Li responded: 'Your remarks are very important. We are determined to speed up our pace'. As the well-connected China watcher Robert Kuhn has observed, this was an astonishing statement. 'Nowhere else in China was reform moving as fast as it was in Shenzhen. Critics in Beijing often pointed to the city as a case study of what happens when reform moves *too* fast'.[26]

With that final encouragement Deng boarded the boat – a sixty-metre customs boat with a black hull and white two-level cabin – and disappeared from view. He would never set foot in Shenzhen again.

Figure 1 The Hankou 'Bund' or embankment, Wuhan.

Figure 2 Swimming in the Yangtze, Wuhan.

Figure 3 Statue of Deng Xiaoping, Lotus Hill Park, Shenzhen.

Figure 4 View from Lotus Hill Park, Shenzhen.

Figure 5 Billboard of Deng Xiaoping, Shenzhen.

Figure 6 Steps up Luo Sanmei Hill, near Zhuhai, where Deng Xiaoping famously declared he would not turn back.

Figure 7 Statue of Deng Xiaoping, Luo Sanmei Hill.

Figure 8 The 'Fisher Girl' statue and cityscape of Zhuhai.

Figure 9 Detail from an oil painting titled *The Vision*, showing modern-day Pudong in Shanghai, on display at the Longhua Martyrs' Cemetery.

Figure 10 View from the peak of Mount Tai.

Figure 11 The Wordless Stele, Mount Tai.

Figure 12 Front page of the *Shenzhen Special Zone Daily*, 26 March 1992, featuring 'East Wind Brings Spring All Around – On-the-spot Report on Comrade Deng Xiaoping in Shenzhen'.

Chapter 7

WELL WATER AND RIVER WATER

When Deng Xiaoping visited the Huanggang border checkpoint on his first day in Shenzhen, he stood silently for nearly nine minutes gazing from the bridge across the river into Hong Kong's New Territories.

What was he thinking about as he studied the view? There was doubtless much to consider as he surveyed the rural hinterland of this city that was so integral to China's future. '[His] expression when looking at the Hong Kong side is unforgettable,' remembered Xiong Changgen, director of the checkpoint at the time of Deng's visit.[1] Photojournalist Jiang Shigao said that Deng 'looked there with his affectionate eyes without any word. It was a long time before he reluctantly returned to the car'.[2] In a later interview his daughter said that Deng told those with him at the time that his wish was to 'walk on our own land' after 1997.[3] A report in Hong Kong at the time suggested that Deng had told Shenzhen's leaders to expect him back, health permitting, in 1997, and mentioned his desire to visit Hong Kong at the same time.[4]

Hong Kong was no object of speculative fantasy to Deng; he had visited the city several times in his youth, arriving first in mid-September 1920, when on his way from Shanghai to Marseille. But he had not set foot there since the long-distant days of the civil war against the Nationalists; and, indeed, he would never get to see the city's transformation for himself; he would die just 132 days before the official handover of Hong Kong in 1997.

Deng had already expressed his desire to 'stand tall and see far' during his tour. But even from his elevated position on the bridge high above the river, with the city of Shenzhen at this back, his view was limited. Invisible beyond the farmland and dense hills before Deng, the landscape valleyed and peaked towards the southward-pointing triangle of the Kowloon peninsula. There, shop-lined, sign-strewn streets narrowed to a pinnacle and a half-mile of water separating this last dense promontory of mainland from the skyscraper frontage of Hong Kong Island: its screen of rectilinear steel and glass office blocks reaching ever higher towards the green ridgeline of the Peak – exploiting to full advantage their square-metreage of some of the most valuable land in the world.

The border Deng surveyed drew a distinction where, for much of history, there had been no difference. The east-west oscillations of the Shenzhen River marked a line that had only existed since June 1898, when the British diplomat Claude MacDonald signed the Second Convention of Beijing: a ninety-nine-year lease on what became known as the New Territories, which massively increased the area of Hong Kong administered by the British – and which would expire in the inconceivably distant year of 1997.

'We have not asked anything but what was absolutely indispensable for the military and civil necessities of our colony,' wrote one British newspaper shortly after the conclusion of negotiations. 'The Chinese Government, to their credit, have freely recognised the reasonableness of the friendly representations to this effect.'[5] There was little either friendly or reasonable about the British approach to Hong Kong, which was part of a scramble for territory by European powers in the wake of another military defeat, this time in the First Sino-Japanese War (1894–5). A famous French cartoon from the same year, oft-reproduced in China's museums of history as an illustration of international aggression, depicts foreign leaders, including Queen Victoria and Kaiser Wilhelm II, sitting around a cake, knives in hand, discussing and contemplating how to divide the pieces. Behind them, a caricatured Qing official – his skin shaded a uniform yellow and his fingernails long and clawlike – throws up his hands in helpless horror at their actions.

The line drawn in 1898 divided families, communities and networks of trade and kinship that had existed for centuries, cutting across an area that was known at different times as Xin'an or Bao'an County – the remnants of which would later become Shenzhen. Over the course of the first decades of the British lease on the New Territories, as the Chinese imperial era whimperingly faded into a series of experiments in republicanism, the border was more of an administrative inconvenience than significant physical barrier. In the early 1950s, after the CCP had taken charge of China, there were moves on both sides to harden the border. Crossing points were closed, fences erected, and soldiers dispatched to patrol the line. But, even then, as the historian Denise Y. Ho comments, 'everyday life along the frontier was characterised as much by porousness as by a boundary.'[6] Local families continued to cross back and forth across the border – albeit with more bureaucratic hassle than before – whilst smuggling was widespread. Residents of Hong Kong relied on water from the Shum Chun reservoir, completed in 1960 to the north of the border, and food from China's interior.

If the border meant cooperation for a limited few, however, it meant something entirely different to the thousands of mostly young men and women who fought to cross it in the first decades of communist rule. For them it was a trapdoor, through which they could drop out of the People's Republic. In the first two years after the communist victory, hundreds of thousands of people fled across it to escape potential persecution, or simply in fear at what the future promised under Mao Zedong; many were businesspeople and entrepreneurs from cities like Shanghai and Wuxi who would drive Hong Kong's future economic success.

In subsequent decades, migration across the border would peak and trough with the vacillations of life in the People's Republic; 1962, at the tail end of the famine caused by Mao's Great Leap Forward, saw an estimated 140,000 people make the crossing.[7] Some would cross by taking the eastern route across the dense peak of Wutong Mountain, and then through the villages of Luofang or Shatoujiao – the advantage to this route was that the river was a less significant obstacle. Others tried to swim across the bay or river to the west, where patrols had to cover a larger area – the longest route entailed a six-mile swim.

In his memoir *Swimming to Freedom: My Escape from China and the Cultural Revolution* Kent Wong describes the challenges and hardships of attempting to cross the border. During one failed attempt Wong made it a few hundred feet from the shore of Hong Kong, after eight days in the mountains and a nearly six-mile swim from Shekou: 'The first rays of dawn illuminated many white buildings on the Hong Kong coastline,' he wrote. 'Now the sea was calm. The Chinese coast was way behind us. We had passed the midline and were definitely now in Hong Kong waters. The white buildings became clearer and clearer. It would be a sunny and cloudless day, a beautiful day! Hong Kong, here we are!'

But then behind him came the sound of a fishing boat, manned by vigilante Chinese fishermen, paid by the authorities to round up freedom swimmers. 'Grab the pole, or I'll shoot you!' Wong remembers them shouting.[8]

If unsuccessful in attempting to cross, the best outcome was, as happened to Wong, being thrown into a crowded, unsanitary detention centre. No one can say with certainty how many drowned or were shot by guards; local villagers on both sides of the border remember the bodies piling up on the riverbank.

Deng had visited Guangdong in November 1977, the year before his final ascension to the top of the leadership; a trip that is sometimes referred to in official histories as his first Southern Tour. He arrived in Guangzhou on 11 November, and spent nine days in the province, coinciding with 30,000 or so foreigners in town for the Canton Trade Fair. In discussions with local officials, he emphasized the need to narrow the gap between the life in Guangdong and that in Hong Kong, and discussed possible options to achieve this, including increasing the productivity of the countryside and levels of tourism.[9] On the specific issue of the border crossings, Deng asserted that 'there is something wrong with our policy'. The provincial party secretary and later enthusiastic supporter of reform and opening, Wu Nansheng, investigated further after Deng's visit, and discovered that in the village of Luofang – where so many Chinese were attempting to cross the border – the per capita annual income of a villager in the People's Republic was almost one hundred times less than their equivalent across the border.[10] When the village chief of Luofang tried to persuade one young villager not to flee, she told him: 'We people are like birds. We will go and settle wherever we want. I personally think Hong Kong is a good place. There is good money over there and a lot of food to eat. I think Hong Kong is heaven'.[11]

The steps towards a potential solution – one that did not involve simply putting more armed PLA soldiers on the border – were tentative, but clear in direction: Guangdong needed to bolster its economy. In April and May of 1978 a delegation of Chinese officials visited both Hong Kong and Macau to develop a better understanding of the two cities, and subsequently delivered a report to the leadership in Beijing suggesting that the two adjacent mainland areas – Bao'an county and Zhuhai – be developed into production and export centres (with a suggested focus on farming), whilst also encouraging tourism; they were known 'for their picture postcard landscapes, beaches, hot springs and strings of scenic islets'.[12]

In late 1978, Xi Zhongxun would give a speech calling for the province to be given more leeway, to bring in technology from abroad and to be allowed to 'absorb funds from Hong Kong and Macau and from among overseas Chinese'.[13] In April 1979, Deng Xiaoping, now secure at the top of the party, was offering his personal approval to the scheme, which was brought forward by Xi to the Central Working Conference in Beijing. On hearing of the proposal, Deng argued that allowing the people of Guangdong and Fujian to get rich first by accessing investment from abroad wouldn't turn them into capitalists 'because the money won't go into the pockets of Comrade Hua Guofeng or others. Ours is ownership by all the people. I just can't see that things would go wrong if we allow the 80 million people of Guangdong and Fujian to get rich first.'[14]

There was much debate over what these new areas should be called – free trade zones, free ports, export processing zones – but Deng suggested that they be called 'Special Zones', reminding officials that this was the name used for the communists' northern revolutionary base in the 1930s and 1940s. Later, on the insistence of Chen Yun, 'economic' would be added to the name to clarify their purpose, and avoid any suggestion that other types of experimentation might be permissible there.[15]

Though they were approved by the Central Committee in July 1979, Shenzhen and Zhuhai's official birthday is 26 August 1980, when the carefully formulated document setting out the parameters of the SEZs was endorsed by the party leadership. Much debate had gone into just how big these sites of experimentation should be. Zhuhai would be relatively small – it was just 6.8 square kilometres when founded – but the Shenzhen Special Economic Zone, contrary to the example of many such trade zones around the world – was substantial: 327.5 square kilometres. On the day news of government approval arrived in Shenzhen, firecrackers were set off, echoing off the hills and over the river into Hong Kong.

Between 1979 and 1990, nearly 60 per cent of all foreign investment to China came from Hong Kong – much of it funnelling into Guangdong's new SEZs.[16] Shenzhen imported 'Hong Kong's capital, technology, equipment, and management; hotels, office buildings, and supermarkets that rivalled the skyscrapers of Hong Kong towered to the sky, and huge neon lights, luxury dance halls, gaily coloured overpasses embellished the fancies of the people of Shenzhen in a riotous dreamlike blur,' wrote journalist Ma Yijun in 1989.[17] Plenty of money went into property and tourism, to the profit of local landowners, but the main appeal of Guangdong to business people based in Hong Kong (and Taiwan) was low wages. In the early years, Hong Kong companies supplied materials, technology and management in factories staffed by young, mainly female, Chinese workers increasingly from rural areas outside Guangdong, producing toys, electronics, shoes and textiles, which would then be exported via Hong Kong. David Wilson, the penultimate governor of Hong Kong, estimated in 1987 that there were over one million workers in Guangdong producing goods for Hong Kong firms; after announcing this he received a call from the official PRC state press agency correcting him: it was, in fact, *two* million.[18]

The factory employees lived in cramped, dirty, poorly ventilated dormitories of stacked bunkbeds, and worked long hours. In one Shenzhen flower factory, female employees interviewed in 1988 talked of how the Hong Kong boss wished 'he could stop the world from turning so there would be only days without nights. That way we would have to keep on working'. They were already putting in sixteen- or seventeen-hour shifts, with no Sundays or holidays off. 'We are mechanical robots during the day and wooden people at night,' one worker said. When challenged, the Hong Kong investor simply responded that they were running the factory according to the law.[19]

The profitable if exploitative relationship that emerged in the 1980s was always overshadowed by an anticipated future growing ever more real. The deadline of 1997, when the British lease on the New Territories expired, was, even from the first years of reform and opening, distinctly foreground in the minds of politicians and businesspeople in both China and Hong Kong. The outlook for Hong Kong, wrote the economist John Greenwood in 1983, was 'inextricably bound up with the 1997 question', emphasizing the importance of fundamental but intangible concepts such as 'trust between individuals, confidence in the stability of monetary and fiscal policy, and the legal sanctity of contracts'.[20]

When discussions with Deng Xiaoping began over the fate of Hong Kong in 1979, the British representatives raised the issue of the New Territories lease in a circumspect manner, by querying what arrangements should be made for leases on individual plots of land in the territory as the deadline got closer. The British wished to grant leases which legally ran beyond the expiration date of 1997 to maintain confidence, but also to strengthen their own position.

According to British diplomat and ambassador to China (1978–83) Percy Cradock, Deng may not have clearly understood the distinction between the different leases (another account indicates that the Chinese translator made a mistake in the translation),[21] but he did emphasize that 'whatever the political solution, it would not affect investment'. He went on to say that Hong Kong would be respected as a 'special case': 'China needed Hong Kong, and a flexible policy [...] helped socialist reconstruction'.[22]

On the issue of sovereignty, it was clear from early in negotiations to those closely involved that Deng Xiaoping – and therefore China – would not countenance anything but a wholesale return of Hong Kong 'to the motherland'. The question remained, however, as to what the nature of the relationship between Hong Kong and the People's Republic would be after 1997.

Deng had said that Hong Kongers should *fang xin* – put their hearts at ease. But such vague reassurances did little to calm nerves as negotiations continued in the early 1980s between the British government – led by a bullish Margaret Thatcher – and China. The 1980s were a bumpy economic decade in Hong Kong, particularly during the initial phases of negotiations between 1982 and 1984, when markets suffered three significant drops. On 24 September 1983, after months of increasing anxiety over Hong Kong's financial system, and the dramatic depreciation of the Hong Kong Dollar, 'Black Saturday' saw panic selling and a precipitous drop in price, as people desperately tried to get their money into more stable assets or currency. The next month, authorities would peg the Hong Kong Dollar to the US Dollar.

In 1984, Deng attempted to calm nervous Hong Kong investors and businesspeople – most of whom had little faith in promises made by the CCP – by offering more concrete reassurance, telling them that Hong Kong's systems 'will remain unchanged, its legal system will remain basically unchanged, its way of life and its status as a free port and an international trade and financial centre will remain unchanged and it can continue to maintain or establish economic relations with other countries and regions'.[23]

Deng also, however, needed to placate those at home who saw Hong Kong as representing a potential headspring from which capitalism, and other associated social evils, could flow into China. He went on to tell the same audience that

> Our policy towards Hong Kong will remain the same for a long time to come, but this will not affect socialism on the mainland. The main part of China must continue under socialism, but a capitalist system will be allowed to exist in certain areas, such as Hong Kong and Taiwan. Opening a number of cities on the mainland will let in some foreign capital, which will serve as a supplement to the socialist economy and help promote the growth of the socialist productive forces. For example, when foreign capital is invested in Shanghai, it certainly does not mean that the entire city has gone capitalist. The same is true of Shenzhen, where socialism still prevails. The main part of China remains socialist.[24]

In December of the same year, the Joint Declaration resulting from negotiations between the two sides was signed in the Great Hall of the People in Beijing; a treaty which confirmed that Hong Kong would return to Chinese rule in 1997, and that the 'current social and economic systems in Hong Kong will remain unchanged, and so will the life-style' for fifty years, setting out the framework for the 'one country, two systems' approach that had originated as a potential solution by Chinese leaders to the question of Taiwan's future.

Any illusion, however, that anxiety in Hong Kong would be quieted by the agreement between the British and Chinese was shattered on the night of 3 June 1989. 'Tiananmen revived all Peking's neuroses about British duplicity and the external threats to their socialist system,' wrote Percy Cradock. 'It imported a renewed element of "struggle" into a relationship where co-operation was slowly beginning to grow'.[25] Politicians in the People's Republic saw the support given to the protestors by those in Hong Kong as an example of the perils of greater openness – Li Peng called Hong Kong and Macau a 'base of subversion'.[26]

And in Hong Kong, the massacre dramatically heightened fears of the future post-1997; it was a demonstration of ruthlessness and brutality that shook the already limited faith the people of Hong Kong had in the principles of the Joint Declaration. On 5 June, the Beijing-controlled Hong Kong newspaper *Wen Wei Po* uncharacteristically published an editorial deeply critical of the CCP, and Li Peng and Yang Shangkun in particular. 'This cannot but set people thinking: What has gone wrong with our system?' it read; the front page featured a pile of bodies and crushed bicycles. The leadership was controlled, it said, by 'a group of butchers'.[27] The newspaper had already attracted attention by the day after the imposition of martial law, printing an editorial column constituting just four large characters: 'deep grief, bitter hatred'. The president of the newspaper was later forced out, whilst its editor went into exile in America.

On the same day, the Hong Kong stock market dropped by 22 per cent; over the following weeks, capital was rapidly moved out of the city. The possibility of Hong Kongers themselves leaving was more fraught; a high proportion of residents had escaped once from the CCP already, and there was no straightforward option if they decided to flee again. For many, the decision was to continue to wait and see. The massacre inspired a substantial period of fevered speculation, with many commentators in Hong Kong and the West asserting that the CCP would not be able to survive the fallout from the spring of 1989.

In July, the new general secretary Jiang Zemin reaffirmed once more the desire of a clear political delineation between Hong Kong and the PRC. 'The saying has it that "well water must not intrude on river water", he said in a meeting with Hong Kong members of the committee responsible for drafting the new 'Basic Law' that would codify the legal system that the city would exist under after 1997. 'I am not going to introduce socialism in Hong Kong, Macau, and Taiwan, and you must also not bring any capitalist ideas into the interior of China'.[28] Some argued, however, that the river water of the mainland was already seeping through; two other members of the committee – founders of the Alliance in Support of the Patriotic Democratic Movement in China – had been stridently criticized in the *People's Daily* and unceremoniously expelled from the committee. An article in the anti-communist Hong Kong magazine *Cheng Ming* argued in August that these events revealed the CCP's true motivations.

> All their talk of "one country, two systems," "no change for the next 50 years," and "no introduction of socialism to Hong Kong, Macau and Taiwan" is nothing but a pack of lies to deceive people. What can be truly believed is that "river water will continuously intrude on well water," and the more it intrudes, the more malicious, the more frequent, and the more unscrupulous it will become.[29]

By the time Deng arrived on the Hong Kong border on that January day in 1992, the relationship between Hong Kong and the People's Republic had stabilized somewhat – economically at least. There had been ongoing disputes around the building of a new US$16 billion airport, and later that year Hong Kong would welcome its new, final and controversial governor in Chris Patten. But that was a few months, and a lost British parliamentary seat, in the future.

Substantial amounts of money were travelling both ways across the border: in 1991, Hong Kong imported nearly US$40 billion worth of Chinese goods, whilst around US$27 billion went the other way. Investment in property from both sides was also substantial; one estimate suggested that by 1997, 20 per cent of Hong Kong's property could be owned by Chinese firms.[30]

In June of that year, shortly before Chris Patten set out for Hong Kong, the governor that had begun negotiations with Deng Xiaoping, Murray MacLehose, rose from his seat in the House of Lords to offer some advice.

'It will be valuable to use the pause to bring this fresh mind to bear on the elements that favour a smooth transition and those that stubbornly appear to threaten it; those that make for a constructive relationship with China and those that do the reverse,' he said. 'Before he sets out Mr. Patten will have been briefed on all the political difficulties that have made his task what is so often described as awesome. But he will find not a community that is weighed down with political care but one that is most obviously thriving in circumstances of steadily rising prosperity. It is also a community not at all at arm's length with China but, on the contrary, in ever closer economic and social contact with it. Indeed, Hong Kong combines with South China to make up the area of most rapid economic growth in the whole world'.[31]

Chapter 8

'WHOEVER IS AGAINST REFORM WILL BE DRIVEN OUT OF POWER'

The Pearl River Delta opens a deep, crooked notch in the coastline of southern China, the most obviously inviting means of ingress along this stretch of the South China Sea. The delta pulls together the waters from most of Guangdong province, as well as neighbouring Guangxi. Three rivers drawing their names from the cardinal points where they find their source – the East, North and West Rivers – become a tangle of waterways meeting the short Pearl River, which runs through the city of Guangzhou and the narrow strait of the *Boca Tigris* or 'Tiger's Mouth' before collectively spilling into the sea.

With Guangzhou at its zenith, the delta today is flanked by the amorphous spread of once distinct towns running down each side of the widening delta. To the east, the manufacturing city of Dongguan is separated only by the inconvenience of low mountains from the northern reaches of Shenzhen; the urban sprawl slicks around them and down the eastern bank of the river through Humen, where Qing official Lin Zexu, dispatched by the Daoguang Emperor to Guangdong, once oversaw the destruction of nearly 1.2 million kilograms of foreign opium: an act which would kick-start the first Opium War in 1839, and mark the beginning of China's 'Century of Humiliation', as it was termed by nationalists in the early twentieth century.

To the west, the curling, thinning strands of the West River separate to find their way to the delta mouth, delineating the spread of similarly dense cities and towns, most notably Foshan, Jiangmen and Zhongshan, where revolutionary leader Sun Yat-sen – known in Mandarin as Sun Zhongshan – was born, and to which he gave his name the year after his death.

And, at the base corners of the triangle of the delta, sit the two former colonial outposts of Hong Kong, to the east, and Macau, to the west: 36 nautical miles apart. They are adornments which mirror one another not only in their position guarding the opening to the delta, but also in the two Special Economic Zones rubbing up against their borders.

And it was from one to the another that Deng Xiaoping crossed on the next stage of his Southern Tour, in a journey across the mouth of the Pearl River to the city of Zhuhai that took just over an hour; a busy hour of conversation, by all accounts, though he was not too preoccupied to note the remains of an old Qing dynasty customs house as he crossed, a crumbling reminder of the bad old days.

It was the morning of 23 January; Deng was six days into his tour. His trip had already attracted press attention in Hong Kong; the newspaper *Ming Pao* was the first to report on Deng's visit to Shenzhen, printing on page two of its 21 January edition a story titled 'Deng Xiaoping Inspects Shenzhen; Has Tight Schedule, Is in Good Spirits'.

It was a bright day on the delta: accounts tell of blue skies, green trees, the gleaming silver sea. As the boat crossed the river, Deng talked to provincial party secretary and Guangdong native Xie Fei on development beyond the Special Economic Zones. Xie told him that despite the prosperity evident around the Pearl River Delta, much of the mountainous region ringing the edge of the province was still relatively backward. Deng told Xie that Guangdong had a leading role to play in reform and opening, and that it must strive to catch up to the four little dragons over the course of the next twenty years.[1]

The boat pulled into Jiuzhou port on the southeastern tip of the city of Zhuhai, and the waiting convoy drove the short distance from the harbour to the Shijingshan Tourist Centre – a white neoclassical hotel flanked by palm trees, set against a rocky outcrop which leant the hotel its name: *Shijingshan* translates literally as *Stone Scenery Mountain*. After a short break, as in Shenzhen, Deng set out to see the changes to the city for himself.

Work had been done in advance of his visit to 'make sure Mr Deng's eyes fell on nothing untoward' during his time in Zhuhai. An official crackdown on brothels had been launched about a week before his arrival, shutting down massage parlours for 'renovation'; prostitution was a persistent challenge for authorities in the city, as it was in Shenzhen. Taxi drivers were also frustrated by a new insistence that they park legally, stopping them from being able to pick up passengers returning across the checkpoint with Macau. 'I hope he will leave as soon as possible,' one driver grumbled.[2]

Deng was impressed by the change he noted. At a point near the old theatre, he recalled how in 1984 there had been just one big stone house, and now it was all new buildings. It was not just the development that Deng noted, however. This self-styled 'garden city' was beautiful, Deng said, and had its own characteristics. 'If I was a foreign businessman,' he said, 'I would come here to invest'.

Zhuhai's character was determined by its long coastline, with arcing bays embellished with hundreds of small islands, many clustered in archipelagos. Once, Zhuhai had been all and only islands; over centuries the alluvium carried in the river water from inland was deposited to form verdant valleys, with the islands becoming low hills.[3] Deng's route took him along the edge of this landscape, curving along the new coastal road around the bay, where the green waters of the delta lapped the shore and from which, on rare clear days, you could make out the outline of Hong Kong's Lantau Island.

Zhuhai was not just geographically distinct from its sibling across the delta mouth. The area given over to the Special Economic Zone in Zhuhai had grown from diminutive beginnings, but even by 1992 was still only just over a third of the area of Shenzhen, mostly hugging the western bank of the broad delta. In population, too, the Zhuhai SEZ was overshadowed by its near neighbour; its permanent population when Deng visited was a little under 300,000.[4]

Its development had been more limited for two main reasons. Firstly, and most prosaically, it lacked the transport connections – and in particular the deep harbour – that benefited Shenzhen: in 1991, Shenzhen received just over fourteen million tonnes of cargo; Zhuhai about two and half million.[5] But as Shenzhen had found both money and an international market via Hong Kong, Zhuhai had had to make do with the more limited possibilities afforded by its neighbour.

Macau was not without a significant and storied role in international trade – but it was a role that had now lapsed into historical memory. In the sixteenth century, Macau had become a Portuguese trading post; the Ming Emperor allowed a permanent settlement to be built on the peninsula in 1557 for a yearly rent of about 20 kilograms of silver. It quickly became the gateway to China for traders and missionaries, and a prosperous, fortified city built in the image of the Europe its settlers had left behind. This golden age was brief, however; by the middle of the following century, the main trade route it relied upon was severed after the Japanese became increasingly unhappy with the interference of Catholic missionaries from Spain and Portugal, and the Ming dynasty had been overthrown by the Manchus from the north.

Once Hong Kong, with its deep harbour, was established as a port by the British in the mid-nineteenth century, Macau descended into relative irrelevance; a curiosity notable more for its unlikely blend of European and Chinese architecture than for its role in international commerce.

By 1992, the small appendage of Macau was embracing its future as a playground for the wealthy, from the mainland, Hong Kong and further afield: a self-styled sin city, greeting millions of tourists each year. New hotels were thrown up, often on land reclaimed from the sea; as its population swelled to around 450,000, the bland, tall apartment blocks that characterized mainland cities became a feature of the skyline, looming over ornate rooflines and crumbling baroque façades of patchy pastel colours: pistachio, peach, pink. An international airport – the city's first – would open in 1995 as the Portuguese colony prepared for its return to China in 1999. The names of its nine casinos alone tell a story of Macau's swirling colonial heritage: the *Jockey Club, Lisboa, Palacio de Macao, Mandarin Oriental, Kam Pek, Kingsway, Westin, Hyatt Regency* and the *Jai Alai Stadium*: in their noisy, smoky rooms, over 100 billion Hong Kong dollars was gambled annually on Baccarat and Blackjack, and Chinese games like Fan Tan and Pai Kao.

The Chinese rhetoric around Macau, and its return to the 'motherland' was often almost indistinguishable from that deployed in discussions of Hong Kong – officialdom generally referred to 'Gang-Ao' in reports, joining the final syllable Hong Kong's Chinese name with the first of Macau's. In an interview in December of 1991, Guo Dongpo, director of the *Xinhua* Macau branch – and therefore speaking on the government's behalf – told a reporter that 'Macau will make full use of its advantages of being adjacent to the mainland and having extensive economic relations with the outside world, and will gain great benefit from its cooperation with the mainland on the basis of mutual benefit. It will be an important window and bridge for the Chinese mainland's foreign exchange during the process of modernization'.[6] But despite this optimistic framing, and its success in relieving Hong Kong's businessmen of their dollars, Deng and the rest of the leadership knew that Macau could never emulate Hong Kong's economic role in developing China.

Zhuhai had initially tried to draw on its neighbour's specialism by positioning itself as a tourist city, a Chinese Riviera, as it would brand itself. The hotel where Deng was staying, the Shijingshan Tourist Centre, had resulted from the first Sino-foreign agreement to build a tourist hotel as part of a deal between the Zhuhai government and a Macau businessman named Ng Fok, whose Lee Fok (Holdings) Ltd had investments in casinos and ferry services in the Portuguese colony.⁷ However, this early plan of avoiding industrialization resulted in sluggish growth, particularly when compared to Shenzhen, and so from 1984, the city began to try to emulate its sister city, and other manufacturing towns around the delta, in attracting low-end, labour-intensive manufacturing. As well as causing environmental problems, this approach also floundered on Zhuhai's noted lack of good transport connections and easy access to international money and markets, and by the time of Deng's visit, the city had returned to a plan of developing Zhuhai as a Singapore-style garden city integrating hi-tech factories which were less polluting, making circuit boards, televisions, air-conditioning units and other electronics. A member of the House of Lords who had been invited on an official visit the previous year noted the rapid pace of development of this type:

> For mile after mile – and I only saw a relatively small corner – factories are being erected, together with blocks of flats, to service a development zone which will supply goods of every description through the new deep-sea port at present under excavation and the new airport proposed to serve the zone.
>
> I should just say here that as one drives through the economic zone there are bulldozers flattening and clearing countryside where very soon there will be factories appearing as if from nowhere. Moreover, in no time at all they will be operational.⁸

Deng's ostensible focus during his time in Zhuhai – he would stay for a week – was on this hi-tech industry, and he threw himself into a busy schedule of factory visits. He toured the city in a motorcade including four minibuses, escorted by a pair of police motorcycle escorts at the front and rear. He would visit pharmaceutical and electronics factories, using the opportunity to reiterate the importance of developing China's scientific and technological industries. 'Only when we promote science will there be hope,' he said. 'In the past decade or so, China's scientific and technological progress has been great, and it is hoped that it will progress faster in the 1990s'. He also emphasized the important role of young people, particularly those who have studied abroad, in increasing China's expertise in hi-tech fields: 'The gate of the motherland is always open to our students abroad,' he said. 'The motherland welcomes you back after your studies'.⁹

On the morning of the 25th, Deng visited the revolving restaurant at the top of the twenty-nine-storey Fangyuan Building, then the tallest building in the city, overlooking Macau and Zhuhai – a scaled-down imitation of the International Trade Centre in Shenzhen. Here, he spoke in general terms: 'Guangdong is the leading force for the economic development of the whole country,' he said. No matter what, China must stick to the principle of stability: 'to keep stability, we must boost the economy; and Guangdong should set a good example in this regard'.[10] At 11.35 am, as Deng descended in the elevator, his daughter told him that a crowd of several thousand had gathered outside the building. 'He was able to see them, the people of the special zone who had used their hands to put bricks and tiles in place in this once barren beach, their sentiments, and their confidence in carrying on reform and opening up. Applause and shouting never ceased ... ' one account hyperbolically recorded.[11]

Missing, however, from official accounts of Deng's visit is perhaps the most significant moment of his whole Southern Tour. Accounts of exactly what happened differ. One version goes like this: on the evening of 25 January, at the Yuanlin Guesthouse just a small distance towards the coast from Deng's own, politicians and military personnel from around the country congregated. The hotel was sealed off to the public and 'lit up like a Christmas tree'.[12] The meeting was chaired by Yang Shangkun, then vice-chairman of the Central Military Commission (as well as President of China), and an ally of Deng, who had accompanied him on the Southern Tour so far. In attendance was Yang's owlish half-brother, Baibing, then secretary general of the Central Military Commission, who had led the military crackdown on 4 June; together, the Yang brothers had secured effective control over the PLA for the last decade. Also present was Qiao Shi, in charge of public security affairs and the man who rumour said might be Jiang's replacement as General Secretary – before Jiang's nomination for the top job, many had seen pro-reform Qiao as the heir-apparent. Qiao had during this period referenced some leading party figures 'who feign support for reform; he advised them to step down from power'.[13] There were also 'commanders from the different military regions, districts, and services'.[14] Deng was, according to this report, not in attendance at this substantial meeting; he instead met the following morning with Yang, amongst others, at his hotel where they reported to Deng on how the conference had proceeded. Another account has Deng leaving his hotel on the afternoon of the 25th to meet with Yang and Qiao at the Yuanlin Guesthouse, where Yang was staying.[15]

What contemporary reports – all published by Hong Kong newspapers and magazines – confirm is that Zhuhai saw a congregation around 25 January of some of the most important military leaders in China, including two vice-chairmen of the Central Military Commission, China's top military decision-making and command organization. One figure was notably absent, however: the chairman, Jiang Zemin. As the most detailed report from Hong Kong would put it: 'It is maintained by some people that, through this conference, Deng Xiaoping wanted to explicitly show that his reform line enjoys strong support within the Army, a demonstration which will be of immense significance in his efforts to shake off the harassment from party conservatives since 4 June and regain real authority'.[16] Another account quotes sources close to CMC vice-chairman Liu Huaqing, who was apparently 'especially interested in the joint efforts by the people and army units in promoting economic construction'. They should support local people in their economic construction, he said.[17]

The message was clear: Jiang needed to firm up his often less-than-unequivocal support for more ambitious reform and opening, and not be swayed by others in the leadership, including hardliner Premier Li Peng, in continuing to dial back growth targets and resist the calls for greater marketization and foreign trade.

Deng had directly addressed the slowdown of the last few years during one of his tours of the city. The years between 1984 and 1988 were, he said, 'very lively and a convincing process of development. We can say that our country's wealth increased enormously in that period, and the national economy as a whole scaled a new height'. He said he had agreed with the rectification which began in 1989, because it was 'indeed necessary'. But its main contribution could only be regarded as stability, he argued. 'In our development, it seems we should seize an opportune moment in a certain stage to accelerate development for a few years and, when problems are identified, promptly straighten them out and then continue advancing'.[18]

If that framing of the last few years was not clear enough, Deng went further whilst talking in the revolving restaurant atop the Fangyuan Building. 'Whoever is against reform will be driven out of power. The present central leadership has done a good job. Of course, there are still many problems, but problems exist at any time,' he added, in a commentary that would not have been entirely reassuring to Jiang.[19] The meeting of the military in Zhuhai seemed designed to imply – none-too-subtly – the consequences of non-compliance. 'Those who take the post of CPC General Secretary will certainly come to no good end,' went a favourite phrase of party cadres at this time; Jiang must have been wondering if this saying might be about to be proved true once again.[20]

That nervousness and uncertainty still ruled back in Beijing was implicitly confirmed by the continuing lack of mainland media attention to Deng's tour. Remarkably, China's news agency Xinhua had managed, on 25 January, to report on the visit of Yang Shangkun to Shenzhen without once mentioning the presence of Deng Xiaoping; the details reported included Yang's visit to the city's Xianhu Botanical Garden, and his planting of a tree – again entirely omitting the presence of the most important man in China and his family at the event.[21]

On the afternoon of 29 January, after a week of factory tours and handshakes – punctuated by that clandestine meeting of the Central Military Commission – Deng prepared to leave Zhuhai. Before his departure, the staff of the Shijingshan Tourist Centre posed for a group photo with 'Grandpa Deng' outside his villa. At 3 pm, he and the rest of the family set out by car on the 130-kilometre drive northwards to the provincial capital of Guangzhou. They passed by the Zhongshan Hot Springs Hotel, its villas nestled amongst the dense greenery at the foot of Luo Sanmei Hill, on which Deng had declared his refusal to turn back in 1984. They passed through the town of Zhongshan itself, alive with the noise and bustle of building work. Around four o'clock in the afternoon, Deng's bus arrived at the Zhujiang Refrigerator Factory. It was a sunny afternoon, and the factory had rolled out the red carpet in anticipation of his visit. The factory had started as a township enterprise, but now sold around half a million Rongsheng brand fridges a year, both in China and abroad.[22] Another factory, another briefing by factory bosses in an anonymous meeting room, another pageant of performative clapping and handshaking from the workforce who lined up to express their 'respect and thanks to the chief designer of China's reform and opening up program'.

It would be his last stop on this trip through Guangdong, but as he progressed towards Guangzhou and his waiting train, he saw from his window the spread of low factories and new industry in market towns that had become industrial satellites: places like Beijiao, a centre of electrical fan manufacturing; Chencun, famous for its flower industry; and Panyu, which was growing into a hub for jewellery making and gem cutting.

Deng crossed the Luoxi Bridge over the Pearl River and into the southern reaches of Guangzhou. At 6 pm, Deng and the family were reunited with his private train at the city's East Railway Station; they clambered aboard after ten days in Guangdong. The train pulled out slowly from the station, through the borderlands of the spreading city, and out of Guangdong.

Chapter 9

THE YEAR OF THE MONKEY

Deng's train cut back north through the valleyed gaps of the Nanling mountain range which, spreading eastward, divides Guangdong from the provinces on its northern border. For centuries these mountains walled off the far south, which was thought of as beyond the civilized world that pooled around the eastern reaches of the Yangtze, and was known as Lingnan, or south of the mountains. Retracing the route of eleven days prior, the train passed back into Hunan province, then headed east along the Yuanhe River valley into landlocked Jiangxi province, through the spreading small factories of towns like Pingxiang and Xinyu. It was a rainy Thursday, cold and overcast, and the valley was swathed in a mix of mist and pollution.

At 3.30 pm, Deng arrived in the town of Yingtan, a railroad hub which sits on a U-shaped curve of the Xin river, about halfway along a north-easterly line drawn between Guangzhou and Shanghai. Waiting on the station platform were Jiangxi's party secretary, Mao Zhiyong, and the governor, Wu Guanzheng. Deng knew the party secretary well from his days in Hunan province, and quizzed him on the usual points of interest – the pace of development and the income of local people – pressing the same message he had brought from Guangdong. 'The swift economic progress achieved in the years since 1984 represents a leap,' he said. 'Peasants are now bringing home more money, electrical appliances have entered peasant households, and many new houses have been built in the rural areas. [...] We must act more boldly and freely.'[1]

There were new tall buildings flanking the grid of streets around the station, and the previous year the town had welcomed 1500 visitors for a 'Dragon and Tiger Culture' festival – named after the nearby mountains where Taoism was born – to attract investment to the town. Deng was not here to laud Yingtan as an exemplar of reform and opening, however; he had more personal matters in mind. 'Father feels very attached to Jiangxi,' Deng Nan told the officials on the platform.

'He never stopped talking about Jiangxi on the train.' 'I do feel attached to Jiangxi,' he told Mao and Wu. 'I have spent more time in Jiangxi than the two of you.'[2]

Deng had spent two extended periods in the province. For the first, he had been just a young revolutionary, in his late twenties. He arrived in the remote city of Ruijin, which sits in the mountains bordering the east of Jiangxi, in August of 1931. Ruijin would later become known as the 'cradle of the Chinese revolution'; here a new state would centre itself. Ruijin would become the capital of the Chinese Soviet Republic, a separate state within Nationalist China, established under Mao Zedong and run by the CCP. Deng involved himself enthusiastically in the development of this new experimental republic.

He would, however, find himself on the wrong side of a factional divide in the party, attacked in 1933 by 'leftists' opposed to Mao Zedong, who Deng had supported, and dismissed from his post. This 'heavy political burden' was not the only consequence of the conflict in the party for Deng; it also resulted in the loss of his wife to a political opponent.[3] In October 1934, Deng and the Communists would embark on the 6000-mile journey known as the 'Long March' to settle in a new base in northern Shaanxi province. But his loyalty to Mao in Jiangxi would repay him, over thirty years later, as the revolution Deng had helped to forge turned on its own.

In the autumn of 1969, three years into the Cultural Revolution, Deng returned, involuntarily, to Jiangxi, after being 'sent down' to work as a lathe operator in a tractor factory near the city of Nanchang. Deng, his wife, Zhuo Lin, and his stepmother would be kept in relative comfort: their house, two-storey, grey brick, had large, well-furnished rooms and a broad carved balcony and was sheltered behind a high gate and tall cassia trees. They lived on the top floor, whilst their guards lodged below them: a persistent reminder of the strictures under which they existed. Each day, Deng and his wife would daily set out on foot for a morning's work at the factory: care was taken not to over-strain the sixty-five-year-old, and he was generally finished by 11 am.

The path to and from the factory was circuitous, though, and involved crossing a busy road; the walk took them over forty minutes each way. Realizing there was a quicker route, Deng talked to those in charge at the factory, and eventually a more direct path was built, halving the time it took to walk to work. Today, tourists can follow the path themselves, and visit a statue and museum opened there in 2002 intended to encourage 'young people to stand up to frustrations with optimism, like Deng did'.

After Lin Biao's death, Deng wrote to Mao, in a letter marked by a performative pragmatism remarkable given the struggles he had been forced to endure:

> I have no requests for myself, only that some day I may be able to do a little work for the party. Naturally it would be some sort of technical job. My health is pretty good. I can put in a few more years before retirement […] I am longing for a chance to pay back by hard work a bit of what I owe […] Chairman, I sincerely wish you long life. Your long and healthy life ensures the greatest happiness for the whole Party and all our people![4]

His plea eventually had the desired effect, though his return to the capital resulted from a mixture of sentimentality and pragmatism on Mao's part. The Great Helmsman needed Deng to take over for the country's premier, Zhou Enlai, who was seriously ill. But Mao also remembered Deng's loyalty to him in the early 1930s in Jiangxi province. On 14 August 1972, Mao wrote a note regarding Deng: he had made serious mistakes, but should be differentiated from Liu Shaoqi. 'He was under attack in the Central Soviet Area,' Mao wrote of Deng's time in Jiangxi. 'He was one of the four guilty persons […] the head of the so-called Maoist faction.'[5] Whatever his recent transgressions, in Mao's eyes that early fealty to his emerging leadership in the communist party counted for something.

Before Deng left, he toured some of the sites in Jiangxi that he remembered from those early revolution days, returning to the city of Ruijin and other parts of the old Central Soviet. 'Although he was still the country's number two "person-in-power taking the capitalist road" and had not been rehabilitated, the cadres and masses of the Jiangxi old revolutionary base area still received him warmly', an article in the *Jiangxi Daily* later recorded.[6] He also stopped at the town of Jingdezhen, the porcelain capital of China, where he was presented by workers with gifts including a coloured vase bearing a motif representing three goats – an image referencing the arrival of spring, and drawn from the *Yijing* or *Book of Changes*, the rising sun heralding good fortune to come. This vase would be put on display in a cabinet in his office following his rehabilitation.

Deng left Jiangxi on 21 February 1973, boarding an ordinary train travelling from Fuzhou to Beijing; the authorities had, however, ensured that Deng and the other nine members of his family had a sleeping car to themselves. 'The engine emitted a great cloud of steam,' wrote Deng's daughter, 'the whistle blew, the big wheels began to roll. The Jiangxi farewell-wishers quickly faded into the distance. The black mountain ridges, the undulating red hills, the endlessly eastward flowing rivers gradually vanished from view'. The next day, the train pulled into platform one of Beijing Railway Station, and Deng and his family spilled out into the capital's cold air, to take their seats in the waiting vehicles that would carry them along Chang'an Avenue and past Zhongnanhai to their new quarters in the west of the city.[7]

Shortly after Deng's return, Mao met him for the first time in six years. Grasping him by the hand, Mao told Deng: 'Work hard and stay healthy.'[8]

It was not quite that simple.

By the time of Deng's recall to Beijing, both Deng and Mao were old men; Deng nearly seventy and Mao nearly eighty. Mao, beset by health problems, would die in the autumn of 1976 – but not before Deng had been subjected to one final round of political persecution.

However useful Deng was politically, he had acquired a powerful enemy in Mao's wife, Jiang Qing. Jiang had orchestrated much of the Cultural Revolution, under Mao's sometimes-tacit, sometimes-vocal, direction, and alongside a group of acolytes who collectively became known as the 'Gang of Four'.

In April 1976, a few months after Premier Zhou Enlai finally succumbed to cancer, there occurred an outpouring of public emotion centred, as it so often has been over the years in China, on Tiananmen Square. Hundreds of thousands of Beijingers came to the square and piled mounds of flowers, wreaths and poems around the base of the 'Monument to the People's Heroes', a granite and marble obelisk reaching nearly forty metres at the square's northern end.

The poems expressed grief at Zhou's passing, but also vitriol towards Jiang Qing and the rest of the 'Gang of Four':

I mourn, but in my ears demons shriek,
I weep, but wolves and jackals grin.
Though tears commemorate the hero
My eyes flash and my sword is drawn.[9]

In the early evening of 5 April, a loudspeaker in Tiananmen Square blared out a warning: the activities on Tiananmen Square were counter-revolutionary, and all those remaining on the square should leave immediately. A few hours later, armed police arrived, and violently cleared the square. Jiang Qing would lay the blame for these 'counter-revolutionary' protests squarely and spuriously at Deng Xiaoping's door, whom she had already been targeting for some months. Deng replied that his only trip anywhere near Tiananmen had been for a haircut at the Beijing Hotel.

Deng had already been stripped again of any meaningful authority, having barely had chance to properly re-establish himself after his return to Beijing in 1973. (He and his family had got so used to the vacillations of his political fortunes that they could pack up their belongings in under two hours: they moved house a dozen times during these years.)[10] In the aftermath of the April protests of 1976, Deng would be relocated, with his wife, to a house just east of Tiananmen Square, leaving his family behind again. He was dismissed from all of his roles in the party.

'Even though I was in difficult circumstances, I always believed that things would change,' he would say in 1984 of his long years of political exile. 'A few years ago some foreign friends asked how I was able to survive that period. I told them that it was simply because I was optimistic. That is why I am still in good health. If you are worrying all the time, how can you get through the days?'[11]

On 6 October 1976, just slightly less than a month since the death of Mao Zedong, a Politburo meeting was scheduled at Huairen Hall to discuss issues deeply pertinent to Mao's legacy – including the building of a grand memorial hall for the Chairman in Tiananmen Square. Wang Hongwen, Zhang Chunqiao and Yao Wenyuan – three of the 'Gang of Four' – arrived at the hall for the 8 pm meeting and were duly arrested by guards. Jiang Qing – the fourth member of the gang – was simultaneously detained at her residence in Zhongnanhai. The four would be accused of forming an anti-party clique, scheming to usurp party and state power.

The door was slowly opening to Deng's return to the party leadership. In July of the following year, Deng would be restored to all the positions he had held before his last ouster the prior year. A joint editorial published in the *People's Daily*, *Red Flag* and the *Liberation Army Daily* lauded the success of an 'historic meeting': 'Chairman Mao long ago made a clear and all-round assessment of Comrade Deng Xiaoping,' it said. 'The plenary session's decision to restore Comrade Deng Xiaoping to all his posts both inside and outside the party embodies the wishes of the mass of party members and of the people. It is yet another proof that the party Central Committee headed by Chairman Hua [Guofeng] is of one heart with the masses'.[12] Deng would, over the course of the next eighteen months, carefully manoeuvre to replace Chairman Hua, advocating a shift away from Maoist dogma, and towards a politics of claimed objectivity; only if comrades 'uphold the principle of seeking truth from facts, of proceeding from reality and of linking theory with practice, can our party smoothly shift the focus of our work, correctly work out the concrete path, policies, methods and measures for carrying out the four modernisations'. So read one section of the communiqué of the Third Plenary session of the Central Committee, adopted on 22 December 1978 – by which time Deng had secured himself in authority.

From Yingtan, east along the valley, threading a needle through the mountains which cut with emerald sharpness across the horizon in every direction. Past the city of Hangzhou, the landscape began to flatten once more, and the view became a patchwork of small towns and factories, compact fields, narrow waterways and raised roads. Eventually, the familiar silhouette of Shanghai appeared, and Deng's train rattled through its western reaches.

Everywhere in the city – from the tree-lined streets of the former French Concession to the winding shadowy lanes of the old city; from the shops of Nanjing Road to the markets of Hongkou – city-dwellers were busy making their final preparations to welcome in the Year of the Monkey. Tons of extra pork had been ordered in to ensure there was sufficient supply for dumpling making; shops were stuffed with boxes of cigarettes and bottles of the potent spirit *baijiu*. Eagerness for the festivities to begin was felt perhaps most acutely by young couples, many of whom had held off trying for a baby in the Year of the Sheep which had now almost passed. Children – particularly girls – born in the Year of the Sheep were expected to have a life of bitterness and bad luck – those who arrived in the Year of the Monkey by contrast were predicted to be blessed by good fortune.

On the eve of the new year, Chinese television carried footage of Deng Xiaoping and Yang Shangkun shaking hands with local officials who had gathered to greet the Year of the Monkey. The two senior officials addressed Deng and Yang, saying that on behalf of the thirteen million people in Shanghai, they wished everyone a happy Spring Festival, health and long life.

Deng was three days into his stay in Shanghai; his fourth consecutive annual visit to the city at Lunar New Year. The city had been the site of his initial attempts to accelerate the pace of reform and opening; the development of Shanghai itself had been a key part of that ambition. 'Comrade Deng Xiaoping has placed high expectations on Shanghai's opening in the 1990s,' one of the 'Huangfu Ping' editorials that Deng had placed in Shanghai's *Liberation Daily* the previous year asserted. 'Shanghai must hold still higher the banner of reform and opening, and the development of Pudong must be faster, better, and bolder. [...] To take a big step forward in opening up during the 1990s, Shanghai must adopt a series of brand new ideas, have the courage to take risks, and do pioneering work.'[13]

In the intervening year, however, the pace had not reached the levels Deng expected. Looking like a rocket being readied for launch, the Oriental Pearl Tower in Pudong was gradually emerging from the nest of scaffolding at its base; even incomplete it towered over the rest of the low-rise warehouses, factories and houses that spread on the eastern bank of the Huangpu River. But there were few other signs of the speedy development that Deng had been advocating. He would complain about this slow progress repeatedly during his stay in 1992, expressing the hope that Shanghai would be 'faster, better, and bolder' in its reform, opening and economic construction. 'The 1990s is the last opportunity for Shanghai's development; we must not let it slip by,' he would say. 'We must boldly make a foray, not be afraid of making mistakes. As long as we can correct ourselves if we have made a mistake, it will be okay.'[14]

In the bright sunny days around the New Year festivities, Deng made no more public appearances. On 7 February, as the weather grew overcast and cold, he resumed his itinerary, visiting first the Nanpu Bridge, completed the previous year and bearing Deng's own calligraphy on its crossbeam, and then the Yangpu Bridge currently under construction; he would return the following year to walk across it. Both were symbolic in their joining of Puxi – west of the Huangpu, where the city was currently centred – and Pudong, east of the Huangpu; the Nanpu cutting into the southern corner of the triangle of Pudong formed by the curve of the river, and the Yangpu connecting the north.

Three weeks previously, Jiang Zemin had been on his own inspection tour of the city with a very similar itinerary, including his own visits to the bridges.[15] He had called Deng shortly after his arrival in Shanghai, to offer his good wishes for the new year, and had given a speech on 4 February to thousands of party cadres which echoed many of the talking points from Deng's speeches to party officials in Wuhan and the south: 'The whole year's work depends on a good start in spring,' he said. The party should 'further emancipate our minds, make explorations boldly, speed up the pace of reform and opening to the outside world,' Jiang declared.[16] The same day, the front-page story of Shanghai's *Liberation Daily* was a long article repeating Deng's Southern Tour ideas almost verbatim.

As Deng Xiaoping had been leaving Guangdong, Li Peng was in Davos, Switzerland, attending the World Economic Forum. The task of improving the economic order in China – of rectification – had been basically accomplished, Li said. And improvement and rectification 'have created even more favourable conditions for furthering reform and opening the country wider to the outside world'.[17] It was a self-justification – the tightening Li had advocated had, he argued, meant that now reform could be pursued more ambitiously (though that ambition should be pegged at 6 per cent growth, in his view) – but Deng cared little for the rhetorical detail. Momentum was starting to build – even if, for now, the national media continued to hold back from reporting on Deng's speeches.

Opposition continued to be led by Chen Yun. On 2 February, Deng and Chen reportedly met at the Xijiao State Guesthouse, in the west of Shanghai, where Deng generally stayed during his visits to the city. During the meeting, Deng had suggested that he, Chen and Yang Shangkun should together send their New Year greetings to the Shanghai people – but Chen refused, and in the end it would be only Deng and Yang who appeared on television.

Four days later, the pair would meet again; again they apparently failed to agree on the party's direction, with Chen advocating ideological construction as the party's main task. The battle between them had become white-hot, close combat according to the same correspondent.[18] 'The meaning of Chen Yun's words is clear,' a report said. 'You, Deng Xiaoping, know only construction and opening up and you will eventually cause peaceful evolution in China as happened in the Soviet Union, and destroy socialism'. Peaceful evolution was a phrase first used by US Secretary of State John Foster Dulles in the 1950s suggesting that socialist states could be peacefully transformed from within via the slow drip feed of foreign ideas; it was a notion that China's leaders had become increasingly sensitive to since June 1989, and which figures like Deng Liqun would argue was an increased threat as a result of the policies of reform and opening.

Over the course of the rest of his stay, Deng would continue to tour the city, taking a night-time boat ride along the Huangpu River and visiting factories, including Belling Microelectronics, a Sino-Belgian venture. Here, he again reiterated that such enterprises were not surnamed 'capitalism' – they were capitalist tools now serving socialism.

His most famous excursion came on the evening of 18 February, the date of the Lantern Festival which draws a close to new year festivities.

9. The Year of the Monkey

At around 8 pm, Deng arrived at Shanghai's No. 1 Department Store on Nanjing Road. He took the elevator up to the third floor, where crowds of people quickly congregated around him. 'How do you do, Comrade Xiaoping!'; 'How are you, Grandpa Deng!' they shouted. Noticing a glass-topped stationery counter on the floor, he walked over and asked for pencils and erasers for his grandchildren. As he was presented with them, shopworkers, reporters, photographers and ordinary Shanghainese crowded around Deng, who looked small and frail in an oversized black Mao jacket. His daughter, Deng Rong, having paid for the stationery, led Deng back out to the crowded corner of Nanjing Road. Later, when asked about his visit, Deng would comment that all he had seen was a sea of people.

Chapter 10

RETURN TO THE CAPITAL

Deng's train departed Shanghai once again at 3 pm on Thursday 20 February, heading for the capital he had not seen for over a month. The train made a brief twenty-five-minute stop at Nanjing station where he talked to local officials and delivered for a final time his pleas for greater speed in developing the economy; it would also pause at the city of Bengbu in Anhui province. But then it was back on board for the overnight haul to Beijing Railway Station and the familiar platform number one. It was a freezing morning that grew more overcast as it progressed, and the greenery and warmth of the south seemed a world away from the capital's narrow grey streets.

A week after Deng's return, the 'full text' of his remarks during the tour was distributed to party cadres. 'Comrade Deng Xiaoping's important remarks not only serve as essential guidelines for the reform and construction at present and for the 14th CCP National Congress [to be held that autumn] to proceed smoothly, but are also of great and far-reaching significance to the cause of socialist modernization as a whole,' a prefatory note from the party's Central Committee asserted. 'Every party member and, in particular, every leading cadre, no matter of which level must conscientiously study Comrade Deng Xiaoping's important remarks, comprehensively and thoroughly master the spiritual essence of the remarks, and implement in real earnest the guidelines embodied in them.'[1]

An editorial in the *People's Daily* on 21 February had begun to drip feed some of Deng's rhetoric – though did not mention the tour – whilst on 9 March, Jiang convened a meeting of the Politburo at which the important guiding role of Deng's southern talks (they were referred to as such so as to avoid using the imperial title of *nanxun*) was emphasized in preparations for the Party Congress.[2] It would not be until 31 March, however – more than two months after Deng had first set out on his Southern Tour – that it was covered in detail by the national media. That evening, a documentary ran on television relaying highlights of the tour; on the same day, the *People's Daily* reprinted 'East Wind Brings Spring All Around – On-the-spot Report on Comrade Deng Xiaoping in Shenzhen', which had been published the week before in the southern city.

In June of that year, Jiang's support was signalled more widely in a speech to the graduating class of the Central Party School which repeated Deng's key Southern Tour talking points and criticized those who failed to consider the important role of the market. 'Deng's *nanxun* was indeed a test for Jiang,' wrote his biographer Robert Kuhn, 'and his Party School speech was his final exam'.[3]

There was, though, nothing like consensus. In an edition of the magazine *Dangdai Sichao* (*Contemporary Trends of Thought*), closely linked to Deng Liqun, a commentary cautioned that China's socialist system would fall to the West if the struggle against 'leftists' was carried too far. Referring back to Zhao Ziyang's leadership, with all the implicit criticism of Deng that such a reference carried, it argued that 'the plague of liberalization had never been placed under control […] [Zhao] directed the struggle against the leftists […] which led to further spread of liberalization and eventually to the political storm which almost overthrew socialist China in 1989's spring'.[4]

But, such theoretical debate held little interest in truth for those beyond Beijing's restless factions. Beginning with the very first explorations of private enterprise in the countryside in the late 1970s, most of the policies of reform and opening had been driven by experiments at the local level. Deng's Southern Tour imperatives became unignorable not because there was consensus at the top, but because, once word got out of his Southern Tour speeches, provincial and city-level officials wanted the freedom to pursue the policies he was advocating, and bombarded officials in Beijing with letters and cables expressing support for Deng's calls to increase the speed of economic development. Every city wanted its own development zone – and often leaders went ahead and set them up without explicit permission from central government. There was obvious self-interest at play here, too; the policies of faster opening – founded on the leasing of urban land – offered cadres an easy way to make a lot of money.

Vice-Premier Tian Jiyun had even pointed out the hypocrisy of some of those who were bad-mouthing the policy – noting that they had themselves derived immense material benefit from it. He proposed critics be sent to a special zone

> where policies favoured by the leftists will be practised. For example, no foreign investment will be allowed there, and all foreigners will

be kept out. Inhabitants of the zone can neither go abroad nor send their children overseas. There will be total state planning. Essential supplies will be rationed and denizens of the zone will have to queue up for food and other consumer products.[5]

*

Deng's next public appearance was in late May, when he arrived early one morning in a green and white Toyota minibus at the enormous iron and steel works that sits in the shadow of the western hills out to the west of Beijing. Accompanying him once more was his wife, Zhuo Lin, and his daughters Deng Rong and Deng Nan. Capital Iron and Steel was a sprawling articulation of the great unresolved problem of the Chinese economy – barely referenced during Deng's Southern Tour: what to do with the country's enormous, inefficient state-owned enterprises.

And Capital Iron and Steel was certainly enormous: the corporation at the time consisted of 7 large companies, 104 factories, 25 Sino-foreign joint-ventures and 8 joint-ventures overseas, spread across twenty-four provinces and three countries. The site in the west of Beijing alone employed over 200,000 people, providing them with housing, food, healthcare and education for their children.

During his tour, however, Deng would laud the organization as a model for others to emulate. A demonstration of his approval was found in Capital Iron and Steel being granted greater autonomy in the months following his visit, including permission by the State Council to open its own bank. Deng called during his time at Capital Iron and Steel for a national drive to reinvigorate state-owned enterprises, arguing that they should not be restricted in their development, 'but rather they should be given greater decision-making power'.[6] It was an intervention as pointed as any he had made during his trip to the south earlier in the year.

During his visit, Deng said that 'The current leadership do not know economics. Zhu Rongji is the only one who understands economics'.[7] The decisive, forceful, hatchet-faced Zhu had already been tasked with beginning to sort out China's State-Owned Enterprises; ten days after Deng's visit, Zhu would drag party cadres from a swathe of different ministries to Capital Iron and Steel, where, following in Deng's slipstream, he argued that if the government continued to 'impose restrictions on enterprises, exercise management over minor issues rather than major ones, and meddle in everything, it will be difficult for enterprises and workers to be masters of their own affairs. Moreover, production and development will not be ensured'.[8]

Zhu had intervened to try to dismantle the knot of debt which bound the state-owned enterprises – debt accumulated nationally was at an astonishing 300 billion yuan in mid-1991. The state-owned enterprises' share of this debt came from mounting deficits as a result of either substandard products or as a consequence of the fixed prices they were required to sell at not being sufficient to cover production costs. Zhu pumped government money into the state-owned enterprises to clear the debts and to grease the gears of the national economy, and by the end of the year he would laud his own 'remarkable results'.[9] But the problems had been displaced, not resolved.

In the middle of October, 2000 delegates arrived at the Great Hall of the People for the fourteenth National Congress of the CCP. It was the first such meeting for five years: since before Tiananmen, before Zhao Ziyang's ousting, before the dominoes of the Soviet Union had begun to fall.

In the months running up to the party congress, Chen Yun had attempted to intervene to block the adoption of Deng's ideas, issuing a ten-point rebuttal in August. It contended that a 'high growth rate with poor efficiency is destructive' and lamented that the study of communist ideals, party rules, socialist morality and patriotism had been 'weakened or abolished'.[10]

In early September, Chen would make another statement of similar force, noting additionally how the agenda was being driven by local officials in search of rapid economic success: '[T]hey put money and materialism first. Regionalism and individualism are rampant,' he said. 'They encourage purely high growth rates, high targets, and high output. The thought that "political study is useless" exists and decadent practices are widespread within the party'.[11]

Despite Chen's forceful rhetoric, the six-day-long party congress would confirm the success of Deng's Southern Tour in decisively shifting the party onto a course of ambitious growth.

In his report, Jiang Zemin would deem Deng the architect of reform and opening up 'as well as of the modernization endeavours related to socialism in China' and in his introduction referenced the 'important talks Comrade Deng Xiaoping delivered during his inspection tour of south China at the beginning of this year' which he said had enormously encouraged cadres. Jiang would affirm Deng's argument that the Special Economic Zones he visited during his tour were surnamed 'socialist' and not 'capitalist'.

10. Return to the Capital

The party now had, he announced, a good opportunity to accelerate development; this should be their primary focus. One of the most significant changes ratified by the congress was the shift from a 'socialist planned commodity economy' to a 'socialist market economy', a phrase which Chen Yun had described as unscientific and unrealistic. Jiang would use the phrase fourteen times in his report. 'The socialist market economic system we want to build is such that the market is allowed to play a fundamental role in the allocation of resources under the macroscopic regulation and control of the socialist country'. He would also echo Deng's constant refrain from his Southern Tour that the party must guard against 'leftist' tendencies, 'particularly among the leading cadres': a pointed message to those in the upper echelons of the party who still wished to attack the central task of economic construction. 'The mistakes which occurred in the twenty years starting from 1957' – namely the Great Leap Forward and the Cultural Revolution – 'were primarily "leftist" in nature', he said.

Jiang was clear that key to the pursuit of Deng's economic line was political stability, without which, he said, there would be social unrest. It was necessary, he said, to uphold the four cardinal principles, and 'resolutely remove all factors which could lead to chaos and even rebellion in China'. Or, as *The New York Times* put it, 'Mr. Deng is willing to free prices but not the press, to loosen controls over companies but not citizens. The Communist Party Congress [...] underscored Mr. Deng's readiness to abandon central planning in the economy but not in politics and society'.[12]

Deng would not attend the congress, though he would make a brief appearance the day after its conclusion. After watching Jiang's speech on TV, he commented: 'This is a good speech; I want to applaud this report'.[13] Chen Yun would also not be present; rumours in Hong Kong were that he was in Beijing's 301 hospital suffering from blood cancer. At the congress, it was also announced, in line with prior agreement, that the Central Advisory Commission, which Chen chaired, would be disbanded; this would mark Chen's official retirement.

There was one apparent concession to Chen, though. Both Deng's ally Yang Shangkun, who had accompanied him on much of his Southern Tour, and Yang's half-brother Baibing would be essentially stripped of power over the military. Yang Shangkun retired – and with the Central Advisory Commission disbanded there was no gerontocratic home for him now – whilst Yang Baibing, who had declared that the military was the 'protector and escort' of reform, and who had been a key attendee of the meeting of the military in Zhuhai seen as a warning shot to Jiang regarding potential replacement, lost both his official positions. The reason given for this clear out was that Yang had organized another meeting of the military leadership in September 1992, in which again a future without Jiang Zemin in charge had been discussed. 'Deng Xiaoping made a compromise with Chen Yun,' one Hong Kong newspaper reported at the time.[14] Deng refused Chen's exhortation that the 'socialist market economy' should not be mentioned, but apparently agreed that '[T]he influence of Yang Shangkun and his brother Yang Baibing on the party be curtailed'.

One very conspicuous winner, however, was Jiang's fellow 'Shanghai Gang' comrade Zhu Rongji who completed his rapid political ascent by becoming a member of the Politburo Standing Committee, alongside the forty-nine-year-old Hu Jintao – who would, in 2002, succeed Jiang Zemin.

Unmentioned – unmentionable – was Zhao Ziyang. Shortly before the party congress, it was announced that the investigation of his case was to be terminated. On 8 October, Zhao had been called to Huairen Hall in Zhongnanhai where he was told that the Central Committee had decided to end his investigation 'while upholding the political and administrative judgement against me'. In his response, Zhao asked that his personal freedom be restored. He was warned that during the party congress there would be many foreign reporters in Beijing. 'They hoped I would observe Party discipline and take into account the big picture,' he wrote. He offered to avoid going out during the party congress. 'Upon hearing this, they seemed to relax'.[15] Zhao would spend the years before his death in 2005 in a tragicomic dance with the authorities, perpetually uncertain of the limits to his freedom. When allowed, he would periodically journey to the south to aid his respiratory system which was troubled by the dry Beijing winters. For reasons that were not made clear to him, he was never permitted to visit Guangdong province.

Zhao's former chief of staff Bao Tong was, as the party congress unfolded in central Beijing, being held in solitary confinement in Qincheng Prison, to the north of the city, after a show trial that summer had sentenced him to seven years in jail for 'leaking state secrets' and 'counterrevolutionary propaganda and instigation'. In an interview marking the ten-year anniversary of the Tiananmen massacre, Bao would tell CNN that if economic reform was not accompanied by political reform, 'then the economic reforms will have to be forced forward single-handedly by a small group of people. Single-handedly

10. Return to the Capital

carrying out economic reforms cannot be successful. Whoever is responsible for doing it single-handedly can only create another tragedy.'[16]

As the cold winter arrived in Beijing once more, Deng and his wife headed south to the city of Hangzhou, and its tranquil West Lake. It was a city that he had great affection for; his twenty-one-day stay there in December and January would be his sixteenth visit to the city. It had been a place of refuge too for Mao Zedong, who viewed it as his second home and a place to ponder political decisions of consequence. For Deng that winter, the sprawling State Guesthouse on the western bank of the lake offered rest and recuperation after an unrelenting year; this was the trip which marked in practical terms the beginning, finally, of his retirement.

Whilst staying there, he was notified that he had been chosen as the *Financial Times*' 'Man of the Year' for 1992. 'Through a simple visit in January to the most prosperous, fast-growing parts of the south, Deng sparked a nationwide renewal of enthusiasm for free-market reforms,' Alexander Nicoll wrote on page ten of the 29 December edition. Deng's actions over the course of the year had substantially increased the likelihood of the reforms being long-lasting; the foreign capital was pouring in, and the economic power of provinces had reduced the influence of Beijing. But, the article pointed out, reform was 'only as deeply rooted as the officials who promote it'. The article noted critically Deng's brutal response to the protests of 1989, and his responsibility for 'countless' abuses of human rights. But he remained a transformative, resilient figure, key to the country's present and future. 'Saddest for China,' the article concluded, 'is that the most important question remains: what will happen after he dies?'

Chapter 11

THE STORY OF SPRING

From the highest point of Shenzhen's Lotus Hill Park, Deng Xiaoping looks out across a future he did not live to see. Striding forward, his burnished six-metre, six-ton bronze form embodies, according to the statue's creator, the idea that 'the steps of reform and opening should be bold'.[1] From his feet, an invisible line runs down the hill, along a north to south axis that mimics the prescribed urban plan of the imperial past, pulling the eye southward into Shenzhen's Futian Central Business District. At the centre of the view is the city's vast Civic Centre, its roof two arcing blue metal wings mimicking the mythical Dapeng, a great bird similar to a roc, above which loom flanking skyscrapers stretching down to the Shenzhen River, including the narrowing steel and glass pinnacle of the 115-storey Ping'an International Finance Centre – currently the fifth tallest building in the world. This is the new Shenzhen that emerged in the decades after Deng's Southern Tour; even in 1995, the view from the top of Lotus Hill was still of a blank grid of newly laid roads, separating building lots of scrubby, sandy grass.

Nestled in among today's skyscrapers on the western side of the axial line is the Shenzhen Museum. Amongst the artefacts on display in the museum's exhibition of reform and opening are the 'Flying Swallow' spade Deng used to plant the tree in 1992 – 'MADE IN CHINA' stamped proudly on the wooden handle; the 'office goods and furniture' of his hotel room; the white Toyota bus with pink velour interior which he toured the city in. Of his visit, a display declares that 'His speech in South China brought another spring of emancipating minds to the country'.

To the east of this incarnation of a city centre, on a busy junction of Shenzhen's main Shennan Boulevard, an enormous billboard stretches bearing a smiling picture of Deng, with the Central Business District behind him. First erected in 1992, it had initially born the slogan 'The development and experience of Shenzhen prove that our policy of establishing the Special Economic Zones is correct'. That incarnation was felled by a typhoon later the same year, and it was replaced with a starker warning that 'Failing to adhere to socialism, failing to reform and open up, failing to develop the economy and improve people's lives can only be a dead end'. Its visuals have also been updated subsequently as the cityscape has evolved. Today's billboard reads 'Adhere to the party's basic line for a hundred years, with no vacillation'.

Meanwhile, on the other side of the Pearl River, Luo Sanmei hill – where Deng had declared, in 1984, he would not turn back – has been transformed into a tourist site, opened in 2011 at a cost of 30 million yuan. A sign declares that the park 'is not only the teaching materials of traditional Chinese virtues, but also the reflection of the Chinese road to prosperity'.

Broad stone steps cut a zig-zag to the peak, and back down to the valley – there is little chance of missing your footing these days. Stelae situated at intervals display, with black painted characters on grey stone, a selection of Deng's sayings – included his most frequently misquoted aphorism: 'Let some areas and some people get rich first, to spur and assist other areas and other people, and gradually achieve common prosperity,' he said in 1985. In the West's parsing it became: 'To get rich is glorious'.[2]

At the top of the hill, another statue of Deng: this time mimicking an official portrait of his 1984 visit to Guangdong. In the painting on which it is modelled, he stands atop the modest peak, hands on hips, in a blue jacket, cream waistcoat and white shirt, surveying the valley below like an explorer who has discovered a new land. His Shangri-La? An indistinct urban panorama punctuated by cranes, sprawling along the valley behind him.

All along the path to the top of the hill, hidden speakers blare a bombastic orchestral ballad called 'The Story of Spring'. First performed as part of a television gala in winter 1994, it would go on to become a huge national hit and the anthem of China's economic transformation. Recounting Deng Xiaoping's efforts to make Guangdong the engine of this process, the lyrics of the song mythologize two pivotal years: 1979 and 1992.

The year of 1992
That was yet another spring
There was a great man
Writing a magnificent poem in Shenzhen
Spreading splendour all over China like a spring breeze.

*

11. The Story of Spring

The process of refining and polishing the official story of Deng Xiaoping's Southern Tour had begun with the national publication of the newspaper article 'East Wind Brings Spring All Around' at the end of March 1992, and would continue over the subsequent years as Deng's pronouncements were transmuted into party dogma.

Adherence to the line put forward by Deng became proof of suitability for leadership. As the *People's Daily* would comment in the year following the tour, a rigorous test of the 'political quality, leadership level, and work ability' of a party cadre was whether they were aware of the opportunity for development advocated by Deng Xiaoping, 'and whether he or she is able to cherish and seize the opportunity and transform it into conscious and fruitful action'.[3] Deng's official speeches from the tour – minus some of the more confrontational statements he had made – would form the final section of the last volume of his 'Selected Works', published in 1993. Jiang Zemin referred to the book's publication as 'a major event in the political life of our country and our Party. Coupling Marxism with Chinese reality, it is the guiding flag of the socialist cause and the spiritual pillar of our people's revitalization'.[4] 1994 was Deng's ninetieth year, and it would see diverse commemorations of the patriarch, including a photographic exhibition in Beijing celebrating his life, as well as the publication of a swathe of books cementing the centrality of Deng's Southern Tour in party historiography: *The Course of Deng Xiaoping*; *The Spiritual Pillar of Contemporary China – Discussions on Deng Xiaoping's Thinking*; *Chronicle of Important Activities of Deng Xiaoping During the New Period*.[5] It was the sort of deifying propaganda that had not been seen since the Mao era.

The developing myth of the Southern Tour, which cemented Deng's legacy as the 'architect of reform and opening', helped to occlude two related, inconvenient truths for the party. The first was Deng's role in the events of June 1989; the Southern Tour meant his biography would ever have a different epilogue than that written on the streets of Beijing on the night of 3 June. 'I think he was lighting a lamp with the political wisdom of an eighty-eight-year-old man,' said Deng Rong of the Southern Tour. 'It may have been the last lamp of his life, but it should also be said that it was the most brilliant lamp of his life'.[6] The second was the central role of Zhao Ziyang in developing and implementing the policies of ambitious opening to the outside world, which Deng was reviving in 1992.

If Deng had not embarked on his Southern Tour, China would still have likely moved back towards a model which emphasized faster growth. In 1991, work had already begun on attempting the restructuring of state-owned enterprises – a project which the leadership broadly acknowledged as necessary, with their inefficiency and lack of profitability an anchor on the national economy. There were also increasing rhetorical references to the conclusion of the phase of 'rectification'. Even before Deng had left on his tour, on 11 January 1992, Li Peng was agreeing that the 'task of improving the economic environment and rectifying the economic order' had basically been completed, even if the watchword for him was still stability: 'We should maintain both a vigorous and a firm and steady attitude toward the reform', he would say, somewhat tautologically. Two days after Deng's departure south, the State Statistics Bureau released their report showing the nation's 'noticeable economic improvement, the accomplishment of major economic readjustment objectives, and the normalization of economic operations' during 1991.[7]

But the theoretical pronouncements Deng made during his tour, dictating what socialism could mean, were crucial; these were interventions that no one else had the authority to make. This was Deng as a *deus ex machina*. He did not finally resolve the tensions or inconsistencies at the top of the party, but he provided a theoretical framework which meant all sorts of mechanisms for the generation of wealth, identified by Deng as crucial to the continued legitimacy of the party, could be framed as socialist, not capitalist.

The effect of the greater economic liberality that followed Deng's tour was seismic. Official growth figures ran at around 13 per cent in both 1992 and 1993,[8] with the private sector growing rapidly – increasing by 72 per cent in 1993 according to state media[9] – and foreign investment flooding into the coastal areas. Nationally, foreign investment reached twenty-five billion US dollars in 1993.[10] The level of investment in Pudong, the most significant site of new development in China, had increased dramatically; on a single day in April 1993, sixty foreign investment deals were reportedly signed in Pudong, bringing investment of half a billion US dollars.[11]

But already by May of that year, Zhu Rongji, though expressing full confidence in the Chinese economy, was commenting that 'investment has heated up, inflationary pressure gradually accumulated, financial and monetary markets grown relatively tight, and disparity between regions in terms of economic development widened to some extent'.[12]

There were over 6000 new development zones across the country, but no centralized strategy, with local cadres enthusiastically following Deng's instruction to experiment. Many of these were left as undeveloped land, with the crops ploughed under. There was, quite simply, not enough money to develop the 24 million *mu* that these new zones covered; it would cost an estimated 4,500 billion yuan to build on this land.[13] Later in the year, the State Council would intervene to drastically reduce the number of new developments zones being set up, and return land to crop growing; Hu Ping, the director of the Special Economic Zone office, said that as of August 1993 only one-tenth of such local economic zones had turned out to be beneficial to the local economy.[14]

Zhu Rongji expressed his concern at seeing agricultural land repurposed like this. 'If we give up agriculture,' he said, 'we will give up everything'.[15] In simple terms of land use and employment, farming remained a central pillar of China's economy and national life. But making a living from the land had already grown increasingly challenging. Having kick-started reform, and benefitted enormously from it, farmers were now the big losers as their incomes shrank as costs ramped up, prices fell and levies ate away at what little profit might be left. When farmers did get paid, it was often in promissory notes – essentially IOUs – rather than real money. The gap between rural and urban would widen over the years following Deng's Southern Tour, with many young workers in the countryside forced to abandon their land, and pulled into low-skill, low-wage work in the new factories that were replacing the farmland on the edge of China's towns and cities.

Such imbalanced development was not the only problem that followed Deng's Southern Tour. Double-digit inflation had also returned. In October of 1993, state media published results of a survey which, despite a near one-fifth increase of the official cost-of-living index in thirty-five cities, 'excluded the possibility of major social instability in the near future'. But, it warned, 'a total of 49 per cent are still haunted by the memories of 1988' – as, no doubt, were the party's leadership, current and retired.[16]

Earlier in the year, as these problems had begun to emerge – many of which had been predicted by those 'leftists' who had been subject to such criticism during the Southern Tour – Deng Xiaoping had reportedly commented on the concerns. 'Is [the economy] being overheated?' he asked. 'Is it "in chaos"? Must it be rectified and stopped?'. Referencing the pace of development in Shanghai, where he had been staying after his sojourn in at the West Lake in Hangzhou, he told officials that they should not waste time arguing about such comments: 'instead, we should seize the opportunity, emancipate our minds, expand the scope of reform, and speed up the pace of economic construction'.[17] For Deng, there was no turning back; he left those now in charge – in particular Zhu Rongji – to attempt to engineer a 'soft landing'. Zhu's role was expanded, and he became governor of the People's Bank of China in the summer of 1993. Zhu would impose measures – he came up with a 'sixteen-point plan' – to centralize government control and gradually reduce inflation whilst avoiding slowing growth in a manner displeasing to Deng, restricting credit and development, and attempting to reduce property speculation.

With the country awash with new money, and with Deng's vocal encouragement of experimentation and speedy development, it is not surprising that the persistent issue of corruption worsened after the Southern Tour. Jiang Zemin, in August of 1993, would describe corruption as a 'virus invading the body of the party and state. It will bury our party, our people's regime, and socialist modernization if we do not attack it seriously and allow it to spread unchecked'.[18] Deng himself would acknowledge that cadres were exchanging power for money 'and debauchery'.[19] An increasing issue was officials insisting on bribes to facilitate property and business deals; Guangdong saw a near 20 per cent increase in such cases in 1993. One Shenzhen official, Zeng Lihua, took bribes worth up to eight million yuan, as well as a fake passport (she planned to flee overseas) and a $20,000 Rolex.[20]

In 1995, accusations of corruption would come to personally affect the Deng family. Jiang Zemin had launched a campaign to eradicate corruption in 1994, which, wrote Jasper Becker in the *South China Morning Post*, 'soon evolved into personal vendettas'. Deng's youngest son, Zhifang, then in his early forties, was caught up in the campaign, which turned its focus onto Capital Iron and Steel – the state-owned enterprise based in western Beijing that Deng had visited, and lavishly praised, shortly after his Southern Tour.

Deng Zhifang had studied Physics at university in America, and seemed destined for career in the field beloved of his father: science and technology. He ended up, however, enmeshed in the complex web of economic relations between Hong Kong and the mainland, acting as the managing director of a subsidiary of Capital Iron and Steel listed in the colony and involving himself in real-estate deals. As the investigation rumbled on, the head of the company, an elderly and long-standing ally of Deng Xiaoping named Zhou Guanwu, stepped down, and his son – who was chairman of the Hong Kong subsidiary which Deng Zhifang worked for – was arrested. Only when Deng Xiaoping's wife, Zhuo Lin, was admitted to hospital – some rumours suggested she had tried to commit suicide, so anxious was she about the unfolding scandal – did Jiang relent and halt the investigation.

Deng Xiaoping had, it was reported, been unable to intervene 'because since December he has barely been able to speak'; that he had not been able to protect his old friend from the revolution, Zhou Guanwu, testified to his dwindling power, both physical and political.[21]

When asked of their father's health by journalists, Deng's children repeatedly insisted in the years immediately subsequent to the tour that he was in good health, with news reports mentioning that he was continuing to attempt two twenty-minute walks each day – with the help of at least one nurse. He was not seen in public after February 1994, and on National Day (1 October) of the same year, Deng arrived at the Diaoyutai State Guesthouse in western Beijing – a lavish compound of lakeside pavilions where dignitaries and foreign leaders are generally billeted on their visits to Beijing – to meet with political and military leaders. Descending from his car, he was seated with help in a wheelchair: the first time he had been seen by the leadership unable to walk independently.

At the meeting he apparently told party elder Bo Yibo that he hoped that 'in a short period of time, the central and provincial leading bodies will unify their thinking, make firm their determination, and closely unite around the party central leading body with Comrade Jiang Zemin at the core. There can only be one centre and one central leading authority'.[22]

Ten years previously, on 1984's National Day, Deng had stood proudly on the balcony of the Gate of Heavenly Peace to witness his first parade as leader, marking the thirty-fifth anniversary of the People's Republic of China. It was the year of his first Southern Tour, and the zenith of this first phase of reform and opening. Deng had given a speech in which he noted that the economy had developed more vigorously than ever before: 'Today, all our people are full of joy and pride', he said. On the rostrum with Deng were Zhao Ziyang and Hu Yaobang; together they watched as the parade began with 100,000 school students and workers forming the national emblem of China and '1949–1984' with bunches of flowers. As well as the float featuring the 'Time is Money, Efficiency is Life' motto made famous that year, and which was shaped in the form of the mythical roc, wings spread as if to fly, there were floats celebrating infra-red laser radar and a Chinese made computer able to do 100 million calculations a second. Paraders held slogans aloft as they passed by the Gate of Heavenly Peace: 'Reunify the motherland!'; 'Quadruple the gross annual value of industrial and agricultural production of 1980 by the end of this century'.

Now, ten years later, Deng sat in a chair in the grounds of Diaoyutai, this former imperial recreation ground, depleted by age and illness. The last available photo of Deng shows him in the chair, wrapped in a blanket against the autumn chill, flat-capped, his face thin and tight – as behind him fireworks lit up the dark Beijing sky.

Like Mao, who talked of 'going to see Marx', Deng Xiaoping preferred not to directly speak of dying, instead saying that he was 'going to see the premier' – meaning his old comrade, Zhou Enlai. By 1996, in the face of continuing rumours of Deng's hospitalization and even death, his son Pufang acknowledged, during a visit to Shenzhen, the inevitability of what was coming. 'We are communists and materialists,' he would say. 'As his son, it is quite natural that I expect him to have a long life. However, we must accept the laws of nature and accept anything that may happen,' he said. 'An old man of over ninety will have to take this road'.[23]

On a cold day in late February 1997, with the capital swathed in freezing smog, a motorcade of thirty-five vehicles processed slowly from Tiananmen Square down the Avenue of Eternal Peace, past thousands of mourners who had turned out to line the street and witness the last journey of Deng Xiaoping. In the vast plaza in front of Beijing Station, train workers and the general public had also assembled, many with white flowers pinned to their lapels, in front of an enormous television screen mounted between its two pagoda clock towers, to watch coverage of the ceremony.

A blue and white Toyota minibus, draped with yellow and black ribbons, bore his coffin west. It passed the intersections at Xidan, where in 1978 'Democracy Wall' had been plastered with posters calling for greater individual freedoms, before Deng's intervention brought the protests to a forced end, and then, further down the road, Muxidi, which had seen some of the first of the killing on the night of 3 June. It headed out into the city's western suburbs, where a modest hill rises from the northern edge of the avenue: Babaoshan, or 'eight-treasure hill'. Babaoshan Revolutionary Cemetery had been established in the 1950s as the final resting place for China's political and military 'martyrs'. Over the decades, many of the country's leaders had been cremated or interred here, including Premier Zhou, whose ashes would be scattered over Beijing, the Miyun reservoir north of the capital, and the Hai and Yellow rivers. In April of 1995, the cremation of Chen Yun took place at Babaoshan, ending the fevered guessing as to which of the two patriarchs would die first. Chen was described in his obituary as 'a great proletarian revolutionary and statesman' and 'an outstanding Marxist'.

Across the lower reaches of Babaoshan stretch orderly lines of gravestones commemorating rank-and-file heroes of the revolution; further up the hill, under the spreading branches of large pines, marble and bronze tombs and effigies memorialize political and military leaders of greater importance – including Chen Yun. At the base of the hill is a suite of imperial-style buildings including a columbarium and a crematorium, in front of which Deng's family and an array of political dignitaries congregated as his coffin was unloaded from the minibus.

Deng died at 9.08 pm on 19 February 1997 from complications resulting from Parkinson's disease, which he had been suffering with since the mid-1980s, and a lung infection. He was ninety-two years old. The authorities' nervousness was signalled by the tightening of security on university campuses, though the correspondent for *The New York Times* found a weary realism amongst students concerning protest. 'It's not that everyone is so happy,' one student at Beijing University told the reporter, 'but even a small action would be blocked immediately, so we all know there is no point in trying'. Most students, he said, spent their free time either playing computer games or discussing ways to make money.[24]

Deng's official obituary instructed that the Chinese people should study Deng Xiaoping's theory of building socialism with Chinese characteristics, and referenced his 'scientific attitude and creative spirit in applying a Marxist stand, viewpoints and methods to studying new problems and solving new problems'. It omitted any mention of Hu Yaobang or Zhao Ziyang, and only euphemistically referenced the Tiananmen massacre, mentioning vague 'political disturbances'. It did, however, comment in glowing terms on his Southern Tour, which, it said 'profoundly answered many key questions for understanding, which had been perplexing and binding people's minds for a long time, especially the questions concerning the relationship between socialism and [the] market economy'.

Many obituaries outside China, however, also noted the fraught economic situation that his tour had bequeathed. By the time of Deng's death, Zhu Rongji had seen success in bringing inflation under greater control, but the economy remained imbalanced. Inequality between the urban and rural, and between the coastal and inland provinces remained a significant structural problem. Despite Jiang's strident rhetoric, corruption too remained pervasive. In *The Independent*, Derek Davies wrote that

While his apologists can claim that his abandonment of a command economy put China, however belatedly, on the road to prosperity, the loss of so many state controls has complicated the task of his proteges in dealing with problems caused by the growth he triggered: an overburdened infrastructure, an overheated economy, inflation and an outflow of capital, plus a massive growth of corruption and criminal gangs.[25]

Socialist Review would comment that Deng's 'victory' in 1989 'was a hollow one: while his regime survived, it was at the cost of losing all support for his reforms in the cities. Since then the crisis of the system has deepened: the economy goes from boom to bust, and while conditions in the cities have improved slightly, opposition to the regime has spread to the villages'.[26]

Deng's ashes were scattered in the Yellow Sea, with Zhuo Lin emptying the urn from an aeroplane into the choppy waters below. China's official news agency suggested that the sea might wash them to Hong Kong and Macau – or even further afield. 'The waves would perhaps carry his ashes to the Pacific Ocean, the Indian Ocean and to the Atlantic Ocean,' it said, 'for he does not only belong to China, but also to the world'.[27]

Though Deng did not live to see the transfer of sovereignty of Hong Kong, Zhuo Lin would be at the ceremony on 1 July 1997. Her grey hair thinning and walking with the aid of a stick, she was seated in the second row of dignitaries. There also were Jiang Zemin and Li Peng; Jiang became the first leader of the People's Republic of China to set foot in the territory. In his speech, Hong Kong's first Chinese Chief Executive Tung Chee-hwa began by addressing Deng's role in engineering the handover, arguing that in the 1980s 'Mr. Deng stepped forward decisively and created a blueprint for Hong Kong after 1997, under the imaginative concept of "One Country, Two Systems"'. He went on to pay tribute to Zhuo – who stood up and received the long ovation of the audience on behalf of her husband.

Chapter 12

THE NEW ERA

In the summer of 1992, the *South China Morning Post* reported that party cadres in Fujian were expected to be fired or sent elsewhere as a result of the sluggish development of the province – especially when compared to next door Guangdong. 'During his tour of Southern China early this year, Deng made it a point not to go to Fujian', a source told Hong Kong journalist Willy Wo-lap Lam. 'And Fujian is never mentioned in the many speeches on reform that the patriarch has recently delivered'. It was reported, however, that one local official might be in line for a promotion, 'in view of his deserved reputation as a reformist'.[1] This was the son of party elder Xi Zhongxun, and then party boss of provincial capital Fuzhou: Xi Jinping.

Xi spent seventeen years in Fujian, a province that, despite its perceived lack of ambition in 1992, was at the forefront of China's modernization drive. He would subsequently serve as party chief of wealthy next-door Zhejiang, where he oversaw the expansion of the private sector and a move away from heavy industry. His father had also, of course, been a pioneer of the policies of reform and opening, advocating for Guangdong's opening in the first years of Deng Xiaoping's rule. So, when Xi came to power in 2012, many commentators, particularly in the west, believed he might be the man to reinvigorate China's economic reform process. Nicholas Kristof, writing in *The New York Times*, predicted that 'The new paramount leader, Xi Jinping, will spearhead a resurgence of economic reform, and probably some political easing as well. Mao's body will be hauled out of Tiananmen Square on his watch, and Liu Xiaobo, the Nobel Peace Prize-winning writer, will be released from prison'.[2] In the *South China Morning Post*, the paper's former editor Wang Xiangwei wrote of the 'lost decade' of Hu Jintao's collective leadership between 2002 and 2012 which lacked 'meaningful economic or political reform' and saw the state-sector strengthening its hold on the economy, in a piece headlined 'Xi Jinping might be the strong reformer China needs – to surprise of the West'.[3]

It was a conviction that was strengthened when, in 2012, Xi made his high-profile first trip as the party's new General Secretary, heading to Shenzhen in December in a visit seen in the media as an obvious homage to Deng's Southern Tour of twenty years earlier. During a five-day stay in Guangdong, Xi laid a wreath at the foot of Deng's bronze statue at the top of Lotus Hill, and planted an alpine banyan tree in the park. It was during this visit too that he stopped at Fishermen's Village to inspect the memorial to Deng's first Southern Tour and meet with villagers – some of whom recalled Deng's visit in 1984.[4] The carefully choreographed trip seemed intended to position Xi as Deng's heir. He had even explicitly invoked the Southern Tour in a speech the prior month, albeit in referencing the unfinished business he was now taking in hand: 'The Chinese socialist system needs to improve to keep in step with the development of the socialist cause with Chinese characteristics. During his inspection tour of southern China in 1992 Deng Xiaoping pointed out, "It will probably take another thirty years for us to develop a more mature and well-defined system in every field"'.[5]

Reform and opening up, Xi said during his visit, was a guiding policy that the Communist Party must stick to. 'We must keep to this correct path,' he added. 'We must stay unwavering on the road to a prosperous country and people, and there must be new pioneering'.[6] In another speech to cadres in Shenzhen that was not made public, however, he revisited the concerns of the late 1980s, questioning the reasons behind the Soviet Union's collapse – one of Xi's great preoccupations as he took office. One important reason was, he said, that 'their ideals and beliefs had been shaken. In the end, "the ruler's flag over the city tower" changed overnight'.[7]

Where Deng had come to see economic growth as a panacea, Xi argued that the country needed to uphold its ideals and beliefs, asserting that 'if we lose sight of our vision as communists, we will lose our direction and succumb to utilitarianism and pragmatism'. The reference to 'pragmatism' was telling – it was a term which had been closely associated with Deng – and as the Chinese journalist Gao Yu wrote in early 2013, the speech seemed to indicate that predictions of Xi as a reformer were wrong: 'With the new southern tour speech, Xi Jinping clearly intended to give the CCP ideology a renewed status'.[8]

This pivot towards ideological work, based on the holistic notion of revival encompassed by Xi's 2012 notion of the 'China Dream' – the 'great rejuvenation of the Chinese nation', as he put it – would set the tone for the initial phase of his rule. Xi would remain rhetorically vague in his early speeches about how he might approach the substantive issues that existed in the Chinese economy: 'We should comprehensively promote socialist economic, political, social and ecological advancement, further reform and opening up, boost balanced development, and continue to lay a solid material and cultural foundation for realizing the Chinese Dream',[9] he would say in a speech to the National People's Congress in March 2013 – but the specific detail – the *how* of such expansive ambitions – remained lacking.

Even back in 2007, though, China's premier Wen Jiabao had described the economy as 'unstable, unbalanced, uncoordinated, and unsustainable' – and that was before the 2008 financial crisis, which saw the government pump unprecedented amounts of money into it. By the time of Xi's Shenzhen visit in 2012, it was clear that the economy faced mounting problems. The double-digit growth figures that the old model had so reliably encouraged looked to be becoming historical: China's annual GDP would drop to 7.8 per cent in 2012, at the beginning of a slow decline that would continue for the next eight years.

State-Owned Enterprises, despite Zhu Rongji's reforms of the 1990s, had returned to the centre of the economy, after forced mergers and closures resulted in huge internationally listed conglomerates holding monopolies in key industries, requiring large state subsidies – and operating with significant inefficiency. Coastal provinces still relied on exploiting young migrant workers, who gravitated to cities from a countryside now startlingly absent of prospects, in manufacturing for the export and domestic market – but the supply of workers was dwindling, and the substantial and consequential increases in wages meant China was no longer the cheapest place to make low-value goods.

Property and infrastructure spending had, along with export trade bolstered by China's entry into the World Trade Organisation in 2001, sustained China's growth, with local land sales and eye-watering levels of debt funding the development of ever-more sprawling Chinese cities of half-empty shopping malls, glossy Central Business Districts and identikit eight-block apartment compounds, built to satisfy the seemingly insatiable demand for private property that had emerged in the Jiang Zemin era. Home ownership rates had jumped to nearly 90 per cent by 2007.[10] These cities were ringed by multi-lane highways and linked by sleek and very expensive high-speed rail stations and airports built out in the cities' edgelands. But the sense was that this model was close to being exhausted; the government wanted to shift the economy away from its reliance of infrastructure and property spending and the shrinking export market by increasing household consumption, but the figures for household spending in 2012 and 2013 were disheartening.

Corruption – 'a matter of life and death for the party' – as Hu Jintao put it in 2011, remained endemic and it was here Xi initially focussed his attention. He had developed a reputation during his time in both Fujian and Zhejiang as being tough on corruption: in 2004, he had warned cadres to 'Rein in your spouses, children, relatives, friends and staff, and vow not to use power for personal gain'.[11] US diplomatic cables from before Xi was elevated to leadership of party and country identify Xi's disdain for both the specific issue of corruption and the moral laxity – the 'spiritual pollution', one might say – he sees it as reflective of:

> Xi knows how very corrupt China is and is repulsed by the all-encompassing commercialization of Chinese society, with its attendant nouveau riche, official corruption, loss of values, dignity, and self-respect, and such 'moral evils' as drugs and prostitution, the professor stated. The professor speculated that if Xi were to become the Party General Secretary, he would likely aggressively attempt to address these evils, perhaps at the expense of the new moneyed class.[12]

In a speech to the Politburo in 2012, he noted the influence corruption had in inspiring the popular uprisings of the 'Arab Spring' the year before. 'Worms can only grow in something rotten,' he said. 'In recent years, long-pent-up problems in some countries have led to resentment among the people, unrest in society and the downfall of governments, with corruption being a major culprit'.[13] In the back of his mind, again, was the fall of the Soviet Union, and, of course, the protests in Tiananmen.

Though there were initial doubts from the commentariat both within and outside China – had Deng, Jiang and Hu not similarly condemned corruption in the party? – Xi wasted little time in demonstrating his resolve. Two days before Xi arrived in Shenzhen to pay homage to Deng, an investigation was opened into the deputy party leader of Sichuan, Li Chuncheng, who was accused of, in various familiar ways, trading power for money. Li's arrest was the first major move of what would become Xi's flagship campaign and would preface the investigation the following year of Li's ally and former boss in Sichuan, Zhou Yongkang, who had until 2012 been one of the most powerful men in China: a member of the Politburo Standing Committee, and in charge of China's formidable security apparatus. Zhou's career had offered plentiful opportunity for graft; he had earned his stripes in the massive state-administered oil industry, before moving on to run Sichuan province, and then becoming Minister of Public Security. It was a career trajectory that had also seen him establish a diverse and potentially threatening power base. Zhou would ultimately be arrested and expelled from the party, subject to a fate that even Zhao Ziyang had managed to avoid; not since the Gang of Four had a member of the Standing Committee been exposed to such public humiliation. 'We need to advance the anti-corruption drive through the investigation of Zhou's serious violations of Party discipline,' an editorial in the *People's Daily* would assert. 'We must stick to the attitude of no tolerance, the resolve of strong treatment, the courage to scrape poison from the bones, and the measure of severe punishment.'[14]

One year into his rule, with his campaign to crack down on corruption well underway, Xi convened the Third Plenum of the Eighteenth Central Committee at the Great Hall of the People in Beijing. Third Plenums – simply meaning the third meeting of the Central Committee since its members were chosen – are often focussed on economic issues, and evoke the memory of both the important meeting of December 1978, posited as the birthday of reform and opening, and that of 1993, which set out the reform measures that would be pursued by Zhu Rongji over the next half decade. This meeting in November of 2013 seemed, from the official communiqué issued afterwards, to promise to be a similarly significant moment: this was Xi apparently acknowledging the 'lost decade' of Hu Jintao's rule and grasping the nettle of economic reform; he had, it seemed, a plan to revive China's slowing economy. 'We must deepen economic system reform by centering on the decisive role of the market in allocating resources,' the communiqué announced in one significant section.[15] Elsewhere, it argued that to adapt to the globalized world, it must promote 'domestic openness together with openness to the outside world', and proposed relaxing control over investment access, speedier construction of free trade zones and opening inland and border areas. It seemed to observers to signal a pivot to a Dengist revitalization, suggesting that Xi, having established his ideological footing, might now initiate a new era of reform and opening.

*

Eight years after his first visit as leader and seven after the promise of the Third Plenum, Xi Jinping returned to the peak of Lotus Hill in Shenzhen, armed with another enormous wicker urn filled with pink lilies and adorned with red ribbon which he set once more beneath the bronze statue of Deng Xiaoping.

It was October 2020, and he was in the south to mark the fortieth anniversary of the establishment of the Special Economic Zones (he had been back in 2018, too). Whilst in town, he would give a speech in which he lauded their contribution to China's modernization – and speak also of the economic challenges the country was facing.[16]

The establishment of the Special Economic Zones had been, he said, a great innovation carried out by the party and the state. Shenzhen was a miracle in the history of world development, one that had been created by the Chinese people. It had led the way in integrating the international and domestic markets, achieving an average annual import-export growth rate of 26.1 per cent. Echoing Deng, he said that the party's decision on the establishment of the SEZs was 'completely correct' and they should continue, but also be better and attain a higher level.

He laid out ten principles to guide their future development – the first of which was that all must adhere to the Party's leadership in the construction of the Special Economic Zones. Others touched one rhetorical favourites of Xi such as ensuring success in the global scientific and technical revolution, adhering to the rule of law, and developing in a sustainable and ecological way.

Xi would move on to warn that the world was in a period of turbulent change accelerated by Covid-19, which had emerged in Wuhan at the end of the previous year. 'China is in a critical period to realize the great rejuvenation of the Chinese nation,' Xi said, 'and its economy has changed from a stage of rapid growth to a stage of high-quality development'. The speech did not contain any revelatory policy pronouncements, and paid lip-service to the idea that Shenzhen would remain integrated into the global economy. But his first instruction to the city was to focus on innovation and production for the domestic market. It was a directive echoed during a factory visit in Guangdong a couple of days prior to his speech. 'We must rely on independent innovation. We are experiencing a great change, unprecedented in the last century, and we need to take the road towards a higher level of self-reliance'.[17]

It was notable too that, in a long speech, Xi managed to mention Deng Xiaoping's name only once, referencing his – relatively minor – decision to call the new areas 'Special Zones'. In the same paragraph of his speech, he credited 'the person in charge' of the Guangdong Party Committee for putting forward the suggestion to the Central Committee to establish an export processing zone. He did not need to say his father's name – everyone in the audience understood Xi's implication.

As with other speeches aimed, at least in part, at a global audience, Xi again referenced broader ambitions of reform and opening 'at a higher starting point' (he used the word reform over fifty times in the speech). But in the intervening seven years since the 2013 Third Plenum, few of the reforms itemized after that meeting had been implemented. The market had not taken on the decisive role stated in the communiqué, with Xi instead preferring to maintain central control of the economy, and funnel funds towards the development of state enterprises and technological and economic self-sufficiency.

Influential Chinese economist Wu Jinglian had, the year before Xi's Shenzhen speech, commented of his rhetorical nods to reform, saying that 'We won't be able to accomplish the goals by just chanting two slogans – "reform and opening up". Instead, many detailed issues need to be analysed and lessons should be learned'. He criticized the shift towards 'state capitalism', arguing that 'It's inconsistent with our reforms. We have made it clear that we will pursue a market economy … rather than state control of the national economy'.[18]

But supplementary to the zero-Covid restrictions imposed by the Chinese government – which remained in place until December 2022 – state control would continue to tighten, with the reforms mooted in 2013 appearing in retrospect one example of the rhetoric of Xi's rule often having little to do with its reality.

In searching for an articulation beyond speeches and communiqués of Xi's vision for the Chinese economy, one does not need to venture far south from the capital. About eighty miles outside Beijing, a new urban area, constructed in Xi's image, is continuing to emerge from the flat fields and wetlands of Hebei province.

The city of Xiong'an – its name is a portmanteau of the characters for 'brave' and 'peace' – began as part of a project to relieve pressure on the capital, and was from its very inception closely associated with Xi. 'General Secretary Xi Jinping has planned for, made decisions on and promoted (Xiong'an) in person, devoting painstaking efforts,' read a 2018 Master Plan;[19] in announcing the project he called it a 'demonstration area for innovative development'.[20] It is part of a project to mirror the mega-city of the 'Greater Bay Area' (intended to unify Guangdong, Hong Kong and Macau) with Xiong'an one hub within 'Jing-Jin-Ji': a combination of Beijing, Tianjin and an old name for the province of Hebei. By high-speed train the city is just fifty minutes from Beijing West Railway Station.

Xi Jinping initially appointed Shenzhen's former mayor and party chief, Xu Qin, as governor of Hebei province, where the city is being built. State media has referred to Xiong'an as the 'Shenzhen of the North' while, according to its master plan, the project is intended to become 'a model city in the history of human development'. Press coverage declared that 'Compared with Special Economic Zones in Pudong and Shenzhen, Xiong'an is designed to represent China's vision of its next stage of development in several areas. It is expected to become a modern high-level city that is green, low-carbon, intelligent, and livable by the end of 2035'.[21]

Where Shenzhen arose in a haphazard, experimental manner, however, driven by the industriousness and enterprise of those who came to live there, and benefitted by its proximity to Hong Kong, Xiong'an is a top-down, state-planned new city reliant on huge amounts of public investment. Attempting to profit from land and real estate deals – a driver of Shenzhen and Pudong's development – has been effectively outlawed, and the city, distant as it is from China's coastline, is not courting international investors: it will be a home for China's domestic corporations – and its state-owned enterprises.

In 2021, however, the *Financial Times* reported that project had become 'bogged down by disputes over costs and companies' reluctance to move to the area'; unemployment had soared as the small factories of the region that made clothes, insulation and plastics had been forced to close for being too polluting and unsightly.[22] These may be short-term challenges, but as the researcher Andrew Stokols noted in 2023, Xiong'an has no viable short-term prospect of generating revenue; its continued development and success will rely on the faith of Xi Jinping and the consequential economic support of the central government.[23]

*

Whilst Zhongnanhai's pavilions and halls have, over the decades, provided a backdrop appropriate to the climactic moments of court drama during China's communist era, its quiet denouements have found a similarly suitable setting in an unremarkable cluster of buildings that sit in the far western suburbs of the capital on an intersection of the busy fourth ring road: the 301 Hospital, or the General Hospital of the PLA. A dedicated wing of the hospital has treated and cared for China's leaders as they suffered with periods of ill-health, and it was where many of them died – including Zhou Enlai, Chen Yun and Deng Xiaoping.

On 5 December 2022, Xi Jinping stood front and centre of an ordered brigade of identically dressed CCP leaders in a large, marble-tiled and brightly lit room at the hospital. Wearing black suits, black ties, black overcoats – embellished with a single white chrysanthemum – and sporting almost uniformly dyed black hair, the group stood facing the dead body of Jiang Zemin. He lay on a crisp white pillow, in a black suit and red tie, his body half covered in the red hammer-and-sickle flag of the Communist Party of China. He was ringed by flowers and cypresses, and a banner hung above him read 'Eternal Glory to Jiang Zemin'. His family stood to one side in front of circular white floral wreaths, with silk ribbons hanging down their front: one of them read 'You will live in our hearts forever'. At 10.20 am, Jiang's body was carried, covered in a clear glass lid, out to the waiting white minibus adorned with yellow ribbons by PLA soldiers in full dress uniform, before setting off westward down the Avenue of Eternal Peace – lined with onlookers – to Babaoshan Revolutionary Cemetery. His ashes would be taken to Shanghai, to be scattered near the mouth of the Yangtze River.

In a speech the next day, Xi Jinping would laud Jiang as 'a great Marxist, a great proletarian revolutionary, statesman, military strategist and diplomat, a long-tested communist fighter, and an outstanding leader of the great cause of socialism with Chinese characteristics'. He praised Jiang's achievements in stabilizing the situation for China's reform and development, in the face of 'severe political disturbances [...] in the international arena and in China' during the late 1980s and early 1990s. Perhaps most interesting was Xi's framing of Jiang's role in economic reform. Deng himself goes unmentioned in the speech – there are two mechanistic references to his 'theory' – but Xi talks of how Jiang 'led us in defining building a socialist market economy [and] led the establishment of a basic economic system for the primary stage of socialism under which public ownership is the mainstay and diverse forms of ownership develop together'.[24] The crucial role of the market, and of individual enterprise and entrepreneurship, in driving the economic growth of the 1990s had been effectively erased from the official story.

Perhaps most notable amongst the orchestrated grieving for Jiang was the presence, lined up next to Xi at the 301 hospital, of his predecessor, and Jiang's successor: seventy-nine-year-old Hu Jintao. It was the first time that Hu had been seen in public since, a month and a half earlier, he had been very publicly escorted out of the closing ceremony of the Twentieth Party Congress, held in mid-October at the Great Hall of the People, looking confused and a little distressed. The congress had already been the most closely scrutinized by observers of the People's Republic for decades, marking the beginning of Xi's 'unprecedented' third term as China's leader. As soon as Hu had departed stage right at the Great Hall, social media outside China exploded with fevered speculation as to what this might mean. Was Hu ill? Was this a very public purge?

Moments like Hu's sudden departure from the Party Congress, and Jiang's death a month later feel particularly significant as Xi's rendering of the party and country's past – the sanctioned version of which leader did what and why – tells us something about its potential future under his rule.

Those searching for more detailed insight into Xi's attitude to his predecessors can consult a document produced by the party in 2021, titled the 'Resolution of the Central Committee of the Communist Party of China on the Major Achievements and Historical Experience of the Party over the Past Century'.[25] This resolution constitutes the official history of the party since its founding in Shanghai in 1921; it is only the third such document published since then. The last had been Deng Xiaoping's assessment of the Cultural Revolution in 1981: the very act of producing the resolution puts Xi in a select club alongside Mao and Deng.

When analysing the 2021 Historical Resolution, many commentators totted up the number of times Xi's predecessors were mentioned. Mao Zedong is referenced eighteen times – though six of these predate the establishment of the People's Republic. Deng gets six mentions, and his Southern Tour is mentioned not at all (Hu Jintao and Jiang Zemin get one each). Xi Jinping is referenced twenty-five times. But with many of these references, the allusion is not to the individual, but the political ideology that bears their name: to 'Mao Zedong Thought'; 'Deng Xiaoping Theory' and 'Xi Jinping Thought'.

In reading the account of the pre-Xi Jinping era, it is not the individual leaders of the past who take the starring role. It is, as the title of the resolution has already suggested, the party itself, mentioned 556 times, that is credited with collective responsibility for the 'great transformation' of the country: 'It has united and led Chinese people of all ethnic groups in working tirelessly to achieve national independence and liberation, and then to make our country prosperous and strong and pursue a better life. The past century has been a glorious journey'. It is a journey, unfinished and continuous, towards the 'rejuvenation of the Chinese nation'. The party must carry with them 'the determination to never let up until we reach our goals and the attitude that the last leg of the journey only marks the halfway point'.

12. The New Era

Too much focus on Deng would undermine this idea of the continuous historical progress of the party; the idea is that both Mao and Deng led the country forward on this unfinished journey, not that Deng revitalized a country that had been brought to its knees by Mao's political excesses. In 2013, Xi introduced the idea of the 'Two Undeniables': '[We] must not use the period of history after reform and opening to deny the period of history prior to reform and opening; [we] must not use the period of history prior to reform and opening to deny the period of history after reform and opening'.[26]

There is no doubt that the resolution plays down Deng's individual role, including removing reference to Deng as the 'core' of the party (a title now reserved for only Mao and Xi, when before both Jiang and Deng had been referred to using the term): 'The Party Central Committee with Comrade Xi Jinping at its core has implemented the national rejuvenation strategy within the wider context of once-in-a-century changes taking place in the world,' it says in a section on China's 'new era', emphasizing Xi's own historical importance.

Xi does likely see Deng's removal of Zhao Ziyang in 1989, his criticism of the leadership between 1989 and 1991 and his backstage pulling of political levers, having nominally handed over to Jiang Zemin, as deeply problematic, both in contradicting the notion of the party as eternally right, and in potentially undermining Xi's own leadership. When a high-budget, forty-eight-episode drama about Deng's life was broadcast in 2014, it stopped at the point of Deng's *annus mirabilis*: 1984. The scriptwriter would go no further, he said, because the history was 'too difficult to write'; he was assuredly not just referring to the challenge of portraying the protests of 1989.[27]

The nostalgia, too, for the ferment of the 1980s, when the question of what China would become was far from fixed, and the nation's rapid economic rise of the 1990s, makes Deng a dangerous figure to centre in the Xi Jinping era; unlike the rule of Mao Zedong, it is still recent history for middle-aged Chinese people. When Jiang Zemin died, censors on Chinese social media worked hard to ensure that official grief and nostalgia for the Jiang era did not tip over into protest against the current regime.[28]

It was telling that the thirtieth anniversary of Deng Xiaoping's Southern Tour came and went in January 2022 with no acknowledgement in national state media – unlike ten years earlier, when it had been widely covered. Instead, on the anniversary, it was announced that the National Development and Reform Commission had established the 'Xi Jinping Economic Thought Research Centre', to explore and promote 'Xi Jinping Thought on [the] Socialist Economy with Chinese Characteristics for a New Era', which features 'innovative, coordinated, green, open and shared development'.[29]

A few days before the anniversary of Deng's departure, a middle-aged man dressed in tan jacket and trousers unveiled a banner on a street corner in Luohu, Shenzhen. 'Down with Xi Jinping,' it read. 'Defend reform and opening, and oppose amending the constitution and abolishing term limits for the president'. The man was soon swarmed with police, armed with cattle-prods and plastic shields, who pinned him to the ground. As they did so, the man shouted out that 'If the correct line of reform and opening is denied, China will be finished'.[30]

EPILOGUE: A SOUTHERN TOUR

On a grey and sweltering July day in 2019, I clambered aboard a sleek, white, air-conditioned train at Beijing's West Railway Station. Clanking over switch points, the train passed out of the city on elevated tracks, cutting between postmodern office towers and the pastel-shaded, Soviet-style housing blocks which still dominate the capital's suburbs. It slipped from the city's orbit and into its tattered edges; elevated above this half-urban, half-rural world, I watched it being remade: construction workers scurrying, cranes sweeping in slow silence, bulging piles of rubble and dirt covered in green netting to keep the dust down. A digital read-out above the carriage door said 146 km/h, and then a minute later held steady at 296 km/h. The train was travelling on one of the 'Eight Verticals' of China's high-speed rail network, which over the last fifteen years had reached out into almost every corner of the country. By 2025, there will be 50,000 kilometres of high-speed track in China, funded by ever-increasing levels of debt – nearly US$900 billion as of the end of 2021.[1] This journey of about 700 miles between Beijing and Wuhan, deep in the country's middle, would take around five hours.

Flat farmland extended either side of the tracks, a line of poplar trees or a raised yellow-dirt round marking the boundaries of the fields. The summer sun fought with the pollution haze to make the sky a thin greyblue; the screen flicked over to display an outside temperature of 35 degrees Celsius.

I was heading south in the footsteps of Deng Xiaoping. In the course of a month's travel, I would retrace his journey of 1992. I ate an overpriced dim-sum lunch atop the International Trade Centre in Shenzhen; I climbed the 650 steps of Luo Sanmei Hill just outside Zhuhai; in Shanghai, I took an elevator up to the third floor of the Shanghai No. 1 Department Store and hovered near the counter where Deng had bought stationery for his grandchildren. But my journey was not just a pursuit of his journey; it was also an attempt to understand its legacy in the new China that had emerged over the intervening twenty-seven years.

For much of my trip, I was travelling in and between the cities of the Pearl River Delta. By boat, bus, train, taxi, and on foot, I saw the urban spread as if a fragmentary timeline of China's modernization. The arteries of the Delta – the big, ten lane highways and elevated rail line – permit a view of a landscape still significantly occupied by older low-rise factories and their attendant dormitories: three, four, five squat storeys of various shades of off-white – cream, pink, peach – their blandness exacerbated by the smog which swathes them. The rest of these compounds are made up of the patched blue metal roofs of windowless factory sheds, and, lining the paths and narrow perpendicular roads, flashes of rich, dense green trees – a reminder of the riotously fertile landscape this spread of industry has replaced. Some of the obviously older factories: the two storey, white-tiled versions which emerged here in the late 1980s and 1990s, have been abandoned, many vacated by manufacturers who have moved production to cheaper areas of Asia, and sit, hollow-eyed and crumbling, waiting for the inevitable.

Above and around this topography of graft, signs and symbols of China's individual economy have emerged: looming ranks of sleek apartment towers to house the more than 120 million inhabitants of the country's most populous province, with roadside hoardings picturing the imagined life of future dwellers there: a woman stands, in a backless red dress, facing the sunset in the landscaped compound garden, currently still a mud-filled crater. Or a sharply dressed executive strides, smartphone glued to his ear, supersized in front of a blue-sky saturated vista of this future urban landscape. Metallic shopping malls and the occasional skyscraper also stand out against the sprawl and low hills – and these suggestions of change become more persistent on the approach to Shenzhen.

The city is increasingly dominated by landscaped plazas, orderly lines of sleek office towers and hotels, and vast, almost-uncrossable urban highways, but even here, in China's most modern, technological city, you can still take a turn down a side street and find yourself in the narrow alleys of one of the city's 'urban villages'. Dwindling in scale, and shifting in purpose from the 1990s when they provided low-cost housing in the seven or eight storey pastel and white 'handshake' buildings hastily constructed for those moving to the city to find manufacturing jobs, they remain, full of the noise of life and the smell of tobacco and hot oil, as a shadow-self of the new city, an increasingly suppressed memory of what Shenzhen used to be; of how it got made.

Shenzhen should today be facing its future with optimism given its status as the pioneer of the sort of technological innovation Xi Jinping is so keen to promote. Tencent, which builds the ubiquitous Swiss Army knife app Weixin, is headquartered here, as is internationally controversial telecommunications giant Huawei, alongside countless other tech firms, large and small. But the relationship between China's tech giants and the state hardened in the second term of Xi's rule. A crackdown on different fronts which began in 2021 – attempts to stop monopolization by these huge companies, by way of significant fines, the imposition of stricter data security laws and a general campaign against what would come to be referred to as the 'disorderly expansion of capital' – would, in combination with China's zero-Covid approach, slow the growth and moderate – sometimes forcibly – the ambitions of China's Big Tech, compelling them to align their vision with the government's. Tencent was even accused of peddling 'spiritual opium' in the form of online games like the wildly popular 'Honor of Kings'. It was a claim with notable historical resonance – particularly for a company based only about thirty-five miles down the estuary from the spot where Lin Zexu oversaw the destruction of foreign drugs that would kick-start the first Opium War.[2]

I took the *Vibrant Express* from Shenzhen to Hong Kong, a high-speed train line opened the previous year to no small controversy, partly because the line's terminus, a fragmented wave-shaped station which crests and falls onto the brink of Victoria harbour, incorporates joint immigration checkpoints – which means that part of the station is effectively mainland Chinese territory.

I wandered from the station through underpasses covered in coloured post-it notes, looking like some corporate planning exercise gone awry; these were the so-called 'Lennon Walls', a visual articulation of the public dissent that had exploded in recent months in Hong Kong. The protests had begun in response to a proposal that February of an extradition bill which would allow criminal suspects to be transferred to countries with which Hong Kong didn't have established treaties – including mainland China. The widespread fear was that the bill – nominally introduced in response to a murder case concerning a Hong Konger who killed his girlfriend in Taiwan before returning to the city – would allow for the removal to the mainland of political dissidents and others who had displeased the increasingly assertive mainland government. A wave of protests, beginning in March, saw hundreds of thousands of Hong Kongers on the streets, violent clashes between police and protestors – and profound divisions opened in Hong Kong society.

In mid-June, a protest march had drawn nearly two million people, uniformed in black t-shirts, with some holding signs saying 'Stop Killing Us' – a reference to the death of a protestor, Marco Leung Ling-kit, the previous day, who had fallen seventeen metres to his death from scaffolding that he had climbed to hang a protest banner. Having initially begun in response to the extradition bill, the protests now grew in scope as well as size, and the demands would expand to a list of five. In addition to killing off the extradition bill, the protestors asked that the term 'riots' cease being applied to their protests, that arrested protestors be released, that an independent commission be established to investigate police conduct during the protests – and that Carrie Lam Cheng Yuet-ngor, the Hong Kong chief executive widely seen as a Beijing stooge – resign, with universal suffrage implemented for subsequent elections. The authorities had, thus far, shown little willingness to accede to the wide-ranging demands, merely pausing the legislation and offering a vague apology.

Three days before my arrival in the city, in Yuen Long, a town just across the bay from Shenzhen in north-western Hong Kong, a mob of men wearing white shirts and carrying wooden poles and sticks had begun attacking people in and around the local subway station, seemingly targeting those wearing black. Despite thousands of calls, police took nearly forty minutes to respond to the attacks, by which time the mob had left the station.

Earlier that same evening, in the centre of Hong Kong, police had unleashed rounds of tear gas, and fired rubber bullets at protestors who had gathered at the liaison office of the Chinese government in the city, and defaced the crest of the Chinese government, throwing black ink and eggs. Carrie Lam would later say that the damage had 'hurt the nation's feelings'; of the attacks in Yuen Long, she offered a deliberately ambiguous response, saying that 'violence is not a solution to any problem. Violence will only breed more violence'.[3]

State media on the mainland would frame the protestors as radicals, and assert, in an echo of the 'peaceful evolution' warned against in the aftermath of Tiananmen, that 'anti-China forces in the West have colluded with local anti-China forces who intend to mess up Hong Kong'.[4] The chief spokesmen for the PRC's Ministry of National Defence would caution that 'The behavior of some radical protesters challenges the central government's authority, touching on the bottom line principle of "one country, two systems". That absolutely cannot be tolerated'.[5] It was seen by many as an implicit threat that China was ready to send in the military if the situation worsened.

In a phrase oft-repeated during the protests of 2019, the Joint Declaration of 1984 signed between the British and Chinese government had asserted that the Hong Kong Special Administrative Region would enjoy a 'high degree of autonomy' and that its lifestyle, and its social and economic systems, would remain unchanged for fifty years after the transition in 1997. A 2019 report by the Foreign Affairs Committee of the House of Commons asserted that it believed 'that the Chinese government's approach to Hong Kong is moving closer to "One Country, One System" than it is to maintaining its treaty commitments under the Joint Declaration'.[6] Well water and river water – the political and legal levee was at least cracking, even if it had not yet been fully breached.

Against the backdrop of this unrest, the Chinese government were pushing ahead with their ambition for the city to become more integrated economically with the mainland as part of a large-scale project, unveiled a few months earlier in 2019, in which Hong Kong would act as one of the hubs of the new 'Greater Bay Area'. This 'megacity' would combine the Hong Kong Special Administrative Region, the Macau SAR, as well as much of Guangdong to either side of the Pearl River, including Shenzhen and Zhuhai. Altogether, it covers a total area of 56,000 square kilometres, and incorporates a population of over seventy million people. The two major drivers of the economic success of this region were, of course, to be Shenzhen, with a 2021 GDP of around US$450 billion, and Hong Kong – which Shenzhen overtook in economic performance in 2018.[7]

The Chinese government wants, by 2035, to make the Pearl River Delta into a pioneer area of high-tech, ecologically sustainable development: a super-sized Silicon Valley. The plan is broad in scope, and grand in ambition: it talks of the markets becoming 'highly connected, with very effective and efficient flow of various resources', with the effect that the people become richer. But there is also an openly stated political aspiration here, too. 'The level of social civility should reach new heights,' the plan states, with 'Chinese cultural influence broadened and deepened, and exchange and integration between different cultures further enhanced'.[8] It is hard not to read the plan as an attempt to diminish Hong Kong's separateness; it is to be pulled more tightly into the close embrace of the motherland.

The plan faces many challenges, however. Despite slick, high-profile projects like the Vibrant Express, there is still nothing like freedom of movement between Hong Kong and the mainland. And though Beijing's legal and political incursions into Hong Kong are of increasing concern to many in the city, the frameworks within which business is conducted remain fundamentally different – even without the complexity introduced by having to deal with three separate currencies: the Chinese Yuan, the Hong Kong Dollar and the Macanese Pataca. The transition from the old model of Guangdong as a low-wage, low-skill export engine to what Xi Jinping terms 'a demonstration zone of high-quality growth, and a pacesetter of Chinese-style modernisation' requires highly trained, innovative workers from the mainland and beyond, and for successful companies to provide employment for them. As the Chinese economy continues to falter in 2023, foreign investment drains away from China's technology sector and unemployment rates soar, the gap between rhetoric and reality in the party's vision for the Greater Bay Area remains wide.

Having arrived on a half-empty ferry from Hong Kong into Zhuhai across the choppy mouth of the Pearl River estuary, the first thing I heard on my taxi driver's radio was a condemnation of the protests in Hong Kong and in particular the 'vandalism' done to the liaison office.

Despite the combative relationship that was developing, however, an evening stroll along Zhuhai's Lovers' Road, which sweeps past man-made beaches of yellow sand around the curving east coast of the city, offered evidence in steel and concrete of the government's ambitions in uniting the 'Greater Bay Area'. Hovering above a horizon of placid blue waves, about a kilometre or so out from the busy esplanade, is the solid grey line of the Hong Kong-Zhuhai-Macau Bridge: the longest sea-crossing bridge in the world, with a total length of thirty-four miles. Opened in 2018, it cost around US$20bn: a flashy feat of engineering that took nine years to build, and which means the journey between Hong Kong and Zhuhai and Macau can now be done in forty minutes.

Like that glittering wave of a railway station in Kowloon, many in Hong Kong saw the bridge as a political symbol rather than a logistical necessity – especially as the ferry ride from Hong Kong only took an hour. One critic had compared it to an umbilical cord. 'You see it,' leading opposition figure Claudia Mo Mon-ching told *CNN*, 'and you know you're linked up to the motherland'.[9] (In early 2021, Mo would be arrested, along with forty-six other prominent campaigners and politicians; accused of 'conspiracy to commit subversion', as of the summer of 2023 she remains in jail.) The bridge has not had the transformative impact envisioned on connecting Hong Kong to the mainland, and helping to encourage the less developed western side of the delta, however. Covid-19 would effectively close the border between Hong Kong and the mainland for two years, but even before the impact of the pandemic was felt, only 4000 vehicles a day were using the bridge – well below the estimated 9,200 the authorities had planned for in its second year.[10]

The destination for those walking Lovers' Road, past solitary fishermen and elderly ladies dancing and clapping in their evening exercise troupes, is marked by the crowds of visitors who congregate at the emblem of this increasingly tourism-conscious city: Zhuhai's 'Fisher Girl'. A near-nine-metre figure of golden stone, with hips cocked, and holding a pearl aloft above her head, it alludes to a local legend in which a daughter of the celestial Dragon King disguised herself as a fisher girl – so bewitched was she by the beauty of Zhuhai. The panorama which spreads behind the statue and the bay exemplifies the modest development of this city of just two and a half million; a mix of pastel and blue glass apartments, hotels and offices set against the smooth round blue edges of the lush hills which frame Zhuhai: a study in contrast to the metallic canyons of Shenzhen. 'As one of China's first Special Economic Zones, the city has continuously prioritized ecological development, enjoying one of the best environments in China,' Zhuhai's official website declares today. 'Local lands have been reasonably developed, low-end industry is kept in check, and the population count is kept in balance with its overall quality of living.'[11]

Looking to the west, an outcrop of sand-coloured rocks half-falling from the side of a hillside marks the site of the Shijingshan Tourist Centre, the lavish, neoclassical hotel where Deng had stayed during his visit. I strolled from the crowds through a quiet twilight park to find it an abandoned shell, its swimming pools full of murky green water, its rooms a chaos of dusty overturned furniture, the faded gold lettering above its pillared entrance half missing. I asked a local walking his dog nearby what had happened, and he told me it had closed five or six years ago – outcompeted by the new mirrored glass hotels that have multiplied on the southern edge of the city, looking out across the border to Macau.

I headed back north, through Guangzhou and then on the slow train to Shanghai. There are no statues of Deng Xiaoping in Pudong, but the emergence of China's most famous skyline – its timelapse development replicated *ad nauseam* in Shanghai's museums and exploited relentlessly in the promotion of China's modernization – is a memorial of sorts to his decisive interventions in the early 1990s, and confirmation of his prediction that the city would turn out to be China's 'trump card'.

Burgeoning behind the Oriental Pearl TV tower that was in the process of being constructed during Deng's Southern Tour visit is now a screen of ever-taller skyscrapers flanking a long, straight avenue which stretches out to the east. From the hotel bars which crown the tallest of these buildings, you can drink overpriced cocktails and look down into the egg-shaped old city of Shanghai on the other side of the Huangpu River and see its old lane houses being razed in real time.

If the old and new of Shanghai co-exist with increasing uneasiness, it is only really in the city's museums where the ideological tensions over its transformation are still evident. 'Shanghai is the birthplace of the Communist Party of China, the sacred land of China's revolution,' as one museum exhibition frames it; historically, it says, the city was 'the cradle of the working class' of China. In the post-liberation period, the people of Shanghai 'adopted forceful measures to crack down on financial speculation', whilst in the new period of reform and opening up, 'Shanghai people took the lead to forge ahead and made use of the new opportunity of Pudong development [...] thus enabling Shanghai to take on an entirely new look and gradually change into an internationally economic, financial, trade, and navigation centre'. This is the story of Shanghai presented by a new and lavish museum exhibition at the Longhua Martyrs' Cemetery, which opened after refurbishment five years into the Xi Jinping era, part of a large-scale project to renew China's existing museums, and open new ones at a startling rate of one every two days.[12] In the grounds here, Deng Xiaoping's first wife, Zhang Xiyuan, is buried; her grave marked by a small maroon headstone, which Deng visited with his daughter Rong during his Shanghai sojourn of 1990. In the museum itself, whether on the placards relating Zhang's biography, or the later development of Shanghai, there is no mention of Deng Xiaoping.

It would be an easy four-hour high-speed train ride back to the capital from Shanghai – but I decided on a whim to break my journey and make one final detour on this final leg of my southern tour.

From a busy train north, I was the only passenger to disembark onto the hot empty platform of the station at Tai'an. Cutting on quiet roads through dusty building sites and anonymous beige-tiled apartment compounds, I was deposited by my taxi at the top of 'Reaching to Heaven' Street, at the centre of this city of six million, beside a richly ornamented stone archway which led to the crenelated walls of a busy temple compound. I was here to climb Mount Tai, the bulbous, spreading mass of tan stone smothered with green trees looming to the north of this Song-dynasty temple, which marks the traditional starting point of pilgrimages up the mountain. The mountain, visited so consistently by those emperors who established the tradition of the Southern Tour, is not as high as some of China's other sacred mountains, rising to only 1500 metres from the surrounding plateau, but it is still the highest mountain in eastern China, and is preeminent amongst the country's five venerated peaks.

The emperors who made the pilgrimage to the peak of Mount Tai were carried up the mountain in a covered sedan chair, accompanied by hundreds of attendants. Today, millions of tourists each year climb the 6500 steps up the mountain, encouraged partly by the promise, repeated to me by my taxi driver, that those reaching the top on foot will live to one hundred.

The associations of the mountain are with the cycle of life, but also, by virtue of its breadth and heft, timelessness and strength. Like many other Chinese leaders, Deng Xiaoping had invoked Mount Tai's symbolism in his rhetoric. When in March 1990, he had called the leadership together at his house to reiterate the need for growth he had just made in Shanghai, he told them that though 'we have to strengthen ideological and political work and stress the need for hard struggle, we cannot depend on those measures alone. No matter how the international situation changes, so long as we can ensure appropriate economic growth, we shall stand firm as Mount Tai'.[13]

The climb is initially benign, punctuated by small temples nestled in the pines, stelae and rock carvings. A little higher up the broad stone path is the 'Imperial Tent Pitching Spot', a rare section of level ground where the Song emperor Zhenzhong instructed his camp to be established. I was heading up and down in a day, and fuelled my ascent with bottles of Coca-Cola kept cool on this sweltering morning in plastic containers filled with running water diverted from the mountain's streams. The bottles got more expensive the higher I climbed.

Bridges and ceremonial archways mark your progress: there is the 'Bridge which crosses the Rainbow', the 'Bridge of the Sinuous Dragon', the 'Bridge of Snowflakes'. One notable arch commemorates the story of the First Emperor, Qin Shi Huang, conferring in 219 BC the title of 'Grand Officer of the Fifth Degree' to a pine tree which had sheltered him from a sudden storm.

From the Halfway Gate to Heaven, the ascent becomes increasingly vertiginous through the Path of Eighteen Bends to the false peak of the South Gate of Heaven. It feels like an arrival, but there is still a slow incline to the actual summit along a road-like path past small shops selling bottles of Nong Fu Spring water, iced tea, Red Bull, ice creams – and ranks of souvenirs, including faux-bronze Mao figurines and idealized pottery representations of the mountain and its inscriptions. There were other signs of the modern world, too, including a few weather-beaten plastic signs, their red characters stripped of colour, outlining the 'Twelve Core Socialist Values', which had been unavoidable in China since early in Xi Jinping's reign as part of a campaign to instil a common social code: the values include 'democracy', 'freedom', 'equality', the 'rule of law' and 'patriotism'.

More diverting, and seemingly more resilient, were the written records of the tours of China's emperors which surrounded me as I approached the peak, carved into every accommodating vertical face of the mountain. Perhaps most famous is that by the Tang dynasty emperor Xuanzong, dating from 1300 years ago. It takes up most of a sheer thirteen-metre-high stone rock face, and expresses great uncertainty about his capacity for rule: 'For fourteen years I have occupied the high position of emperor. I am, however, troubled by my lack of virtue; I am ignorant of perfect reason. The duties which I have to fulfil are hard to fulfil; the calm which I should preserve is hard to preserve'.[14]

The Temple of the Jade Emperor which sits at the true peak was almost deserted, and I walked round to the northern wall to look out at the view. In a side room, two elderly caretakers were sitting watching a game show on TV, their mops threaded through the window's metal grating to drip dry.

'Stand tall, see far', went the saying Deng Xiaoping was fond of. Mao Zedong had, according to myths that swirl around his biography, been struck by epiphanic inspiration on this peak – looking out at the sun and declaring 'The East is Red'.

Confucius climbed to the top and felt the world looked smaller, a sense of perspective echoed by the lines of Tang dynasty poet Du Fu:

One day I shall reach its highest peak
And hold the mountains below in a single glance.

But the view today was obscured by draped cloud and mist, out of which, just occasionally, the long limbs of the mountain appeared, stretching out towards valleys beyond of the same rich green. If I had hoped to gain some perspective from this hard-won vantage point, the gods clearly had different ideas.

In front of the temple was a huge stele of yellow stone. Unlike the rest of the peak, which was covered in imperial graffiti, this tablet was completely blank. No one knows the true history of this monument or why it is wordless: one theory is that the emperor responsible for its erection was dissatisfied by the suggestion of his scribes, and opted instead to leave the meaning of the monument for the imagination of those that gazed upon it. Others contest that long centuries of wind, rain and ice have worn the calligraphic inscription from the face of the stone – so that whatever account had once been engraved here was now lost to time and memory.

TIMELINE

10 November 1965 — An article by Yao Wenyuan criticizing the play *Hai Rui Dismissed from Office* is published in Shanghai.

16 May 1966 — The 'May 16 Notification' is issued representing the first major political declaration of the Great Proletarian Cultural Revolution. It condemns '[t]he representatives of the bourgeois who have infiltrated the Party, the government, the army, and various cultural sectors' as 'a group of counterrevolutionary revisionists. Once the conditions are ripe, they will seize power and transform the proletarian dictatorship into a bourgeois dictatorship.'

16 July 1966 — Mao Zedong swims in the Yangtze River at Wuhan.

5 August 1966 — Mao issues a *dazibao* or 'big character poster' titled 'Bombard the Headquarters' condemning 'leading comrades' as 'poisonous'; it was widely seen as a direct condemnation of President Liu Shaoqi and Deng Xiaoping.

8 August 1966 — The 'Sixteen Points' are adopted by the party, setting down guidelines for the Cultural Revolution. They declare that 'our objective is to struggle against and overthrow those persons in authority who are taking the capitalist road, to criticize and repudiate the reactionary bourgeois academic "authorities" and the ideology of the bourgeoisie and all other exploiting classes and to transform education, literature and art and all other parts of the superstructure not in correspondence with the socialist economic base.'

August 1966 — Red Guards, made up mainly of students, target and violently persecute those they consider to be class enemies, torturing and murdering teachers, academics, intellectuals and others. In Beijing, this phase becomes known as 'Bloody August', and violence spreads in other Chinese cities. 'Whoever opposes Chairman Mao will have his head smashed into 10,000 pieces!' one Red Guard slogan declares. Mao Zedong reviews the Red Guards from Tiananmen eight times between August and November; an estimated eleven million Red Guards will take part in these mass gatherings in Tiananmen Square.

Timeline

23 October 1966	After increasing attacks, and the abolition of his official post, Deng Xiaoping makes a self-criticism declaring that he should have been more modest and reported to, and asked for instructions, from Mao.
29 July 1967	Deng is denounced by the 'revolutionary masses', and placed under house arrest in Zhongnanhai. Deng and his wife, Zhuo Lin, are subject to criticism and denunciation by the rebels, physically removed from their house and forced to kneel whilst the rebels condemn and question them.
August 1968	Deng Pufang, Deng Xiaoping's son, is paralysed after falling from a fourth storey window, having been subject to relentless persecution by Red Guards.
22 October 1969	Deng, Zhuo Lin and Deng's stepmother are sent to Jiangxi province. Deng works half days in a tractor factory, to learn from labour.
August–September 1970	The Second Plenum of the Ninth Central Committee is held at Lushan in Jiangxi province. Here, despite Mao's clear objections, Defence Minister and *de-facto* heir Lin Biao proposes that the position of state chairman, a mainly ceremonial role, be retained. Mao believes this is a tactic to allow Lin to claim the position when Mao continues to refuse it. It causes an irrevocable split between Mao and Lin.
August–September 1971	Mao sets off on a Southern Tour criticizing the actions of Lin Biao and his supporters, visiting Wuhan, Changsha, Nanchang, Hangzhou and Shanghai.
13 September 1971	Lin Biao dies when an aircraft carrying him and several members of his family crashes in Mongolia.
22 February 1973	Deng Xiaoping returns to Beijing and assumes the post of deputy premier.
October 1974	Deng is appointed as deputy chairman of the Central Military Commission and as Chief of the General Staff of the PLA.
April 1976	After Premier Zhou Enlai's death in January, public commemoration of Zhou begins in March, with the laying of a wreath in Tiananmen Square. On 4 April, the eve of the Qingming, or Tomb-Sweeping, Festival, more than one million people converge on Tiananmen to publicly honour the premier and criticize the 'Gang of Four'. The square is cleared, with authorities using force to remove the last

	protestors; on 7 April Deng Xiaoping is removed from all posts and placed under house arrest.
9 September 1976	Mao Zedong dies.
6 October 1976	The 'Gang of Four' is arrested at Zhongnanhai.
17 July 1977	'The Decision Concerning the Return of Comrade Deng Xiaoping to Work' is passed, marking Deng's official return to the positions he had held before April 1976.
18–22 December 1978	The Third Plenum of the Eleventh Party Congress takes place at the Jingxi Hotel in Beijing, following on from a work conference held the previous month. The plenum confirms Deng's ascendancy to the leadership of the party.
July 1979	The Central Committee approve the establishment of the first two Special Economic Zones, in Shenzhen and Zhuhai.
September 1980	Zhao Ziyang becomes Premier.
November 1983–February 1984	A campaign against 'Spiritual Pollution' is pursued.
24 January 1984	Deng Xiaoping begins his first Southern Tour.
May 1984	A further fourteen Open Coastal Cities are established.
December 1986–January 1987	Student demonstrations take place in cities across China. Hu Yaobang is forced to resign as General Secretary of the CCP. A campaign against 'bourgeois liberalization' gathers momentum.
October–November 1987	The Thirteenth Party Congress takes place in Beijing. Deng gives up his party and government roles; Zhao Ziyang, now General Secretary, is handed even greater authority.
Summer 1988	Spiralling inflation, exacerbated by suggestions from the leadership that large-scale price reform was about to be implemented, creates a political and social crisis which sees controls reimposed on prices, and a significant shift in policy designed to cool down China's economy.
15 April 1989	Hu Yaobang dies.
22 April 1989	Thousands gather in front of the Great Hall of the People for Hu's memorial service.
26 April 1989	An editorial titled 'It is necessary to take a clear-cut stand against turmoil' is published in the *People's Daily* denouncing the student movement.

Timeline

13 May 1989	Hundreds of students begin hunger strikes in Tiananmen Square.
15 May 1989	Mikhail Gorbachev arrives in Beijing.
19 May 1989	Zhao Ziyang visits students in Tiananmen Square.
20 May 1989	Martial law is declared in Beijing.
3 June 1989	Troops begin to move into Beijing heading towards Tiananmen Square. At barricades established along major routes, the army opens fire, killing and injuring civilians.
9 June 1989	Deng addresses PLA generals at Huairen Hall in Zhongnanhai.
4 September 1989	Deng announces to senior officials that he will retire from his last leadership position (Chairman of the Central Military Commission) in November.
9 November 1989	Deng officially retires.
10 January 1990	Martial law is lifted in Beijing.
21 January 1990	Deng sets out for Shanghai for the Lunar New Year. He will return to Beijing on 13 February.
27 January 1991	Deng again departs for Shanghai.
March–April 1991	The 'Huangfu Ping' articles are published in Shanghai's *Liberation Daily*.

*

January–February 1992	The Southern Tour
17 January 1992	Deng Xiaoping departs Beijing Railway Station at 3.35 pm on his Southern Tour.
18 January	At 10.31 am Deng arrives at Wuchang Railway Station in the city of Wuhan. He stays for around half an hour. At 4 pm on the same day, his train arrives at Changsha Railway Station in Hunan province.
19 January	At 9 am, Deng's train arrives at Shenzhen Railway station. He tours the city and visits Huanggang Port on the Hong Kong border.
20 January	Deng visits Shenzhen's International Trade Centre and the Xianke factory.
21 January	Deng and his family visit the 'Splendid China' and 'China Folk Culture Village' theme parks.
22 January	Deng visits the Xianhu Botanical Garden with his family and plants a tree. In the afternoon he meets with local leaders at his hotel.

23 January	On the morning of the 23rd, Deng crosses the Pearl River Delta from Shenzhen to Zhuhai and surveys the city by road. Over the subsequent days, Deng will visit various factories and meet with officials.
29 January	Deng leaves Zhuhai by car to meet his train once more in Guangzhou.
30 January	Deng's train stops at Yingtan in Jiangxi province.
31 January	Deng arrives in Shanghai for the Lunar New Year holiday.
7 February	Deng visits the Nanpu Bridge site.
12 February	Deng visits the Minhang Development Zone.
18 February	Deng visits the Zhongbaiyi Department Store on Nanjing Road.
20 February	Deng departs Shanghai, via Nanjing and Bengbu, and returns to Beijing.

*

28 February 1992	The Central Committee issues a summary of Deng's speeches during the Southern Tour for distribution to cadres.
31 March 1992	The *People's Daily* reprints 'East Wind Brings Spring All Around – On-the-spot Report on Comrade Deng Xiaoping in Shenzhen'.
9 June 1992	Jiang Zemin gives a speech at the Central Party School titled 'Deeply Understand and Implement Comrade Deng Xiaoping's Important Spirit, Make Economic Construction, Reform and Opening Go Faster and Better'.
12–18 October 1992	The Fourteenth Party Congress is held in Beijing. Jiang Zemin declares that China is building a 'socialist market economy' and growth targets are increased.
10 April 1995	Chen Yun dies, aged eighty-nine.
19 February 1997	Deng Xiaoping dies, aged ninety-two, from a lung infection and complications of Parkinson's disease.
1 July 1997	The Handover of Hong Kong from the UK to the People's Republic of China takes place.

ACKNOWLEDGEMENTS

When I first went to China, nearly a decade and a half ago, I became preoccupied by a desire to understand the country's journey towards its modern incarnation. This book is the result of that continuing preoccupation, and I feel privileged to have had the opportunity to pursue its story, both on the ground in China and in the wealth of primary sources and secondary sources I have consulted in the course of the book's writing. In trying to explain this complex era to myself and to readers, I have relied on the work of scholars who have dedicated their professional lives to the People's Republic, and whose expertise was hugely reassuring to return to when the complexities of modern China threatened to become overwhelming. In particular, the works of Jonathan Spence, Ezra Vogel, Joseph Fewsmith, Barry Naughton, Susan Shirk and Richard Baum have had significant influence on the writing of this book.

For their help in developing my ideas of what this book might look like, I would like to particularly thank Julia Lovell, Emma Finn and James Carter. I first began to explore the story of Deng's Southern Tour in a podcast series, and am grateful to those who so graciously gave of their time and expertise: Julian Gewirtz, Chris Courtney, Juan Du, Dexter Roberts, Adrien Gombeaud, who has written his own book on travelling the route of Deng's Southern Tour, *Dans les Pas du Petit Timonier*, Jenny Lin, Patrick Cranley and Lawrence C. Reardon. I would particularly like to offer my thanks to Chris Reardon, who so graciously and generously offered his time and expertise on China's reforms, as well as reading and commenting on an early draft of the book. Katie Stallard also offered hugely helpful comments and suggestions on the book's first draft. Thanks also to the staff at the British Library, the BBC Archive, NewsBank and the University of Birmingham library. Travelling alone for a month in China meant that, once again, I relied upon the friendliness and hospitality of old friends in China, as well as those I met on my travels. I would like to thank them for the generosity of all kinds that they showed.

David Avital at Bloomsbury and Paul French have editorially shepherded the book along to publication; I am deeply grateful for their insight and encouragement.

I began this project in 2019, and it simply would not have been possible without the support of my wife, Kate, whilst my two children, Clara and Iris, helped to provide much needed perspective when progress seemed elusive.

NOTES

Prologue

1. 'Liaowang Article Details Deng's Shenzhen Visit', *Zhongguo Xinwen She*, 12 February 1984, Translation by the *Foreign Broadcast Information Service, FBIS Daily Report, China 1979–1996*, NewsBank (hereafter *FBIS*).
2. Mary Ann O'Donnell, Winnie Wong, and Jonathan Bach, eds., *Learning from Shenzhen: China's Post-Mao Experiment from Special Zone to Model City* (Chicago: The University of Chicago Press, 2011), 129.
3. 'Liaowang Article Details Deng's Shenzhen Visit', *FBIS*.
4. Juan Du, *The Shenzhen Experiment: The Story of China's Instant City* (Cambridge, MA: Harvard University Press, 2020), 170–1.
5. 'Wealthy Peasants to Embark on Japan Tour', *Xinhua*, 21 June 1984, *FBIS*.
6. For details of Deng's visit to Shenzhen and his 1984 Southern Tour, see *Reforming China: Major Events (1978–1991): Vol.3* (Hong Kong: Enrich Professional Publishing, 2010), 201–7; '习近平视察深圳渔民村 村民生活成调研重点-搜狐新闻', 14 December 2012, news.sohu.com, http://news.sohu.com/20121214/n360402921.shtml; 邓小平年谱, *1975–1997*, vol. 下册 (中央文献出版社, 2004), 954–61.
7. Deng Xiaoping, 'The Army Should Subordinate Itself to the General Interest, Which Is to Develop the Country', *Selected Works of Deng Xiaoping. Volume III*.
8. 'Thriving Shenzhen Tells Tale of Old Man and the City', *China Daily*, 18 February 2017, https://www.chinadaily.com.cn/china/2017-02/18/content_28251795_2.htm.
9. Kang Zhengguo, *Confessions: An Innocent Life in Communist China*, trans. Susan Wilf (New York; London: W.W. Norton, 2008), 118.
10. Deng Xiaoping, 'We Shall Concentrate on Economic Development', *Selected Works of Deng Xiaoping. Volume III*.
11. Lijia Zhang, *Socialism Is Great! A Worker's Memoir of the New China* (New York: Anchor Books, 2009), 14.
12. See Lawrence C. Reardon, *A Third Way: The Origins of China's Current Economic Development Strategy* (Cambridge, MA: Harvard University Asia Center, 2020), 18–27; Barry Naughton, *Growing out of the Plan: Chinese Economic Reform, 1978–1993* (Cambridge: Cambridge University Press, 1995), 67–70.
13. Deng Xiaoping, 'The Organizational Line Guarantees the Implementation of the Ideological and Political Lines', in *Selected Works of Deng Xiaoping. Volume II, 1975–1982* (Beijing: Foreign Languages Press, 1995).

14 Naughton, *Growing out of the Plan*, 138–42.
15 Zhao Ziyang, *Prisoner of the State: The Secret Journal of Zhao Ziyang*, ed. and trans. Bao Pu, Renee Chiang, and Adi Ignatius (London: Simon and Schuster, 2009), 142.
16 Gregory C. Chow and Dwight H. Perkins, eds., *Routledge Handbook of the Chinese Economy* (Abingdon: Routledge, 2015), 56.
17 Ezra Vogel, *Deng Xiaoping and the Transformation of China* (Cambridge, MA: Harvard University Press, 2011), 303–4.
18 Robert Lawrence Kuhn, *How China's Leaders Think: The Inside Story of China's Past, Current and Future Leaders* (Singapore: John Wiley & Sons, 2011), 61.
19 Ezra Vogel, *One Step Ahead in China: Guangdong under Reform* (Cambridge, MA: Harvard University Press, 1989), 35–6.
20 Barry Naughton, 'The Third Front: Defence Industrialization in the Chinese Interior', *The China Quarterly*, no. 115 (1988): 351–86.
21 Vogel, *One Step Ahead in China*, 37.
22 '"Back Where We Were": History Repeats for Hong Kong's Freedom Swimmers', *The Guardian*, 28 September 2020.
23 Kuhn, *How China's Leaders Think*, 60.
24 'The Approval and Transmittal of the "Two Reports of the Guangdong and Fujian Provincial Committees Concerning the Implementation of Special Policies and Flexible Measures in Foreign Trade Activities" (Excerpts) (15 July 1979)', *Chinese Law and Government* 27, no. 3 (May–June 1994): 19–44. The island province of Hainan would also be designated as a Special Economic Zone in 1988.
25 Michaela Fontana, *Matteo Ricci: A Jesuit in the Ming Court* (Lanham: Rowman and Littlefield, 2011), 42.
26 Benjamin Couch Henry, *Ling-Nam; or, Interior Views of Southern China* (London: S.W. Partridge, 1886), 30.
27 Vogel, *One Step Ahead in China*, 201.
28 邓小平实录4 1982–1997: 改革开放40周年纪念版 (北京: 北京联合出版公司, 2018), 66.
29 Deng Xiaoping, 'Make a Success of Special Economic Zones and Open More Cities to the Outside World', *Selected Works of Deng Xiaoping. Volume III*.
30 Ibid.
31 Richard Baum, *Burying Mao: Chinese Politics in the Age of Deng Xiaoping* (Princeton: Princeton University Press, 1994), 160.
32 'Chen Yun Supports Constitution, Zhao Report', *Xinhua*, 2 December 1982, FBIS.
33 'Cheng Ming Article Views Deng's Guangdong Trip', *Cheng Ming*, 1 March 1984, FBIS.
34 'Cheng Ming on Deng Xiaoping, Chen Yun Dispute', *Cheng Ming*, 1 October 1985, FBIS.
35 Reardon, *A Third Way*, 96.

36 'A Major Policy Decision for Promoting the Modernisation Drive', *People's Daily*, 28 May 1984, FBIS.
37 Deng Xiaoping, 'Speech at the Third Plenary Session of the Central Advisory Commission of the Communist Party of China', *Selected Works of Deng Xiaoping. Volume III*.
38 'TV Series Illuminates Deng's Achievements', *Global Times*, 13 August 2014, https://www.globaltimes.cn/content/875856.shtml.
39 'Deng Said Behind Huangfu Ping Articles on Reform', *Sing Pao*, 10 May 1991.

Chapter 1

1 It was altogether a more dignified reception than that which saw Nikita Khrushchev forced into the pool for a swim during a meeting in 1958 – with flotation devices provided to assist the floundering Soviet leader.
2 In the early years after the CCP established themselves at Zhongnanhai, the auditorium at Huairen hosted numerous parties, with famous Peking Opera stars summoned to perform for the party elite. The hall later became the main meeting place for China's Politburo, the 'cabinet' who decide the country's political direction. On occasion, it also hosts the smaller Politburo Standing Committee – the core of China's political elite.
3 For the text of the whole speech, see Deng Xiaoping, 'Address to Officers at the Rank of General and above in Command of the Troops Enforcing Martial Law in Beijing', *Selected Works of Deng Xiaoping. Volume III*.
4 Michel Oksenberg, Lawrence R. Sullivan, and Marc Lambert, eds., *Beijing Spring, 1989: Confrontation and Conflict* (London: M.E. Sharpe, 1990), 364.
5 Harrison E. Salisbury, *The New Emperors: Mao and Deng: A Dual Biography* (London: HarperCollins, 1993), 443.
6 'Hu Yaobang Resigns as General Secretary', *Xinhua*, 16 January 1987, FBIS.
7 'Journal on "Hu Yaobang after Resignation"', *Kuang Chiao Ching*, 16 January 1989, FBIS.
8 Oksenberg et al., *Beijing Spring*, 195–203.
9 Ann Kerns, *Who Will Shout If Not Us?: Student Activists and the Tiananmen Square Protest, China, 1989* (Minneapolis: Twenty-First Century Books, 2011), 47.
10 'Further on Expressions of Mourning', *Xinhua*, 17 April 1989, FBIS.
11 Craig Calhoun, *Neither Gods nor Emperors: Students and the Struggle for Democracy in China* (Berkeley; Los Angeles: University of California Press, 1994), 246.
12 Chen Xitong, 'Report to the NPC on Quelling the Counter-Revolutionary Rebellion', in Oksenberg, Sullivan, and Lambert, eds., *Beijing Spring, 1989*, 55–88.
13 Zhao, *Prisoner of the State*, 10.
14 'It Is Necessary to Take a Clear-Cut Stand against Turmoil', *People's Daily*, 26 April 1989.

15   Calhoun, *Neither Gods nor Emperors*, 55.
16   Mikhail Gorbachev, *Memoirs*, trans. Georges Peronansky and Tatjana Varsavsky (London: Doubleday, 1996), 490.
17   Plus Yang Shangkun. See Zhao, *Prisoner of the State*, 27–9 for his account of this meeting.
18   Ibid., 31.
19   Jasper Becker, 'Zhao Ziyang: Chinese Leader Who "Came Too Late" to Tiananmen Square', *The Independent*, 18 January 2005; Kuhn, *How China's Leaders Think*, 54.
20   Zhao, *Prisoner of the State*, 152.
21   'Obituary: Zhao Ziyang', *BBC News*, 17 January 2005.
22   Zhao, *Prisoner of the State*, 135.
23   Deng Xiaoping, 'Our Magnificent Goal and Basic Policies', *Selected Works. Volume III*.
24   Reardon, *A Third Way*, 230.
25   Zhao, *Prisoner of the State*, 145.
26   Ibid., 59–60.
27   Deng Xiaoping, 'Urgent Tasks of China's Third Generation of Collective Leadership', *Selected Works. Volume III*.
28   Celia Hatton, 'What Do Chinese Leaders Do When They Retire?' *BBC News*, 15 March 2013.
29   Deng Xiaoping, 'Answers to the Italian Journalist Oriana Fallaci', *Selected Works. Volume II*.
30   Vogel, *Deng Xiaoping and the Transformation of China*, 556–7.
31   Robert Lawrence Kuhn, *The Man Who Changed China: The Life and Legacy of Jiang Zemin* (New York: Crown, 2004), 173–4.
32   Sheryl WuDunn, 'Communist Chief Is Named Deng's Heir Apparent', *The New York Times*, 11 October 1989.
33   Kuhn, *The Man Who Changed China*, 179.
34   Deng Xiaoping, 'With Stable Policies of Reform and Opening to the Outside World, China Can Have Great Hopes for the Future', *Selected Works. Volume III*.
35   'There Will Be No Change in the General Principle of Reform and Opening up', *People's Daily*, 22 September 1989, *FBIS*.
36   Deng Rong, *Deng Xiaoping: My Father* (New York: BasicBooks, 1995), 1–3.

Chapter 2

1   See 'Recollections at a Great Man's Home', *People's Daily*, 23 August 2004, http://en.people.cn/200408/23/eng20040823_154351.html; Ezra Vogel, *Deng Xiaoping and the Transformation of China*, 378; 'My Father, Deng Xiaoping (Interview with Deng Rong)', *China Newsweek*, 20 August 2004, http://www.china.org.cn/english/NM-e/104645.htm.

2   Baum, *Burying Mao*, 290.
3   Calhoun, *Neither Gods nor Emperors*, 148.
4   Liao Yiwu, *Bullets and Opium: Real-Life Stories after the Tiananmen Square Massacre* (New York: Atria/One Signal, 2020), Apple Books, 275.
5   'Beijing Municipal Government Lifts Martial Law', *Beijing Television Service*, 10 January 1990, *FBIS*.
6   Bruce Gilley, *Tiger on the Brink: Jiang Zemin and China's New Elite* (Berkeley; Los Angeles: University of California Press, 1998), 168.
7   Deng Rong, *Deng Xiaoping: My Father*, 51–3.
8   *The Far Eastern Review* 15 (1919):116.
9   Philip Kerby, *Beyond the Bund* (New York: Payson & Clarke Ltd., 1927), 11.
10 Zhao, *Prisoner of the State*, 102.
11 Richard Hu and Weijie Chen, *Global Shanghai Remade: The Rise of Pudong New Area* (Abingdon: Routledge, 2019), 30.
12 '1990年, 邓小平和夫人卓琳在上海西郊宾馆', 邓小平纪念网, 15 November 2019, http://cpc.people.com.cn/n1/2019/1115/c69113-31457773.html.
13 邓小平年谱, 1975–1997, vol. 下册,1308.
14 Zhu Rongji, *Zhu Rongji: On the Record – The Shanghai Years 1987–1991*, trans. June Y. Mei (Washington, DC: Brookings Institution Press, 2018), Apple Books, 823.
15 Deng Xiaoping, 'The International Situation and Economic Problems', *Selected Works. Volume III*.
16 *China's Economic Dilemmas in the 1990s: The Problems of Reforms, Modernization, and Interdependence: Study Papers Submitted to the Joint Economic Committee*, Congress of the United States (United States: U.S. Government Printing Office, 1991), 111.
17 'Beijing Radio Views Panic Buying in Cities', *Beijing Domestic Service*, 8 August 1988, *FBIS*.
18 Baum, *Burying Mao*, 235.
19 Zhao, *Prisoner of the State*, 234–5.
20 'Chen Yun Denounces Inner-Party Corruption', *Sing Pao*, 10 September 1990, *FBIS*.
21 Zhao, *Prisoner of the State*, 224.
22 Naughton, *Growing out of the Plan*, 275.
23 'Article Views Economic Rectification', *People's Daily*, 9 March 1990, *FBIS*.
24 'Li Peng Gives Speech on Economy 11 Oct', *People's Daily Overseas Edition*, 27 October 1989.
25 'Li Peng Tours Guangdong's Shenzhen, Huizhou', *Xinhua*, 12 February 1990.
26 Deng Xiaoping, 'The International Situation and Economic Problems', *Selected Works. Volume III*.
27 'Approves Pudong Development', *Xinhua*, 18 April 1990, *FBIS*.
28 Zhu, *On the Record*, 1062.

29 Ibid., 1041–50.
30 Deng Xiaoping, 'Remarks Made during an Inspection Tour of Shanghai', *Selected Works. Volume III*.
31 Zhu, *On the Record*, 1123.
32 Joseph Fewsmith, *China since Tiananmen: From Deng Xiaoping to Hu Jintao* (New York: Cambridge University Press, 2008), 49.
33 'Huangfu Ping Article on Cadre Appointments', *Jiefang Ribao*, 12 April 1991, *FBIS*.
34 Fewsmith, *China since Tiananmen*, 49.
35 Quoted in ibid., 61.
36 'Chen Yun Urges Caution in Reform, Opening', *Sing Pao*, 5 September 1991, *FBIS*.
37 'Floods May Ruin Grain Harvest', *China Daily*, 13 June 1991, *FBIS*.
38 Gorbachev, *Memoirs*, 631.
39 Deng Xiaoping, 'Review Your Experience and Use Professionally Trained People', *Selected Works. Volume III*.
40 Baum, *Burying Mao*, 333.
41 Ibid., 337.
42 Salisbury, *The New Emperors*, 461.
43 David Shambaugh, 'China in 1991: Living Cautiously', *Asian Survey* 32, no. 1 (1992): 19–31.
44 Suisheng Zhao, 'Deng Xiaoping's Southern Tour: Elite Politics in Post-Tiananmen China', *Asian Survey* 33, no. 8 (1993): 745.

Chapter 3

1 Four courtiers initially administered his reign, as a result of his youth; he would claim power back at fifteen.
2 Michael G. Chang, *A Court on Horseback: Imperial Touring and the Construction of Qing Rule, 1680–1785* (Cambridge, MA: Harvard University Asia Center, 2007), 7.
3 Jonathan D. Spence, *Emperor of China: Self-Portrait of K'ang-Hsi* (New York: Vintage, 1988), Apple Books, 117.
4 Richard E. Strassberg, *Inscribed Landscapes: Travel Writing from Imperial China* (Berkeley: University of California Press, 1994), 12–13.
5 Lawrence D. Kessler, *K'ang-Hsi and the Consolidation of Ch'ing Rule 1661–1684* (Chicago: University of Chicago Press, 1976), 2.
6 Kangxi was an avid traveller; as Michael G. Chang notes between 1681 and his death in 1722 the Kangxi emperor embarked on a total of 128 imperial tours of various length.
7 Maxwell K. Hearn, 'Recording the Imperial Southern Inspection Tours', *Asia for Educators*, http://afe.easia.columbia.edu/qing/tours.html.
8 Chang, *A Court on Horseback*, 2.

9. Bruce Gordon Doar, 'The Southern Expeditions of Emperors Kangxi and Qianlong', *China Heritage Quarterly*, no. 9 (March 2007), http://www.chinaheritagequarterly.org/features.php?searchterm=009_expeditions.inc&issue=009.
10. Chang, *A Court on Horseback*, 450.
11. Though Qing hunting tours continued for another generation.
12. Yang Jisheng, *The World Turned Upside down: A History of the Chinese Cultural Revolution*, trans. Stacy Mosher and Guo Jian (New York: Farrar, Straus and Giroux, 2021), Kindle edition, 44.
13. Roderick MacFarquhar, ed., *The Politics of China: The Eras of Mao and Deng* (New York: Cambridge University Press, 1997), 248.
14. Deng Rong, *Deng Xiaoping and the Cultural Revolution: A Daughter Recalls the Critical Years*, trans. Sidney Shapiro (Beijing: Foreign Languages Press, 2002), 56.
15. Li Zhisui, *The Private Life of Chairman Mao: The Inside Story of the Man Who Made Modern China* (London: Chatto & Windus, 1994), 454.
16. Daniel Leese, 'Little Red Book/Quotations from Chairman Mao', *The Mao Era in Objects*, https://maoeraobjects.ac.uk/object-biographies/little-red-book-红宝书/.
17. Yang, *The World Turned Upside Down*, Kindle edition, 444.
18. 孟昭庚, '毛泽东险象环生的1971年南巡路', *People's Daily*, 15 April 2014, http://dangshi.people.com.cn/n/2014/0415/c85037-24898922.html.
19. Roderick Macfarquhar and Michael Schoenhals, *Mao's Last Revolution* (Cambridge, MA: The Belknap Press of Harvard University Press, 2006), 335.
20. Deng Rong, *Deng Xiaoping and the Cultural Revolution*, 184.

Chapter 4

1. Deng Rong, *Deng Xiaoping: My Father*, 132.
2. Alexander V. Pantsov and Steven I. Levine, *Deng Xiaoping: A Revolutionary Life* (Oxford: Oxford University Press, 2015), 94.
3. Ibid., 424.
4. 'My Father, Deng Xiaoping' (Interview with Deng Rong).
5. Willy Wo-lap Lam, 'Deng Xiaoping Reaffirms Commitment to Reform', *South China Morning Post*, 3 October 1991.
6. 'GDP Growth (annual %) – China', The World Bank, https://data.worldbank.org/indicator/NY.GDP.MKTP.KD.ZG?end=1992&locations=CN&start=1979.
7. Susan Shirk, *The Political Logic of Economic Reform in China* (Berkeley: University of California Press, 1993), 17.
8. Barry Naughton, *The Chinese Economy: Adaptation and Growth* (Cambridge, MA: MIT Press, 2018), 475.

9   See Carolyn Hsu, 'Cadres, Getihu, and Good Businesspeople: Making Sense of Entrepreneurs In Early Post-Socialist China', *Urban Anthropology and Studies of Cultural Systems and World Economic Development* 35, no. 1 (2006): 1–38.
10 Zhang, *Socialism Is Great*, 32.
11 Shirk, *The Political Logic of Economic Reform in China*, 43.
12 Willy Wo-Lap Lam, *China after Deng Xiaoping: The Power Struggle in Beijing since Tiananmen* (Singapore; New York: John Wiley & Sons, 1995), 58.
13 邓小平实录4, 215.

Chapter 5

1   Alexander V. Pantsov and Steven I. Levine, *Mao: The Real Story* (New York: Simon and Schuster, 2012), Apple Books, 1711.
2   Richard Evans, *Deng Xiaoping and the Making of Modern China* (London: Penguin, 1995), 5.
3   He also visited Tianjin, Jinan, Xuzhou, Nanjing, Nanchang, and Changsha. His itinerary is recorded in 逄先知 and 冯蕙, 毛泽东年谱: 1949-1976 / 第五卷 (北京: 中央文献出版社, 2013), 536–632.
4   Pantsov and Levine, *Mao: The Real Story*, Apple Books, 1480–85.
5   Details for this section on Deng's departure and visits to Wuhan and Changsha are, unless otherwise noted, drawn from 邓小平实录4, 207–10.
6   James Miles, *The Legacy of Tiananmen: China in Disarray* (Ann Arbor: The University of Michigan Press, 1997), 88–9.
7   Chris Courtney, *The Nature of Disaster in China: The 1931 Yangzi River Flood* (Cambridge: Cambridge University Press, 2018), 30.
8   Qtd in William T. Rowe, *Hankow: Commerce and Society in a Chinese City, 1796–1889* (Stanford: Stanford University Press, 1984).
9   Stephen R. MacKinnon, *Wuhan, 1938: War, Refugees, and the Making of Modern China* (Berkeley; Los Angeles, CA: University of California Press, 2008), 5.
10 Laurence Oliphant, *Narrative of the Earl of Elgin's Mission to China and Japan in the Years 1857, '58, '59*, vol. 2, 2 vols (Edinburgh; London: William Blackwood and Sons, 1859), 396.
11 Wang Shaoguang, *Failure of Charisma: The Cultural Revolution in Wuhan* (Hong Kong; New York: Oxford University Press, 1995), 24.
12 Jianquan Cheng and Jie Zhou, 'Urban Growth in a Rapidly Urbanized Mega City – Wuhan, P.R. China', in *Urban Development Challenges, Risks and Resilience in Asian Mega Cities*, ed. R.B. Singh (Tokyo: Springer, 2015), 301–22.
13 *China Daily*, 17 May 1995, p. 4, reprinted in *FBIS*, 17 May 1995.
14 Deborah Davis, 'Urban Consumer Culture', *The China Quarterly* 183 (2005): 692.

15 Edward S. Steinfeld, *Forging Reform in China: The Fate of State-Owned Industry* (Cambridge: Cambridge University Press, 1998), 16.
16 Deng Xiaoping, 'We Shall Expand Political Democracy and Carry Out Economic Reform', *Selected Works of Deng Xiaoping. Volume III*.
17 Naughton, *Growing out of the Plan*, 203.
18 Ibid., 286–7.
19 Miles, *The Legacy of Tiananmen*, 125.
20 Deng Xiaoping, 'Our Work in All Fields Should Contribute to the Building of Socialism with Chinese Characteristics', *Selected Works of Deng Xiaoping. Volume III*.
21 Deng Xiaoping, 'Excerpts from Talks Given in Wuchang, Shenzhen, Zhuhai and Shanghai', *Selected Works of Deng Xiaoping. Volume III*.
22 牛正武, 南行纪 : *1992年邓小平南方谈话全记录* (广州: 广东人民出版社, 2012), 9.
23 James Sterngold, 'Flood Toll in China Nears 1,000', *The New York Times*, 9 July 1991.
24 Nicholas D. Kristof, 'China's Floods of July: Misery Lingers', *The New York Times*, 27 January 1992.
25 Ibid.
26 'Xiong Qingquan Stresses Decreasing Party Formalism', *Changsha Hunan People's Radio Network*, 20 June 1991, FBIS.
27 'Xiong Qingquan Proposes Basic Ideas for 1991 Work', *Changsha Hunan Provincial Service*, 26 February 1991.
28 周帙恒, '邓小平视察南方途经长沙:湖南加快改革开放步伐', 华声在线, 6 May 2021, https://baijiahao.baidu.com/s?id=1699051785507772947&wfr=spider&for=pc.

Chapter 6

1 Details for this section on Deng's visit to Shenzhen are, unless otherwise noted, drawn from 'East Wind Brings Spring All Around – On-the-spot Report on Comrade Deng Xiaoping in Shenzhen', *Shenzhen Tequ Bao*, 26 March 1992, FBIS; 邓小平实录4, 210–20; 'Records of Comrade Deng Xiaoping's Shenzhen Tour', *People's Daily*, 18 January 2002; Peng Sen and Chen Li, *Reforming China: Major Events (1992–2004): Vol. 4* (Hong Kong: Enrich Professional Publishing, 2010), 2–5.
2 '東方風來滿眼春"作者陳錫添: 改革關鍵期 將小平南巡講話傳向世界', *Hong Kong Commercial Daily*, 18 December 2018.
3 Peng and Chen, *Reforming China, Vol. 4*, 2.
4 Yue-man Yeung and David K.Y. Chu, eds., *Guangdong: Survey of a Province Undergoing Rapid Change* (Hong Kong: Chinese University Press, 1994), 463 and Jianfa Shen, 'Urban Growth and Sustainable Development in Shenzhen City 1980–2006', *The Open Environmental Journal* 2 (2008): 71–9.

5   In reality, the percentage was higher than this – see Jianfa Shen, 'Urban Growth and Sustainable Development in Shenzhen City 1980–2006'.
6   See Matt Kennard and Claire Provost, 'Story of Cities #25: Shannon – A Tiny Irish Town Inspires China's Economic Boom', *The Guardian*, 19 April 2016 and Paul Quigley, 'Why Do China's Leaders Love Visiting Shannon?' *The Journal.Ie*, 23 February 2012, https://www.thejournal.ie/why-do-chinas-leaders-love-visiting-shannon-363579-Feb2012/.
7   'What Are the Distinctions between Special Zones and Concessions?' *Xuexi Yu Yanjiu [Study and Research]*, no. 5 (5 May 1985).
8   Suzanne Pepper, 'China's Special Economic Zones: The Current Rescue Bid for a Faltering Experiment', *Bulletin of Concerned Asian Scholars* 20, no. 3 (1 September 1988): 2–21.
9   Miles, *China in Disarray*, 153–5.
10 Zhu Rongji, *Zhu Rongji on the Record: The Road to Reform 1991–1997*, trans. June Y. Mei (Washington, DC: Brookings Institution Press, 2013), 93.
11 Baum, *Burying Mao*, 359.
12 Deng Xiaoping, 'We Are on the Right Track and Our Policies Will Not Change', *Selected Works of Deng Xiaoping. Volume III*.
13 Deng Xiaoping, 'Excerpts from Talks Given in Wuchang, Shenzhen, Zhuhai and Shanghai', *Selected Works, Volume III*.
14 Denise Y. Ho, 'Hong Kong, China: The Border as Palimpsest', *Made in China Journal* 5, no. 3 (2020): 95.
15 'The Kowloon Canton Railway (British Section) Part 4 – The Early Years (1910 to 1940) – The Industrial History of Hong Kong Group', https://industrialhistoryhk.org/kcrc-railway-british-section-3-early-years-1910-1940/.
16 'Japanese Bomb Shumchun', *The New York Times*, 1 August 1939.
17 Trevor Fishlock, 'A Cheerful Crowd on the Slow Train to China', *The Times*, 16 August 1980.
18 Li Hao, 'Pioneer Shenzhen SEZ Boasts "Remarkable" Gains', *Qiushi (Seeking Truth)*, 16 September 1990, in *Joint Publications Research Service* (hereafter *JPRS*).
19 Vogel, *Deng Xiaoping and the Transformation of China*, 673.
20 'DVD Pioneer Looks for Foreign Investors', *South China Morning Post*, 26 June 2004.
21 Joseph Lelyveld, 'Barbecue, Bulls and Stagecoach Help Teng Get Flavor of Texas', *The New York Times*, 4 February 1979.
22 Calhoun, *Neither Gods nor Emperors*, 37.
23 'Recollections at a Great Man's Home', *People's Daily*.
24 Deng Rong, *Deng Xiaoping: My Father*, 374.
25 Carolyn Cartier, 'Transnational Urbanism in the Reform-Era Chinese City: Landscapes from Shenzhen', *Urban Studies* 39, no. 9 (2002): 1513–32.
26 Kuhn, *The Man Who Changed China*, 213.

Chapter 7

1. 'The then-and-now of Deng's Historic Visit', *South China Morning Post*, 2012.
2. 'CPC's Reform and Opening-up Policies Overcome Major Hurdles and Change China, the World', *Global Times*, 12 August 2021, https://www.globaltimes.cn/page/202108/1231304.shtml.
3. Du Wenjuan, 'Deng Rong: Father Would Be Proud', *China Daily*, July 2007, https://www.chinadaily.com.cn/china/2007-06/26/content_902694.htm.
4. 'Deng on Hopes for 1997 Inspection', *Ming Pao*, 23 January 1992, *FBIS*.
5. *The Times*, 10 June 1898.
6. Denise Y. Ho. 'Hong Kong, China: The Border as Palimpsest', 97.
7. 'Million Refugees from China Crowd Housing in Hong Kong', *The New York Times*, 3 May 1964.
8. He would eventually, on his third attempt, be successfully smuggled into Hong Kong. Kent Wong, *Swimming to Freedom: My Escape from China and the Cultural Revolution* (New York: Abrams Press, 2021), Apple Books, 444–5.
9. 邓小平年谱, *1975–1997* vol. 上册 (中央文献出版社, 2004), 237–40.
10. '一代人的命运与一座城市的崛起', 中国共产党新闻, accessed 22 July 2022, http://cpc.people.com.cn/GB/85037/85038/7161467.html.
11. Qtd. in Da Wei David Wang, 'Shenzhen's Urban Villages: Surviving Three Decades of Economic Reform and Urban Expansion' (PhD, The University of Western Australia, 2013), 48.
12. Li Lanqing, *Breaking Through: The Birth of China's Opening-Up Policy*, trans. Ling Yuan and Zhang Siying (Oxford; Hong Kong: Oxford University Press and Foreign Language Teaching and Research Press, 2009), 87–8; 'Guangdong Seaside Counties Renamed, Developed for Tourism', *Xinhua*, 22 March 1979, *FBIS*.
13. Ibid., 90.
14. Ibid., 93.
15. Vogel, *Deng Xiaoping and the Transformation of China*, 402.
16. Sung Yun-Wing, *The Economic Integration of Hong Kong with China in the 1990s: The Impact on Hong Kong* (Toronto: Joint Centre for Asia Pacific, 1992), 11.
17. 'SEZ Temporary Workers Experience Hardships', *Zhongguo Zuojia*, June 1989, *JPRS*.
18. Vogel, *One Step Ahead in China*, 69.
19. 'SEZ Temporary Workers Experience Hardships', *JPRS*.
20. '1997: The Big Question', *The Times*, 26th September 1983.
21. Michael Sheridan, *The Gate to China: A New History of the People's Republic & Hong Kong* (London: William Collins, 2021), Apple Books, 206.

22 Percy Cradock, *Experiences of China* (London: John Murray, 1999), 166.
23 Deng Xiaoping, 'One Country, Two Systems', *Selected Works. Volume III.*
24 Ibid.
25 Cradock, *Experiences of China*, 223.
26 Miles, *China in Disarray*, 247.
27 *Summary of World Broadcasts: The Far East. Part III.* United Kingdom: Monitoring Service of the British Broadcasting Corporation, 1989, 8–9.
28 'Meddling in Hong Kong Affairs Criticized', *Cheng Ming*, 1 August 1989, *JPRS*.
29 Ibid.
30 John P. Burns, 'Hong Kong in 1992: Struggle for Authority', *Asian Survey* 33, no. 1 (1993): 22–31.
31 Hansard HL Deb, vol. 538, cols. 186–225, 17 June 1992.

Chapter 8

1 Details for this section on Deng's visit to Zhuhai are, unless otherwise noted, drawn from 南行纪, 62–117 and 邓小平实录4 1982–1997, 220–5.
2 'Local Authorities "Purge" Zhuhai for Deng's Visit', *South China Morning Post*, 26 January 1992.
3 N. Sheng and U.W. Tang, 'Zhuhai', *Cities* 32 (2013): 70.
4 Yeung and Chu, *Guangdong: Survey of a Province Undergoing Rapid Change*, 463.
5 Ibid., 460.
6 'Xinhua Director Interviewed on Macau's Future', *Tzu Ching*, 5 December 1991, *FBIS*.
7 Sheng and Tang, 'Zhuhai', 72.
8 Hansard HL Deb, vol. 538, cols. 186–225, 17 June 1992.
9 'Zhuhai Mayor Describes Deng's Inspection of SEZ', *Wen Wei Po*, 17 February 1992, *FBIS*.
10 'On Importance of Guangdong, Stability', *Ta Kung Pao*, 26 January 1992, *FBIS*.
11 '"Notes" on Deng Xiaoping's Zhuhai Tour, Remarks', *Wen Wei Po*, 17 April 1992, *FBIS*.
12 'Hong Kong Paper Views Zhuhai Military Conference', *Cheng Ming*, 1 March 1992, *FBIS*.
13 Kuhn, *The Man Who Changed China*, 214.
14 'Hong Kong Paper Views Zhuhai Military Conference', *Cheng Ming*.
15 'Deng, Yang, Qiao Shi Meeting Reported', *Ming Pao*, 26 January 1992, *FBIS*.
16 'Hong Kong Paper Views Zhuhai Military Conference', *Cheng Ming*.

17 'Liu Huaqing Meets Military Personnel', *Ta Kung Pao*, 25 January 1992, *FBIS*.
18 '"Notes" on Deng Xiaoping's Zhuhai Tour, Remarks', *Wen Wei Po*.
19 Kuhn, *The Man Who Changed China*, 213.
20 'Jiang Zemin Said to Suffer "Loss of Favour"', *Kai Fang*, 18 March 1992, *FBIS*.
21 'Yang in Shenzhen; Urges Bolder Reforms', *Xinhua*, 25 January 1992, *FBIS*.
22 'Article Notes Deng's Guangdong Plant Visit', *Yangcheng Wanbao*, 20 March 1992, *FBIS*.

Chapter 9

1 'Account of Deng's Jan 1992 Visit to Yingtan', *Jiangxi Ribao*, 14 August 1994, *FBIS*.
2 Ibid.
3 Deng Rong, *Deng Xiaoping: My Father*, 216.
4 Deng Rong, *Deng Xiaoping and the Cultural Revolution*, 185–7.
5 Deng Rong, *Deng Xiaoping: My Father*, 216.
6 'Account of Deng's Jan 1992 Visit to Yingtan', *Jiangxi Ribao*.
7 Deng Rong, *Deng Xiaoping and the Cultural Revolution*, 238–40.
8 Pantsov and Levine, *Deng Xiaoping: A Revolutionary Life*, 275.
9 Roderick MacFarquhar and John K. Fairbank, eds., *The Cambridge History of China, vol. 15. The People's Republic, Part 2: Revolutions within the Chinese Revolution 1966–1982* (Cambridge: Cambridge University Press, 1991), 807.
10 'Recollections at a Great Man's Home', *People's Daily*.
11 Deng Xiaoping, 'We Should Take a Longer-Range View in Developing Sino-Japanese Relations', *Selected Works. Volume III*.
12 'An Historic Meeting', *People's Daily*, 22 July 1977, *FBIS*.
13 'Jiefang Ribao Article on Shanghai Opening', *Jiefang Ribao*, 22 March 1991, *FBIS*.
14 'New Financial Opening up in Pudong Development', *Wen Wei Po*, 12 March 1992, *FBIS*.
15 'Reports on Jiang Zemin Inspection Tours, Comments; Views Shanghai's Infrastructure', *Jiefang Ribao*, 21 January 1992, FBIS.
16 'Jiang Remarks Cited', *Xinhua*, 4 February 1992, *FBIS*.
17 '"Text" of Li's speech', *Xinhua*, 30 January 1992, *FBIS*.
18 'Article Views Deng-Chen Yun "Confrontation"', *Cheng Ming*, 1 March 1992, *FBIS*.

Chapter 10

1. '"Full Text" of Document No. 2 on Deng Remarks', *Cheng Ming*, 1 April 1992, FBIS.
2. 邓小平年谱, 1975–1997 vol. 下册, 1345–6.
3. Kuhn, *The Man Who Changed China*, 216.
4. 'Hardliners Warn Deng Risks Overthrowing Socialism', *The Standard*, 2 March 1992, FBIS.
5. 'Tian Jiyun Proposes "Special Leftist Zone"', *South China Morning Post*.
6. *Beijing Review*, 17–23 August 1992, FBIS.
7. Laurence Brahm, 'Zhu Rongji: A Rare Talent … ', *South China Morning Post*, 10 March 2003.
8. 'Article Views Reform of State Enterprises', *Liaowang*, 7 September 1992, FBIS.
9. 'Zhu Rongji Summarizes Debt Default Experiences', *Xinhua*, 25 December 1992, FBIS.
10. 'Journal Views Inner-Party Struggle', *Cheng Ming*, 1 October 1992, FBIS.
11. Ibid.
12. Nicholas D. Kristof, 'The New China – A Special Report; Chinese Communism's Secret Aim: Capitalism', *The New York Times*, 19 October 1992.
13. 邓小平年谱, 1975–1997 vol. 下册, 1355.
14. 'Deng Xiaoping, Chen Yun Reportedly Reach Compromise', *Ching Chi Jih Pao*, 19 October 1992, FBIS.
15. Zhao, *Prisoner of the State*, 60–1.
16. Rebecca Mackinnon, 'Former Communist Party Official: Last Decade Wasted"', *CNN*, June 1999, http://edition.cnn.com/WORLD/asiapcf/9906/02/tiananmen/MacKinnon/bao.tong.html.

Chapter 11

1. Zhou Mo, 'Statue Stands Tall as Nation Continues to Make Huge Strides', *China Daily*, 30 November 2021, https://www.chinadaily.com.cn/a/202111/30/WS61a598b3a310cdd39bc7865f_2.html.
2. '鄧小平:讓一部分人先富起來', 一部中国共产党新闻.
3. 'Editorial Calls for Faster Development', *People's Daily*, 11 March 1993, FBIS.
4. Kuhn, *The Man Who Changed China*, 242.
5. '"Craze" for Prediction of Post-Deng Period', *Kuang Chiao Ching*, 16 September 1994, FBIS.
6. '邓楠、邓榕姐妹回忆陪邓小平南巡的情况', 四川在线-华西都市报, 12 February 2007.

7   'Statistics Support Reports of Economic Recovery', *Xinhua*, 19 January 1992.
8   Naughton, *Growing Out of the Plan*, 304.
9   '"Roundup" on "Vigorous" Private Economic Sector', *Xinhua*, 22 December 1993, *FBIS*.
10 Naughton, *Growing Out of the Plan*, 303.
11 'Shanghai's Pudong Attracts Overseas Investment', *Xinhua*, 20 April 1993, *FBIS*.
12 'Zhu Discusses Economic Growth', *Xinhua*, 13 May 1993, *FBIS*.
13 'Zhu Rongji Warns of "Too Many Development Zones"', *Jingji Daobao*, 1 March 1993, *FBIS*.
14 'Coastal Areas Close Several Development Zones', *Xinhua*, 11 August 1993, *FBIS*.
15 'Zhu Rongji Warns of "Too Many Development Zones"'.
16 '"Soaring Inflation" "Has Not Sparked Panic"', *China Daily*, 28 October 1993, *FBIS*.
17 'Article on Deng-Chen Yun Economic "Disagreement"', *Cheng Ming*, 1 March 1993, *FBIS*.
18 'Deng, Chen Factions View Anticorruption Fight', *Cheng Ming*, 1 September 1993, *FBIS*.
19 Ibid.
20 'Guangdong Official on Corruption, Bribery', *South China Morning Post*, 25 July 1993.
21 Jasper Becker, 'Sources View Course of Jiang Zemin's "Purge"', *South China Morning Post*, 18 May 1995.
22 'Journal Analyzes Deng's State of Health', *Cheng Ming*, 1 November 1994. *FBIS*. See also Kuhn, *The Man Who Changed China*, 253.
23 'PRC: Son Describes Deng Xiaoping Illness', *Tung Hsiang*, 15 July 1996, *FBIS*.
24 Seth Faison, 'Campus Mood Is Unlike '89, but Lid Is Kept on Anyway', *The New York Times*, 24 February 1997.
25 Derek Davies, 'Obituary: Deng Xiaoping', *The Independent*, 20 February 1997.
26 'Deng Xiaoping Obituary', *Socialist Review*, February 1997, http://pubs.socialistreviewindex.org.uk/sr206/obit.htm.
27 'Deng's Ashes Cast to Sea', *The New York Times*, 3 March 1997.

Chapter 12

1   'Fujian Cadres Face Dismissal for Reform Failures', *South China Morning Post*, 17 July 1992.
2   Nicholas D. Kristof, 'Looking for a Jump-Start in China', *The New York Times*, 5 January 2013.

3 Wang Xiangwei, 'Xi Jinping Might Be Strong Reformer China Needs – To Surprise of the West', *South China Morning Post*, 19 November 2012.
4 'General Secretary Xi Jinping's Trip to Shenzhen', *Guangming Daily*, 15 December 2012, https://epaper.gmw.cn/wzb/html/2012-12/15/nw.D110000wzb_20121215_1-01.htm.
5 'Study, Disseminate and Implement the Guiding Principles of the 18th CPC National Congress', *The National People's Congress of the People's Republic of China*, 17 November 2012, http://www.npc.gov.cn/englishnpc/c23934/202005/1ea4ce6a31714887a17412cb8f9f30cc.shtml.
6 Edward Wong, 'Signals of a More Open Economy in China', *The New York Times*, 9 December 2012.
7 Gao Yu, 'Beijing Observation: Xi Jinping the Man', *China Change*, 26 January 2013, https://chinachange.org/2013/01/26/beijing-observation-xi-jinping-the-man-by-gao-yu/.
8 Gao would, in 2015, be sentenced to seven years in jail for 'illegally providing state secrets beyond China's borders'. She was released in 2019.
9 'Address to the First Session of the 12th National People's Congress', *The National People's Congress of the People's Republic of China*, 17 March 2013, http://www.npc.gov.cn/englishnpc/c23934/202006/7954b8df92384c729c02be626840daed.shtml.
10 Edward White, 'Xi Jinping's Last Chance to Revive the Chinese Economy', *Financial Times*, 5 October 2022.
11 'Xi Jinping Millionaire Relations Reveal Elite Chinese Fortunes', *Bloomberg*, 29 June 2012, https://www.bloomberg.com/news/articles/2012-06-29/xi-jinping-millionaire-relations-reveal-fortunes-of-elite?leadSource=uverify%20wall.
12 Paul Eckert, 'Special Report: Cables Show U.S. Sizing Up China's Next Leader', *Reuters*, 17 February 2011, https://www.reuters.com/article/us-wiki-china-xi-idUSTRE71G5WH20110217.
13 'Study, Disseminate and Implement the Guiding Principles of the 18th CPC National Congress', *The National People's Congress of the People's Republic of China*.
14 'Corruption Must Be Punished, Discipline Must Be Strictly Upheld: People's Daily', *Global Times*, 6 December 2014, https://www.globaltimes.cn/content/895251.shtml.
15 'Communiqué of the Third Plenary Session of the 18th Central Committee of the Communist Party of China', *China.org.cn*, 15 January 2014, http://www.china.org.cn/china/third_plenary_session/2014-01/15/content_31203056.htm.
16 '习近平:在深圳经济特区建立40周年庆祝大会上的讲话', *Xinhua*, 14 October 2020, http://www.xinhuanet.com/politics/2020-10/14/c_1210840649.htm.
17 '汕头全民"追星"争睹总书记风采', *Ta Kung Pao*, 14 October 2020, http://www.takungpao.com/news/232108/2020/1014/508308.html.

18. Frank Tang, 'Chinese Pro-market Economist Wu Jinglian Warns of "State Capitalism" Dangers', *South China Morning Post*, 21 January 2019.
19. 'China Publishes Master Plan for Xiong'an New Area', *xiongan.gov.cn*, 21 April 2018, http://english.xiongan.gov.cn/2018-04/21/c_129855751.htm.
20. 'Xiong'an New Area to be "Historic" Development', *China Daily*, 9 April 2017, http://www.chinadaily.com.cn/kindle/2017-04/09/content_28848655.htm.
21. 'City of the Future: Xiong'an Becomes a Model for Urban High-Quality Development under CPC Leadership', *Global Times*, 3 July 2022, https://www.globaltimes.cn/page/202207/1269662.shtml.
22. Sun Yu, '"Invisible Hand" Pulls up the Handbrake on Xi's Pet Project', *Financial Times*, 18 May 2021; also, author's own visits to the area in 2013, 2016, and 2017.
23. Andrew Stokols, 'China's Techno-natural Utopia: A Deep Dive into Xiong'an', *The China Project*, 3 April 2023, https://thechinaproject.com/2023/04/03/chinas-techno-natural-utopia-a-deep-dive-into-xiongan/.
24. 'Full Text of Xi Jinping's Speech at Memorial Meeting for Comrade Jiang Zemin', *Ministry of Foreign Affairs of the People's Republic of China*, 6 December 2012, https://www.fmprc.gov.cn/mfa_eng/wjdt_665385/zyjh_665391/202212/t20221207_10986435.html.
25. 'Full Text: Resolution of the CPC Central Committee on the Major Achievements and Historical Experience of the Party over the Past Century', *English.gov.cn*, 16 November 2021, https://english.www.gov.cn/policies/latestreleases/202111/16/content_WS6193a935c6d0df57f98e50b0.html.
26. David Bandurski, 'The Return of "Socialist Transformation"', *China Media Project*, 3 October 2018, https://chinamediaproject.org/2018/10/03/the-return-of-socialist-transformation/.
27. Chris Buckley, 'Xi Jinping the Hidden Star of a TV Series about Deng Xiaoping', *The New York Times*, 27 August 2014.
28. Kerry Allen, 'Chinese Bypass Censors to Remember Jiang Zemin', *BBC News*, 30 November 2022.
29. 'Research Center on Xi Jinping's Economic Thought Officially Launched', *Xinhua*, 18 January 2022, https://english.news.cn/20220118/a62125251a5f45d08309e807ee2e6b05/c.html.
30. 叶兵, '邓小平南巡30年:"谁不改革谁就下台"还算数吗?' *Voice of America Chinese*, 24 January 2022, https://www.voachinese.com/a/shen-zhen-protester-deng-xiaoping-reform-vs-xi-jinping-clinging-to-power-20220124/6409654.html.

Epilogue

1. 'China Railway's Debt Nears $900bn under Expansion Push', *Nikkei Asia*, 6 July 2022, https://asia.nikkei.com/Business/Markets/China-debt-crunch/China-Railway-s-debt-nears-900bn-under-expansion-push.
2. '精神鸦片" 竟长成数千亿产业 业内人士提醒, 警惕网络游戏危害, 及早合理规范' *Xinhua Finance*, 3 August 2021, https://www.cnfin.com/news-xh08/a/20210803/1996101.shtml.
3. Austin Ramzy, 'Mob Attack at Hong Kong Train Station Heightens Seething Tensions in City', *The New York Times*, 22 July 2019.
4. 'How Violence Has Disrupted Hong Kong over Last 2 Months', *People's Daily*, 18 August 2019, http://en.people.cn/n3/2019/0818/c90000-9606983.html.
5. Lara Seligman and Elias Groll, 'China's Military Threatens Protestors', *Foreign Policy*, 25 July 2019, https://foreignpolicy.com/2019/07/25/chinas-military-threatens-protesters/.
6. 'China and the Rules-Based International System: Sixteenth Report of Session 2017–19', *House of Commons Foreign Affairs Committee*, 4 April 2019, https://publications.parliament.uk/pa/cm201719/cmselect/cmfaff/612/612.pdf.
7. 'Beijing's New Infrastructure Binds Hong Kong to Mainland', *Financial Times*, 27 January 2023.
8. 'Outline Development Plan for the Guangdong-Hong Kong-Macau Greater Bay Area', *www.bayarea.gov.hk*, 18 February 2019, https://www.bayarea.gov.hk/filemanager/en/share/pdf/Outline_Development_Plan.pdf, 10.
9. James Griffiths, 'Chinese President Xi Jinping Opens World's Longest Sea-Crossing Bridge', *CNN*, 23 October 2018, https://edition.cnn.com/2018/10/22/asia/china-hong-kong-macau-bridge-xi-jinping-intl/index.html.
10. Gu Mengyan, 'Underutilized HZMB Finds It Difficult Bridging the Gap', *China Daily*, 26 October 2020, https://www.chinadaily.com.cn/a/202010/26/WS5f967d8aa31024ad0ba8101c.html.
11. 'Overview of Zhuhai', *cityofzhuhai.com*, 7 February 2022, http://www.cityofzhuhai.com/2022-02/07/c_270301.htm.
12. 'Over 1,000 New Museums Open in China during Past 5 Years', *Global Times*, 26 July 2021, https://news.cgtn.com/news/2021-07-26/Over-1-000-new-museums-open-in-China-during-past-5-years-12dxzUq4Y1i/index.html.
13. Deng Xiaoping, 'The International Situation and Economic Problems', *Selected Works. Volume III*.
14. Translated by Édouard Chavannes, *Le T'ai Chan, Essai de monographie d'un culte chinois* (Paris: Annales du Musée Guimet, 1910), 318.

SELECT BIBLIOGRAPHY

Baum, Richard. *Burying Mao: Chinese Politics in the Age of Deng Xiaoping*. Princeton: Princeton University Press, 1994.

Blanchette, Jude. *China's New Red Guards: The Return of Radicalism and the Rebirth of Mao Zedong*. New York: Oxford University Press, 2019.

Calhoun, Craig. *Neither Gods nor Emperors: Students and the Struggle for Democracy in China*. Berkeley; Los Angeles: University of California Press, 1994.

Chang, Michael G. *A Court on Horseback: Imperial Touring and the Construction of Qing Rule, 1680–1785*. Cambridge, MA: Harvard University Asia Center, 2007.

Chow, Gregory C., and Dwight H. Perkins, eds. *Routledge Handbook of the Chinese Economy*. Abingdon: Routledge, 2015.

Courtney, Chris. *The Nature of Disaster in China: The 1931 Yangzi River Flood*. Cambridge: Cambridge University Press, 2018.

Cradock, Percy. *Experiences of China*. London: John Murray, 1999.

Du, Juan. *The Shenzhen Experiment: The Story of China's Instant City*. Cambridge, MA: Harvard University Press, 2020.

Evans, Richard. *Deng Xiaoping and the Making of Modern China*. London: Penguin, 1995.

Fewsmith, Joseph. *China since Tiananmen: From Deng Xiaoping to Hu Jintao*. New York: Cambridge University Press, 2008.

Fontana, Michaela. *Matteo Ricci: A Jesuit in the Ming Court*. Lanham: Rowman and Littlefield, 2011.

Gewirtz, Julian. *Never Turn Back: China and the Forbidden History of the 1980s*. Cambridge, MA: The Belknap Press of Harvard University Press, 2022.

Gilley, Bruce. *Tiger on the Brink: Jiang Zemin and China's New Elite*. Berkeley; Los Angeles: University of California Press, 1998.

Gombeaud, Adrien. *Dans Les Pas Du Petit Timonier: La Chine, vingt ans apres Deng Xiaoping*. Paris: Èditions du Seuil, 2013.

Gorbachev, Mikhail. *Memoirs*. Translated by Georges Peronansky and Tatjana Varsavsky. London: Doubleday, 1996.

Henry, Benjamin Couch *Ling-Nam; or, Interior Views of Southern China*. London: S.W. Partridge, 1886.

Hu, Richard, and Weijie Chen. *Global Shanghai Remade: The Rise of Pudong New Area*. Abingdon: Routledge, 2019.

Jisheng, Yang. *The World Turned Upside down: A History of the Chinese Cultural Revolution*. Translated by Stacy Mosher and Jian Guo. New York: Farrar, Straus and Giroux, 2021.

Kang, Zhengguo. *Confessions: An Innocent Life in Communist China.* Translated by Susan Wilf. New York; London: W.W. Norton, 2008.
Kerby, Philip. *Beyond the Bund.* New York: Payson & Clarke Ltd., 1927.
Kerns, Ann. *Who Will Shout If Not Us?: Student Activists and the Tiananmen Square Protest, China, 1989.* Minneapolis: Twenty-First Century Books, 2011.
Kessler, Lawrence D. *K'ang-Hsi and the Consolidation of Ch'ing Rule 1661–1684.* Chicago: University of Chicago Press, 1976.
Kuhn, Robert Lawrence. *The Man Who Changed China: The Life and Legacy of Jiang Zemin.* New York: Crown, 2004.
Kuhn, Robert Lawrence. *How China's Leaders Think: The Inside Story of China's Past, Current and Future Leaders.* Singapore: John Wiley & Sons, 2011.
Lam, Willy Wo-Lap. *China after Deng Xiaoping: The Power Struggle in Beijing since Tiananmen.* Singapore; New York: John Wiley & Sons, 1995.
Li, Lanqing. *Breaking Through: The Birth of China's Opening-Up Policy.* Translated by Ling Yuan and Zhang Siying. Oxford; Hong Kong: Oxford University Press and Foreign Language Teaching and Research Press, 2009.
Li, Zhisui. *The Private Life of Chairman Mao: The Inside Story of the Man Who Made Modern China.* London: Chatto & Windus, 1994.
MacFarquhar, Roderick, ed. *The Politics of China: The Eras of Mao and Deng.* New York: Cambridge University Press, 1997.
MacFarquhar, Roderick, and John K. Fairbank, eds. *The Cambridge History of China. Vol. 15. The People's Republic, Part 2: Revolutions within the Chinese Revolution 1966–1982.* Cambridge: Cambridge University Press, 1991.
MacFarquhar, Roderick, and Michael Schoenhals. *Mao's Last Revolution.* Cambridge, MA: The Belknap Press of Harvard University Press, 2008.
MacKinnon, Stephen R. *Wuhan, 1938: War, Refugees, and the Making of Modern China.* Berkeley; Los Angeles, CA: University of California Press, 2008.
Miles, James. *The Legacy of Tiananmen: China in Disarray.* Ann Arbor: The University of Michigan Press, 1997.
Naughton, Barry. *Growing out of the Plan: Chinese Economic Reform, 1978–1993.* Cambridge: Cambridge University Press, 1995.
Naughton, Barry. *The Chinese Economy: Adaptation and Growth.* Cambridge, MA: MIT Press, 2018.
Oborne, Michael. *China's Special Economic Zones.* Paris: Development Centre of the Organisation for Economic Co-operation and Development, 1986.
O'Donnell, Mary Ann, Winnie Wong, and Jonathan Bach, eds. *Learning from Shenzhen: China's Post-Mao Experiment from Special Zone to Model City.* Chicago: The University of Chicago Press, 2011.
Oksenberg, Michel, Lawrence R. Sullivan, and Marc Lambert, eds. *Beijing Spring, 1989: Confrontation and Conflict.* London: M.E. Sharpe, 1990.
Oliphant, Laurence. *Narrative of the Earl of Elgin's Mission to China and Japan in the Years 1857, '58, '59.* 2 vols. Edinburgh; London: William Blackwood and Sons, 1859.

Pantsov, Alexander, and Steven I. Levine. *Mao: The Real Story.* New York: Simon & Schuster Paperbacks, 2013.
Pantsov, Alexander, and Steven I. Levine. *Deng Xiaoping: A Revolutionary Life.* Oxford: Oxford University Press, 2015.
Peng, Sen, and Chen Li. *Reforming China: Major Events (1978–1991): Vol. 3.* Hong Kong: Enrich Professional Publishing, 2010.
Peng, Sen, and Chen Li. *Reforming China: Major Events (1992–2004): Vol. 4,* Hong Kong: Enrich Professional Publishing, 2010.
Reardon, Lawrence C. *A Third Way: The Origins of China's Current Economic Development Strategy.* Cambridge, MA: Harvard University Asia Center, 2020.
Rong, Deng. *Deng Xiaoping: My Father.* New York: BasicBooks, 1995.
Rong, Deng. *Deng Xiaoping and the Cultural Revolution: A Daughter Recalls the Critical Years.* Beijing: Foreign Languages Press, 2002.
Rongji, Zhu. *Zhu Rongji on the Record: The Road to Reform 1991–1997.* Translated by June Y. Mei. Washington, D.C: Brookings Institution Press, 2013.
Rongji, Zhu. *Zhu Rongji on the Record: The Shanghai Years 1987–1991.* Translated by June Y. Mei. Apple Books. Washington, D.C: Brookings Institution Press, 2018.
Rowe, William T. *Hankow: Commerce and Society in a Chinese City, 1796–1889.* Stanford: Stanford University Press, 1984.
Salisbury, Harrison E. *The New Emperors: Mao and Deng: A Dual Biography.* London: HarperCollins, 1993.
Shambaugh, David L. *The Making of a Premier: Zhao Ziyang's Provincial Career.* New York; Abingdon: Routledge, 1984.
Sheridan, Michael. *The Gate to China: A New History of the People's Republic & Hong Kong.* London: William Collins, 2021.
Shih, Victor C. *Factions and Finance in China: Elite Conflict and Inflation.* Cambridge: Cambridge University Press, 2008.
Shirk, Susan L. *The Political Logic of Economic Reform in China.* Berkeley: University of California Press, 1993.
Spence, Jonathan D. *Emperor of China: Self-Portrait of K'ang-Hsi.* New York: Vintage, 1988.
Steinfeld, Edward S. *Forging Reform in China: The Fate of State-Owned Industry.* Cambridge Modern China Series. Cambridge: Cambridge University Press, 1998.
Vogel, Ezra. *One Step Ahead in China: Guangdong under Reform.* Cambridge, MA: Harvard University Press, 1989.
Vogel, Ezra. *Deng Xiaoping and the Transformation of China.* Cambridge, MA: Harvard University Press, 2011.
Wang, Shaoguang. *Failure of Charisma: The Cultural Revolution in Wuhan.* Hong Kong; New York: Oxford University Press, 1995.
Weber, Isabella M. *How China Escaped Shock Therapy: The Market Reform Debate.* Abingdon: Routledge, 2021.

Wong, Kent. *Swimming to Freedom: My Escape from China and the Cultural Revolution.* New York: Abrams Press, 2021.

Xiaoping, Deng. *Selected Works of Deng Xiaoping. Volume II, 1975–1982.* Beijing: Foreign Languages Press, 1994.

Xiaoping, Deng. *Selected Works of Deng Xiaoping. Volume III, 1982–1992.* Beijing: Foreign Languages Press, 1994.

Yeung, Yue-man, and David K.Y. Chu, eds. *Guangdong: Survey of a Province Undergoing Rapid Change.* Hong Kong: Chinese University Press, 1994.

Yiwu, Liao. *Bullets and Opium: Real-Life Stories After the Tiananmen Square Massacre.* Apple Books. New York: Atria/One Signal, 2020.

Zhang, Lijia. *Socialism Is Great! A Worker's Memoir of the New China.* New York: Anchor Books, 2009.

Zhao, Suisheng, and Carol Lee Hamrin, eds. *Decision-Making in Deng's China: Perspectives from Insiders.* New York: East Gate, 1995.

Ziyang, Zhao. *Prisoner of the State: The Secret Journal of Zhao Ziyang.* Translated by Bao Pu, Renee Chiang, and Adi Ignatius. London: Simon and Schuster, 2009.

Works in Chinese

牛正武. 南行纪: 1992年邓小平南方谈话全记录. 广州: 广东人民出版社, 2012.

逄先知 and 冯蕙eds. 毛泽东年谱: 1949–1976/第五卷. 北京: 中央文献出版社, 2013.

邓小平实录4 1982–1997: 改革开放40周年纪念版. 北京: 北京联合出版公司, 2018.

邓小平年谱, 1975–1997. Vol. 上册. 中央文献出版社, 2004.

邓小平年谱, 1975–1997. Vol. 下册. 中央文献出版社, 2004.

INDEX

agriculture xvi, 115

Babaoshan Revolutionary Cemetery 118–19,129
Bao Tong 108–9
Berlin Wall 13
bourgeois liberalization 21, 61–2

Canton Fair xix
Capital Iron and Steel (Shougang) 105–6,116–17
Central Advisory Commission 10–1, 107
Central Military Commission 6, 10
  Zhuhai meeting of 90–1
Changsha 32, 35, 44, 51–2
Chen Yun xxiv, 10, 18, 21, 25, 26, 57, 79, 100, 106, 107–8
  background and ideology xx–xxi
  death of 118–19
corruption xxi, 5, 12, 21, 116, 119–20
  in Xi Jinping era 124–5
Covid-19 126, 127, 135, 138–9
Cultural Revolution
  and Deng Xiaoping 33, 36, 94–7
  economic impact xiv–xv
  in Guangdong xvii
  origins of 44–6

Deng Pufang 33
Deng Rong 46, 57, 59, 66, 101, 105, 113
Deng Zhifang 37, 116–17
Diaoyutai State Guesthouse 117–18

'East Wind Brings Spring All Around' 54, 104, 113

Fishermen's Village (Yumin Cun) xii–xiv, xxii–xxiii, 60, 122
floods 1991 25, 51
Four Cardinal Principles 63, 107
Fujian xiii, xviii, 78–9, 121, 124

Gang of Four 96–7, 125
getihu 40, 49
golf 9–10, 58, 64
Gorbachev, Mikhail 7, 25–6
Great Hall of the People 3, 6, 12, 27, 106, 125, 129
Great Leap Outward xv
Greater Bay Area 127, 137–8
Guan Guangfu 46
Guangdong xxii, 35, 40, 41, 79, 92.
  See also Greater Bay Area; Pearl River Delta
  Deng Xiaoping 1977 visit 78
  geography of 85
  history of xviii–xix
  post-Cultural Revolution xvi–xvii
Guangzhou xviii–xix, 53, 55–6, 60, 78, 85, 92
Guo Shuyan 46

Hangzhou 35, 45, 98, 109
Historical Resolution (2021) 130
Hong Kong 60, 75–84, 86, 116. See also Greater Bay Area
  2019 protests 135–8
  border with PRC 56–8, 76–7
  escaping to xvii, 16, 77
  relationship with SEZs 78–80
  return to PRC control 80–2, 120
household responsibility system xvi
Hu Jintao 108, 121, 129–30
Hu Yaobang xxiii, 3–4, 6, 11, 117, 119

Hua Guofeng xiii–xiv, xv, xvi
Huairen Hall (Hall of Cherished Compassion) 2–3, 6, 21, 97, 108
Huangfu Ping 24–5, 45, 99
Hunan 35, 45, 51–2, 93

Inflation xxiii, 5, 20–1, 49–50, 115–16, 119

Jiang Qing 36, 96–7
Jiang Zemin 20, 39, 50, 55, 65, 66, 91
  1992 visit to Shanghai 99
  and corruption 116–17
  death 129–30, 131
  and Hong Kong 82–3, 120
  reaction to Southern Tour 106–7, 113
  rise to power 11
Jiangxi Province 34–5, 93
  and Deng Xiaoping 94–6

Kangxi Emperor 29–32

Lee Kuan Yew 63
Li Hao 54, 59, 61, 62–3, 66
Li Peng 6, 16, 20–2, 23, 25, 40–1, 50, 82, 100, 114
Lin Biao 32, 33–6, 95
Liu Shaoqi 33, 34, 36, 52, 95
long march 8, 94
Luo Sanmei 58–9, 92, 112, 133
Lushan 34–5, 45

Macau xviii, 60, 78, 82, 83, 85, 127, 138. *See also* Greater Bay Area
  history of 87–8
MacLehose, Murray 83–4
Mao Zedong xvii, 10, 52, 109, 130
  1971 Southern Tour 32, 35–6
  conflict with Lin Biao 33–6
  establishment at Zhongnanhai 2

relationship with Deng Xiaoping 43–4, 94, 96–7
  travels in 1965–6 44–6
Mao Zhiyong 93
Mount Tai 30, 31, 140–3

National Day 36
  1984 xxi, 117–18
  1994 117

Open Coastal Cities xxi

Party Congress, 14th 27, 103, 106–8
Patten, Chris 83–4
Pearl River xviii–xix, 55, 60, 85–6, 134, 137–8
People's Liberation Army (PLA) 3, 7, 16, 33, 78, 90–1
price reform 20–1

Qianlong 30, 31–2

Ruijin 94, 95

Shanghai 22–3, 29, 35, 39, 43, 57, 115, 139–40
  Deng Xiaoping 1990 visit 17, 18–19
  Deng Xiaoping 1991 visit 23–4
  Deng Xiaoping 1992 visit 98–101
  history of 17–18, 48
  Mao Zedong 1965 visit 45
Shenzhen 41, 75, 92, 122–3, 126–7, 128, 132
  controversy xix–xxi, 22, 61–3
  Deng Xiaoping 1984 visit xi–xiii, xix
  development xviii, xxii–xxiii, 54, 60–1, 79, 111, 134–5
  economic performance 50, 55, 79–80, 87
  International Trade Centre xi, 59
  Lotus Hill Park 66, 111, 125
  population 54, 61

Second Line xi, xxi, 53
stock exchange 57
tourism 64–5
urban villages 61, 134
Sichuan 8, 17, 25, 124
Soviet Union 12, 25–6, 35, 122, 124
Special Economic Zones (SEZs)
    CCP approval of 78–9
    corruption in xxi
    debate over xx–xxi, xxiii, 27, 56
    Deng Xiaoping support xix, 39, 54
    origins of xviii, 55–6
    and Xi Jinping 126–8
spiritual pollution 61, 124
state-owned enterprises (SOEs) xvi, 21, 49–50, 105–6, 114, 123, 128

Tai Shan. *See* Mount Tai
'The Story of Spring' 112
Third Front xvii, 48
Third Plenum (2013) 125
Tiananmen Protests (1976) 96–7
Tiananmen Protests (1989) 3–5, 6–8, 62, 65, 82, 108, 119, 136
    aftermath 2–3, 16
township and village enterprises (TVEs) 40, 92

unemployment 5, 20, 22
urban reform 49–50

Wen Jiabao 55, 123
World Economic Herald 11
Wu Guanzheng 93
Wu Jinglian 127
Wuhan 17, 35, 65
    Deng Xiaoping's 1992 visit 46–7, 50–1
    history of 47–8
    and Mao Zedong 43–6

Xi Jinping 55, 135, 138
    approach to corruption 124–5
    attitude to Deng Xiaoping 131–2
    as potential reformist 121–3
    and predecessors 128–30
    visits to Shenzhen xxii–xxiii, 125–7
Xi Zhongxun xvii, 78, 121, 126
Xianke Laser Company (SAST) 63–4
Xie Fei 54, 63, 86
Xiong Qingquan 51
Xiong'an 127–8

Yang Baibing 90, 107–8
Yang Shangkun xvii, 6, 82, 90, 92, 98, 107–8
Yangtze River 17, 29, 38, 129
Yellow River 31, 38, 118
Yingtan 93, 98

Zhao Ziyang 104, 117, 119, 125, 131
    economic approach 9, 20–1
    house arrest 9–10, 108
    rise in party 8
    and Tiananmen Square protests 6–8
Zhongnanhai 1–2, 3, 11, 45, 97, 108
Zhou Enlai 10, 35, 46, 95, 96, 118
Zhou Yongkang 124–5
Zhu Rongji 19–20, 23, 24, 25, 52, 55
    post Southern Tour 105, 108, 114–15, 116, 119, 123, 125
Zhuhai 58, 86, 92, 137, 138–9
    Deng Xiaoping 1984 visit xiii, xix
    development xviii, 78–9, 88–9
    geography 87
    military meeting in 90, 108
Zhuo Lin 19, 38, 94, 105, 116–17, 120

www.ingramcontent.com/pod-product-compliance
Lightning Source LLC
Chambersburg PA
CBHW051644230426
43669CB00013B/2440